The Golden Book of
COOKIES

The Golden Book of
COOKIES

First English language edition
for the United States and Canada
published in 2009 by Barron's Educational Series, Inc.

© 2008 McRae Books S.r.l.

The Golden Book of Cookies
was created and produced by McRae Books S.r.l.
Via del Salviatino, 1 – 50016 Fiesole, Florence, Italy
info@mcraebooks.com
www.mcraebooks.com
Publishers: Anne McRae, Marco Nardi

Project Director Anne McRae
Art Director Marco Nardi
Photography Brent Parker Jones (R&R Publications)
Photographic Art Direction Neil Hargreaves
Introduction Carla Bardi
Texts Carla Bardi, Pamela Egan, Brenda Moore, Ting Morris
Food Styling Lee Blaylock, Neil Hargreaves
Layouts Aurora Granata
Pre-press Filippo Delle Monache

All inquiries should be addressed to:
Barron's Educational Series, Inc.
250 Wireless Boulevard
Hauppauge, New York 11788
www.barronseduc.com

ISBN-13: 978-0-7641-6185-8
ISBN-10: 0-7641-6185-7

Library of Congress Control Number: 2008923901

Printed in China
9 8 7 6 5 4 3 2

The level of difficulty for each recipe is given on a scale from
1 (easy) to 3 (complicated).

CONTENTS

INTRODUCTION

Cookies are one of life's simple pleasures. The word itself is a hold-all term that covers a huge range of sweet, bite-sized, baked goods—from crisp wafers, crumbly meringues and macaroons, and light-as-air madeleines, to buttery shortbread, chewy chocolate chip super-cookies, and rich gooey bars and brownies. The fact that cookies can be shaped, flavored, and decorated in so many different ways has given rise to a large number of names for them, including some quite colorful ones such as cat's tongues, Russian cigarettes, and gingerbread people.

The origins of cookie-making are lost in the mists of time. The ancient Romans made cookie-like products by boiling wheat flour and water to a thick paste then frying it in oil and serving with it with lashings of honey. But cookie-making probably began in earnest with the widespread cultivation and processing of sugar. Sugar farming spread from India and China to the Middle East and from there to Europe. Many believe that the earliest cookies were made in ancient Persia (modern Iran) in the 7th century AD. Certainly by the time of the Middle Ages, Italian merchants were dealing in biscotti. This is the word that gave rise to the British term for cookie—"biscuit" (not to be confused with the same word in North America, where it means a thick, savory, scone-like baked good). The Italian word biscotti, or *panis biscoctus*, says it all: the cookies are baked twice, a process which allows them to be kept for much longer periods of time.

Macaroons are another medieval cookie that have survived to the present day. Stiffly-beaten egg whites mixed with flour or nuts and sugar gradually gave rise to modern meringues and sponge-like cookies, such as ladyfingers. By the 17th and 18th centuries, baking was a carefully controlled profession over much of Europe, with guilds regulating the type of cookies to be baked and sold. British and Dutch immigrants took these recipes and standards with them to the United States. In fact it was the Dutch word *koekje*, meaning "little cake" that gave rise to the modern American term cookie.

Subsequent generations of immigrants from all over Europe have contributed to the rich store of recipes in the American tradition and the United States has become the homeland of the cookie. So much so that many American-born "classic" cookie recipes have been exported back to Europe and to the rest of the world. The chocolate chip cookie is a good example of this: as the story goes, this cookie was invented in 1937 by Ruth Graves Wakefield of Whitefield, Massachusetts. Ruth ran the Toll House Restaurant where one of her favorite offerings was the Butter Drop Do cookie, made with bakers' chocolate. Finding herself without the necessary chocolate one day, Ruth chopped up a semisweet chocolate bar thinking it would melt during baking. It did not, but the resulting cookie was so good that she called it the Toll House Crunch Cookie and added it to her repertoire. Word spread and the cookie became so popular that Ruth struck a deal to have the recipe published on the wrapping paper of a chocolate bar made by Nestle. The "Chinese" Fortune cookie is another American invention. These popular little wafer cookies with messages tucked inside were invented somewhere in America (probably in California) by members of the Chinese immigrant community.

INGREDIENTS

BUTTER: Make sure it is fresh; it can spoil in the supermarket or refrigerator, turning rancid from the oxidation of fatty acids. Butter keeps in the refrigerator for 2–3 weeks only. Wrapped in airtight foil, it can be frozen for several months. Use unsalted butter in these recipes; we have indicated where salt should be added. For baking, most brands of butter are fine, but when butter is needed to make frostings always use the highest quality butter available.

EGGS: Always use the freshest of eggs when baking. To keep, they are best stored on the top shelf of the refrigerator rather than in the egg compartment on the door (which is not cool enough). Store them in their cardboard carton, which will stop them from absorbing odors from other foods. Eggs come in different sizes; in these recipes we have used large (2 oz/60 g) eggs throughout. Since eggs often provide most of the liquid in cookie batters, be sure to use the same sized eggs.

FLOUR: Unless otherwise stated, all-purpose or plain flour will produce the best results for these recipes.

SUGAR: Sugar is a fundamental ingredient in most cookie recipes, adding both structure and texture to the finished product. Most recipes call for ordinary granulated sugar; a few make use of superfine (caster) sugar. If you don't have superfine sugar on hand you can make it easily by processing granulated sugar for 20–30 seconds in a food processor. Both light and dark brown sugar are made by moistening granulated sugar with molasses. Raw sugar, or Demerara (named after the place in Guyana where it was originally made), is a partially refined sugar which is usually sprinkled over cookies before baking.

RAISING AGENTS: Many cookies are leavened with just the air bubbles incorporated into the batter when the sugar is creamed with the butter, or beaten with the egg. Others make use of chemical raising agents, such as baking powder. Alkaline baking soda (bicarbonate of soda) is used to leaven cookie batters containing acid ingredients such as honey or brown sugar.

THE GOLDEN RULES OF COOKING MAKING

One of the best things about cookies is that they are so easy to make. A few common ingredients (usually butter, sugar, eggs, and flour), artfully flavored, beaten, and baked, will not only fill your kitchen with delicious aromas, but will spread good cheer among family and friends. Here are a few basic rules:

BAKING SHEETS: Use shiny, light-colored (silver) baking sheets (also called cookie sheets) which heat more evenly than darker ones. They will brown the bottoms of your cookies without burning them. Line with parchment paper to prevent the cookies from sticking to the sheets.

METHOD: Always use softened butter at room temperature when creaming with sugar. Beat by hand or in an electric mixer until light and fluffy. Eggs should also be at room temperature; cold eggs can curdle the batter. Take them out of the refrigerator an hour or two before you start. Modern flour is all pre-sifted, so there is no need to sift it before adding to the batter. Cocoa powder will often benefit from sifting, but to remove the lumps rather than to add air. Solid ingredients such as chocolate chips should always be added last. Stir in by hand or use a mixer on low speed.

CHILLING THE DOUGH: Chilling cookie dough in the refrigerator for 30–60 minutes stops cookies from spreading and becoming too thin during baking.

BAKING: Make all the cookies about the same size so that they bake at the same rate. Leave plenty of space between one cookie and the next when placing on the baking sheets. Two inches (5 cm) is a safe distance. In many ovens you can bake two cookie sheets at a time; remember to reverse their positions top and bottom halfway through baking and to rotate back to front as well, for even baking. Do not place cookie dough onto hot baking sheets as it will spread and bake unevenly. If you like soft, chewy cookies, bake them for 2–3 minutes less than the indicated baking time. Let the cookies firm on the baking sheets for 2–3 minutes after you remove them from the oven. Use a metal spatula to transfer the cookies to wire racks to cool.

CUT OUT
COOKIES

COCONUT COOKIES WITH ROLLED OATS

Preheat the oven to 300°F (150°C/gas 2).
• Butter two cookie sheets. • Mix the flour
and salt in a large bowl. • Use a pastry
blender to cut in the shortening until the
mixture resembles fine crumbs. • Stir in the
coconut, rolled oats, and sugar. • Mix the
water, molasses, and baking soda in a small
bowl. • Stir the baking soda liquid into the oat
mixture to form a stiff dough. Press the
dough into a disk, wrap in plastic wrap (cling
film) and refrigerate for 30 minutes. • Roll out
the dough on a lightly floured surface to a
¼-inch (5-mm) thick. • Use a 3-inch (8-cm)
cookie cutter to cut out the cookies. Gather
the dough scraps, re-roll, and continue
cutting out cookies until all the dough is used.
• Use a spatula to transfer the cookies to the
prepared cookie sheet, placing them 1 inch
(2.5 cm) apart. • Bake until just golden at the
edges, 25–30 minutes. • Transfer to wire racks
and let cool completely

¾ cup (125 g) all-purpose
(plain) flour

⅛ teaspoon salt

½ cup (125 g) vegetable
shortening

1 cup (125 g) shredded
(desiccated) coconut

1 cup (150 g) old-
fashioned rolled oats

½ cup (100 g) granulated
sugar

2 tablespoons cold water

1 tablespoon light
molasses

1 teaspoon baking soda
(bicarbonate of soda)

Makes: 25–30 cookies
Preparation: 40 minutes
+ 30 minutes to chill
Cooking: 25–30 minutes
Level: 1

ALMOND CUT OUT COOKIES

Preheat the oven to 325°F (170°C/gas 3).
• Spread the whole almonds on a large
baking sheet. Toast until lightly golden,
about 7 minutes. • Let cool completely then
chop coarsely. • Mix the flour, baking
powder, cinnamon, cloves, and salt in a
medium bowl. • Beat the butter and sugar in
a large bowl with an electric mixer at high
speed until creamy. • Add 2 eggs, beating
until just blended. • Heat the honey in a
small saucepan over low heat until liquid.
Stir the warm honey, candied lemon and
orange peel, and chopped almonds into the
mixture. • Mix in the dry ingredients to form
a smooth dough. • Press the dough into a
disk, wrap in plastic wrap (cling film), and
refrigerate for 1 hour. • Preheat the oven to
350°F (180°C/gas 4). • Line three cookie
sheets with parchment paper. • Roll out the
dough on a lightly floured surface to ¼-inch
(5-mm) thick. • Use a 2½-inch (6-cm)
cookie cutter to cut out the cookies.
Gather the dough scraps, re-roll, and
continue cutting out cookies until all the
dough is used. • Use a spatula to transfer
the cookies to the prepared cookie sheets,

1 cup (150 g) whole almonds

3⅓ cups (500 g) all-purpose (plain) flour

1½ teaspoons baking powder

2 teaspoons ground cinnamon

½ teaspoon ground cloves

⅛ teaspoon salt

½ cup (125 g) butter, softened

½ cup (100 g) granulated sugar

3 large eggs

¾ cup (180 ml) honey

1 cup (50 g) chopped candied lemon peel

1 cup (100 g) chopped candied orange peel

2 tablespoons flaked almonds

2 tablespoons chopped mixed candied peel

Makes: 50–60 cookies
Preparation: 50 minutes
+ 1 hour to chill
Cooking: 10–12 minutes
Level: 2

placing them about 1 inch (2.5 cm) apart.
• Lightly beat the remaining egg and brush
over the tops of the cookies. • Decorate
with the flaked almonds and candied peel.
• Bake until just golden and crisp around
the edges, 10–12 minutes. • Transfer to
wire racks to cool.

CRISP RAISIN COOKIES

Plump the raisins in hot water in a small bowl for 10 minutes. • Drain well and pat dry with paper towels. • Mix the flour, baking powder, and salt in a large bowl. • Stir in the sugar. • Use a pastry blender to cut in the butter until the mixture resembles coarse crumbs. • Mix in the egg, wine, and lemon zest to form a smooth dough. Knead in the raisins until well blended. • Press the dough into a disk, wrap in plastic wrap (cling film), and refrigerate for 30 minutes. • Preheat the oven to 400°F (200°C/gas 6). • Butter two cookie sheets. • Roll out the dough on a lightly floured surface to 1/4-inch (5-mm) thick.
• Use a 2-inch (5-cm) cookie cutter to cut out the cookies. Gather the dough scraps, re-roll, and continue cutting out cookies until all the dough is used. • Use a spatula to transfer the cookies to the prepared cookie sheets, spacing them 1 inch (2.5 cm) apart.
• Bake until just golden, 12–15 minutes.
• Transfer to racks to cool.

½ cup (90 g) golden raisins (sultanas)

1½ cups (225 g) all-purpose (plain) flour

1 teaspoon baking powder

⅛ teaspoon salt

½ cup (100 g) granulated sugar

⅓ cup (90 g) butter, cut up

1 large egg, lightly beaten

3 tablespoons dry white wine

Finely grated zest of 1 lemon

Makes: about 25 cookies
Preparation: 40 minutes
    + 30 minutes to chill
Cooking: 12–15 minutes
Level: 1

ALLSPICE SUGAR COOKIES

Preheat the oven to 375°F (190°C/gas 5).
• Butter two cookie sheets. • Mix the flour, baking powder, allspice, and salt in a medium bowl. • Beat the butter and sugar in a large bowl with an electric mixer at high speed until creamy. • Add the egg yolk, beating until just blended. • Mix in the dry ingredients, currants, candied peel, brandy, and enough milk to form a soft, but not sticky, dough. • Press into a disk, wrap in plastic wrap (cling film) and refrigerate for 30 minutes. • Roll out the dough to ¼-inch (5 mm) thick. • Use a 2-inch (5-cm) cookie cutter to cut out cookies. Gather the dough scraps, re-roll, and continue cutting out cookies until all the dough is used. Transfer the cookies to the cookie sheets, spacing well. • Bake for 10 minutes. • Beat the egg white lightly.
• Remove the cookies from the oven and brush with the egg white. Sprinkle with the extra sugar. • Bake until lightly browned, 5–10 minutes more. • Cool on the sheets until the cookies firm slightly. Transfer to racks and let cool completely.

1¼ cups (180 g) all-purpose (plain) flour

1 teaspoon baking powder

½ teaspoon ground allspice

⅛ teaspoon salt

⅓ cup (90 g) butter, softened

⅓ cup (70 g) granulated sugar + extra, to sprinkle

1 large egg, separated

⅓ cup (45 g) currants

1 tablespoon finely chopped mixed candied peel

¼ teaspoon brandy

2 tablespoons milk, or more, as needed

Makes: about 24 cookies
Preparation: 40 minutes + 30 minutes to chill
Cooking: 15–20 minutes
Level: 1

SOUR CREAM COOKIES

Mix the flour, baking powder, and salt in a large bowl. • Use a pastry blender to cut in the butter until the mixture resembles fine crumbs. • Stir together the sugar, sour cream, and 1 egg. Stir into the dry ingredients to form a smooth dough. • Press the dough into a disk, wrap in plastic wrap (cling film), and refrigerate for 30 minutes. • Preheat the oven to 425°F (220°C/gas 7). • Line two cookie sheets with parchment paper. • Roll out the dough on a lightly floured surface to ¼-inch (5-mm) thick. • Use a 2-inch (5-cm) cookie cutter to cut out the cookies. Gather the dough scraps, re-roll, and continue cutting out until all the dough is used. • Use a spatula to transfer the cookies to the cookie sheets, spacing them 2 inches (5 cm) apart. Prick all over with a fork. • Beat the remaining egg and brush over the tops of the cookies.
• Bake until golden brown, 10–15 minutes.
• Transfer to racks to cool.

1 cup (150 g) all-purpose (plain) flour

½ teaspoon baking powder

⅛ teaspoon salt

2 tablespoons butter, cut up

3 tablespoons granulated sugar

5 tablespoons sour cream

2 large eggs

Makes: 16–20 cookies
Preparation: 40 minutes
 + 30 minutes to chill
Cooking: 10–15 minutes
Level: 1

VANILLA ROUNDS

Preheat the oven to 350°F (180°C/gas 4).
• Butter three cookie sheets. • Mix the flour, cornstarch, baking powder, and salt in a large bowl. • Use a wooden spoon to mix in the sugar, butter, egg, cream, and vanilla to form a smooth dough. • Press the dough into a disk, wrap in plastic wrap (cling film), and refrigerate for 30 minutes. • Roll out the dough on a lightly floured surface to ¼-inch (5-mm) thick. • Use a 2½-inch (6-cm) fluted cookie cutter to cut out the cookies. Gather the dough scraps, re-roll, and continue cutting out cookies until all the dough is used. • Use a spatula to transfer the cookies to the prepared cookie sheets, placing them 1 inch (2.5 cm) apart. • Bake until just golden at the edges, 10–15 minutes. • Transfer to racks and let cool.

3 cups (450 g) all-purpose (plain) flour

⅔ cup (100 g) cornstarch (cornflour)

2 teaspoons baking powder

⅛ teaspoon salt

1 cup (200 g) granulated sugar

¾ cup (180 g) butter, melted

1 large egg

⅓ cup (90 ml) light (single) cream

½ teaspoon vanilla extract (essence)

Makes: about 35 cookies
Preparation: 40 minutes
    + 30 minutes to chill
Cooking: 10–15 minutes
Level: 1

HONEY COOKIES

34

Mix the flour, baking soda, cinnamon, cardamom, nutmeg, and salt in a medium bowl. • Beat the eggs and sugar in a large bowl with an electric mixer at high speed until pale and thick. • Heat the honey in a small saucepan over low heat until liquid. • Stir the honey and vanilla into the beaten egg mixture. • Mix in the dry ingredients to form a stiff dough. • Wrap in plastic wrap (cling film) and refrigerate for 1 hour. • Preheat the oven to 375°F (190°C/gas 5). • Butter two cookie sheets. • Roll out the dough on a lightly floured surface to ½-inch (1 cm) thick. • Use a 2-inch (5-cm) cookie cutter to cut out the cookies. • Gather the dough scraps, re-roll, and continue cutting out cookies until all the dough is used. • Transfer the cookies to the cookie sheets, placing them 2 inches (5 cm) apart. • Bake until just golden, 15–20 minutes. • Cool on the sheets until the cookies firm slightly. • Transfer to racks to finish cooling. • Dust with the confectioners' sugar.

3 cups (450 g) all-purpose (plain) flour

1 teaspoon baking soda (bicarbonate of soda)

½ teaspoon ground cinnamon

½ teaspoon ground cardamom

¼ teaspoon ground nutmeg

⅛ teaspoon salt

2 large eggs

1 cup (200 g) granulated sugar

1 cup (250 ml) honey

½ teaspoon vanilla extract (essence)

4 tablespoons confectioners' (icing) sugar, to dust

Makes: 24–30 cookies
Preparation: 40 minutes + 1 hour to chill
Cooking: 15–20 minutes
Level: 1

APRICOT CUT OUT COOKIES

36

Preheat the oven to 350°F (180°C/gas 4).
• Butter two cookie sheets. • Beat the butter and brown sugar in a large bowl with an electric mixer at high speed until creamy.
• Add the egg yolk, beating until just blended.
• Mix in the flour, lemon zest and juice, apricots, and pecans. • Press the dough into a disk, wrap in plastic wrap (cling film), and refrigerate for 30 minutes. • Roll out the dough on a lightly floured surface to 1/4-inch (5-mm) thick. • Use a 2-inch (5-cm) cookie cutter to cut out the cookies. Gather the dough scraps, re-roll, and continue cutting out cookies until all the dough is used.
• Use a spatula to transfer the cookies to the prepared cookie sheets. • Bake until lightly browned, 15–20 minutes. • Transfer to racks and let cool completely.

1/3 cup (90 g) butter, softened

1/3 cup (70 g) firmly packed light brown sugar

1 large egg yolk

1 1/4 cups (180 g) whole-wheat (wholemeal) flour

Finely grated zest and juice of 1/2 lemon

1/2 cup (50 g) finely chopped dried apricots

1/2 cup (50 g) coarsely chopped pecans

Makes: about 16 cookies
Preparation: 40 minutes + 30 minutes to chill
Cooking: 15–20 minutes
Level: 1

GINGER CRISPS

Mix the flour, ginger, baking soda, and salt in a large bowl. • Stir in the sugar, candied peel, and lemon zest. • Heat the butter and molasses in a small saucepan over low heat until liquid. • Mix the molasses mixture into the dry ingredients to form a stiff dough. • Press the dough into a disk, wrap in plastic wrap (cling film), and refrigerate for 30 minutes. • Preheat the oven to 350°F (180°C/gas 4). • Butter two cookie sheets. • Roll out the dough on a lightly floured surface to ⅛-inch (3-mm) thick. • Use a 2-inch (5-cm) cookie cutter to cut out the cookies. Gather the dough scraps, re-roll, and continue cutting out cookies until all the dough is used. • Use a spatula to transfer the cookies to the prepared cookie sheets, placing them 2 inches (5 cm) apart. • Bake until just golden, 8–10 minutes. • Cool on the sheets until the cookies firm slightly. • Transfer to racks to cool completely.

1⅔ cups (250 g) all-purpose (plain) flour
2 teaspoons ground ginger
¼ teaspoon baking soda (bicarbonate of soda)
⅛ teaspoon salt
¾ cup (150 g) granulated sugar
1 cup (100 g) finely chopped mixed candied peel
½ teaspoon finely grated lemon zest
½ cup (125 g) butter, cut up
¼ cup (60 g) light molasses (treacle)

Makes: 24–30 cookies
Preparation: 40 minutes + 30 minutes to chill
Cooking: 8–10 minutes
Level: 1

WALNUT CUT OUT COOKIES

Beat the butter, granulated and brown sugars, and maple syrup in a large bowl with an electric mixer at high speed until creamy.
• Mix in the flour, coffee, walnuts, and salt to form a soft dough. • Turn the dough out onto a lightly floured surface and knead until smooth. • Press the dough into a disk, wrap in plastic wrap (cling film), and refrigerate for 30 minutes. • Preheat the oven to 375°F (190°C/gas 5). • Butter and flour two cookie sheets. • Roll out the dough to ⅛-inch (3-mm) thick. • Use a 3-inch (8-cm) cookie cutter to cut out the cookies. • Gather the dough scraps, re-roll, and continue cutting out cookies until all the dough is used.
• Use a spatula to transfer the cookies to the prepared cookie sheets, placing them 1 inch (2.5 cm) apart. • Bake until pale golden brown, 8–10 minutes. • Transfer to racks to cool.

½ cup (125 g) butter, softened

½ cup (100 g) granulated sugar

2 tablespoons light brown sugar

2 teaspoons pure maple syrup

1⅓ cups (200 g) all-purpose (plain) flour

1 teaspoon instant coffee granules

½ cup (60 g) finely chopped walnuts

⅛ teaspoon salt

Makes: about 30 cookies
Preparation: 40 minutes + 30 minutes to chill
Cooking: 8–10 minutes
Level: 1

EVERYDAY ALMOND COOKIES

Beat the butter and sugar in a large bowl with an electric mixer at high speed until creamy. • Mix in the flour, almonds, and salt. • Add the lemon juice to form a stiff dough. • Press the dough into a disk, wrap in plastic wrap (cling film), and refrigerate for 30 minutes. • Preheat the oven to 375°F (190°C/gas 5). • Butter a cookie sheet. • Roll out the dough on a lightly floured surface to 1/4-inch (5-mm) thick. • Use a 2-inch (5-cm) cookie cutter to cut out the cookies. Gather the dough scraps, re-roll, and continue cutting out cookies until all the dough is used. • Use a spatula to transfer the cookies to the prepared cookie sheet, placing them 2 inches (5 cm) apart. • Bake until pale golden, 12–15 minutes. • Cool on the sheet until they firm slightly. Transfer to racks to cool completely.

1/2 cup (125 g) butter, softened
3/4 cup (150 g) granulated sugar
1 1/2 cups (225 g) all-purpose (plain) flour
2/3 cup (100 g) finely ground almonds
1/8 teaspoon salt
Freshly squeezed juice of 1 lemon

Makes: 12–16 cookies
Preparation: 40 minutes + 30 minutes to chill
Cooking: 12–15 minutes
Level: 1

GLAZED VANILLA STARS

Line three cookie sheets with parchment paper. • Beat the egg whites in a large bowl with an electric mixer at medium speed until frothy. With mixer at high speed, gradually beat in the confectioners' sugar, cream of tatar and lemon juice until stiff, glossy peaks form. • Use a large rubber spatula to fold the almonds, vanilla sugar, and vanilla into the beaten egg whites. • Shape the dough into a disk, wrap in plastic wrap (cling film) and refrigerate for 30 minutes. • Preheat the oven to 300°F (150°C/gas 2). • Roll out the dough on a lightly floured surface to ½-inch (1-cm) thick. • Dip a star-shaped cookie cutter into cold water and cut out star shapes. Gather the dough scraps, re-roll, and continue cutting out cookies until all the dough is used. • Use a spatula to transfer the cookies to the cookie sheets, placing them 1 inch (2.5 cm) apart.

• Bake until firm to the touch, 25–30 minutes.

• Cool completely on the cookie sheets.

• Spread each star with vanilla frosting and let set.

3 large egg whites

1½ cups (225 g) confectioners' (icing) sugar

⅛ teaspoon cream of tartar

3 tablespoons freshly squeezed lemon juice

4 cups (600 g) finely ground almonds

2 teaspoons vanilla sugar

¼ teaspoon vanilla extract (essence)

1 recipe vanilla frosting (see page 699)

Makes: about 50 cookies
Preparation: 45 minutes
  + 30 minutes to chill
Cooking: 25–30 minutes
Level: 2

CURRANT AND SPICE DIAMONDS

46

Mix the flour, baking soda, cinnamon, nutmeg, and cloves in a medium bowl. • Beat the butter and ¾ cup (150 g) of sugar in a large bowl with an electric mixer at high speed until creamy. • Add the milk and egg, beating until just blended. • Mix in the dry ingredients, followed by the currants. • Press the dough into a disk, wrap in plastic wrap (cling film), and refrigerate for 30 minutes. • Preheat the oven to 375°F (190°C/gas 5). • Set out three cookie sheets. • Roll out the dough on a lightly floured surface to ⅛-inch (3-mm) thick. • Sprinkle with the remaining sugar. • Use a 2-inch (5-cm) diamond-shaped cookie cutter to cut out the cookies. Gather the dough scraps, re-roll, and continue cutting out cookies until all the dough is used. Transfer the cookies to the cookie sheets, spacing well. • Bake until lightly browned, 8–10 minutes. • Transfer to racks to cool.

1⅔ cups (250 g) all-purpose (plain) flour
1 teaspoon baking soda (bicarbonate of soda)
1 teaspoon ground cinnamon
¼ teaspoon ground nutmeg
¼ teaspoon ground cloves
⅛ teaspoon salt
½ cup (125 g) butter, softened
1 cup (200 g) granulated sugar
2 tablespoons milk
1 large egg, lightly beaten
½ cup (90 g) dried currants

Makes: about 36 cookies
Preparation: 40 minutes + 30 minutes to chill
Cooking: 8–10 minutes
Level: 1

HEARTS OF SPICE

Mix the flour, allspice, baking soda, cinnamon, cloves, ginger, nutmeg, and salt in a medium bowl. • Use a wooden spoon to beat the molasses, brown sugar, and butter in a large bowl until well blended. • Mix in the dry ingredients to form a stiff dough. • Press the dough into a disk, wrap in plastic wrap (cling film), and refrigerate for 30 minutes. • Preheat the oven to 375°F (190°C/gas 5). • Butter two cookie sheets. • Roll out the dough on a lightly floured surface to ¼-inch (5-mm) thick. • Use a 1½-inch (4-cm) heart-shaped cookie cutter to cut out the cookies. Gather the dough scraps, re-roll, and continue cutting out cookies until all the dough is used. • Use a spatula to transfer the cookies to the prepared cookie sheets, placing them 1 inch (2.5 cm) apart. • Bake until golden brown, 8–10 minutes. • Transfer to racks to cool.

1¾ cups (275 g) all-purpose (plain) flour
¼ teaspoon ground allspice
¼ teaspoon baking soda (bicarbonate of soda)
¼ teaspoon ground cinnamon
¼ teaspoon ground cloves
¼ teaspoon ground ginger
¼ teaspoon freshly grated nutmeg
⅛ teaspoon salt
½ cup (125 g) light molasses (treacle)
½ cup (200 g) firmly packed light brown sugar
¼ cup (60 g) butter, melted

Makes: 30–35 cookies
Preparation: 40 minutes + 30 minutes to chill
Cooking: 8–10 minutes
Level: 1

RAW SUGAR AND GINGER COOKIES

50

Mix the flour, baking powder, cocoa, ginger, and salt in a large bowl. Use a wooden spoon to mix in the raw sugar, egg, butter, milk, and vanilla to form a soft dough. • Press the dough into a disk, wrap in plastic wrap (cling film), and refrigerate for 30 minutes.
• Preheat the oven to 350°F (180°C/gas 4).
• Butter two cookie sheets. • Roll out the dough on a lightly floured surface to ¼-inch (5-mm) thick. • Use variously shaped cookie cutters to cut out the cookies. Gather the dough scraps, re-roll, and continue cutting out cookies until all the dough is used.
• Use a spatula to transfer the cookies to the prepared cookie sheets, placing them 1 inch (2.5 cm) apart. Prick all over with a fork.
• Bake until just golden, 8–10 minutes.
• Transfer to racks and let cool completely.

2⅓ cups (350 g) all-purpose (plain) flour

1 teaspoon baking powder

2 teaspoons unsweetened cocoa powder

2 teaspoons ground ginger

⅛ teaspoon salt

1 cup (200 g) raw sugar (Demerara or Barbados)

1 large egg

½ cup (125 g) butter, melted

2 tablespoons milk

½ teaspoon vanilla extract (essence)

Makes: about 25 cookies
Preparation: 40 minutes
+ 30 minutes to chill
Cooking: 8–10 minutes
Level: 1

CARDAMOM STARS

Melt the butter and molasses in a small saucepan. Set aside to cool. • Mix the flour, baking soda, cinnamon, ginger, salt, peppercorns, and cardamom in a large bowl. • Use a wooden spoon to stir in the sugar, molasses mixture, and egg. • Turn out onto a lightly floured surface and knead lightly until smooth. • Shape into a disk, wrap in plastic wrap (cling film), and refrigerate for 30 minutes. • Preheat the oven to 350°F (180°C/gas 4). • Line two cookie sheets with parchment paper. • Roll out the dough on a lightly floured surface to ¼-inch (5-mm) thick. • Use a star-shaped cutter to cut out the cookies. • Gather the dough scraps, re-roll, and continue cutting out cookies until all the dough is used. Transfer the cookies to the cookie sheets, spacing well. • Bake until firm to the touch, 10–15 minutes. • Cool completely on the cookie sheets. Transfer to a rack. • Mix the confectioners' sugar and water in a small bowl. Drizzle over the cookies.

⅓ cup (90 g) butter, cut up

2 tablespoons dark molasses (treacle)

1½ cups (225 g) all-purpose (plain) flour

½ teaspoon baking soda (bicarbonate of soda)

½ teaspoon ground cinnamon

½ teaspoon ground ginger

½ teaspoon salt

3 black peppercorns, crushed

Seeds of 10 cardamom pods, crushed

¼ cup (50 g granulated sugar

1 large egg, lightly beaten

1 cup (150 g) confectioners' (icing) sugar

2 tablespoons boiling water

Makes: about 35 cookies
Preparation: 50 minutes
+ 30 minutes to chill
Cooking: 10–15 minutes
Level: 1

CHOCOLATE DIPPED HEARTS

Mix the flour, baking powder, and salt in a medium bowl. • Beat the butter, sugar, vanilla, and almond in a large bowl with an electric mixer at high speed until creamy. • Add the egg and egg yolk, beating until just blended. • Mix in the dry ingredients and milk to form a soft dough. • Divide the dough in half. Press into disks, wrap in plastic wrap (cling film), and refrigerate for 30 minutes. • Preheat the oven to 350°F (180°C/gas 4). • Line three cookie sheets with parchment paper. • Roll out the dough on a lightly floured surface to 1/4-inch (5-mm) thick. • Use a heart-shaped cookie cutter to cut out cookies. • Gather the dough scraps, re-roll, and continue cutting out until all the dough is used. • Transfer the cookies to the cookie sheets, spacing well. • Bake until just golden, 12–15 minutes. • Transfer to racks and let cool completely. • Melt the chocolate in a double boiler over barely simmering water. • Dip the hearts in the chocolate and let stand until set.

3 cups (450 g) all-purpose (plain) flour
1/2 teaspoon baking powder
1/2 teaspoon salt
1 cup (250 g) butter, softened
1 cup (200 g) granulated sugar
1 teaspoon vanilla extract (essence)
1/4 teaspoon almond extract (essence)
1 large egg + 1 large egg yolk
1/4 cup (60 ml) milk
6 oz (180 g) semisweet (dark) chocolate, coarsely chopped

Makes: about 40 cookies
Preparation: 40 minutes + 30 minutes to chill
Cooking: 12–15 minutes
Level: 1

CARAWAY ROSE CRISPS

Mix the flour and salt in a medium bowl.
• Stir in the sugar and caraway seeds. • Beat
in the egg yolk and egg whites and rose water
to form a stiff dough. • Press the dough into
a disk, wrap in plastic wrap (cling film), and
refrigerate for 30 minutes. • Preheat the oven
to 325°F (170°C/gas 3). • Butter two cookie
sheets. • Roll out the dough on a lightly
floured surface to ⅛-inch (3-mm) thick.
• Use a 2-inch (5-cm) cookie cutter to cut out
the cookies. Gather the dough scraps, re-roll,
and continue cutting out cookies until all the
dough is used. • Use a spatula to transfer the
cookies to the prepared cookie sheets, placing
them 1 inch (2.5 cm) apart. • Bake until
golden brown, 10–15 minutes. • Transfer
to racks to cool.

1½ cups (225 g) all-
  purpose (plain) flour

⅛ teaspoon salt

1 cup (200 g) granulated
  sugar

1 teaspoon caraway
  seeds

1 large egg yolk
  + 3 large egg whites

1 tablespoon rose water

Makes: 24–30 cookies
Preparation: 40 minutes
  + 30 minutes to chill
Cooking: 10–15 minutes
Level: 1

HEARTS OF PROVENCE

Preheat the oven to 400°F (200°C/gas 6).
• Line two cookie sheets with parchment
paper. • Mix the flour, baking powder, and
salt in a large bowl. • Beat the butter and
sugar in a large bowl with an electric mixer
at high speed until creamy. • Add the egg
yolk, beating until just blended. • Mix in the
dry ingredients. • Turn the dough out onto a
lightly floured surface and knead to form a
soft dough. • Roll out the dough to ¼-inch
(5-mm) thick. • Sprinkle the dough with the
lavender flowers, pressing in the heads with a
rolling pin. • Use heart-shaped cookie cutters
to cut out the cookies. Gather the dough
scraps, re-roll, and continue cutting out
cookies until all the dough is used. • Use
a spatula to transfer the cookies to the
prepared cookie sheets. • Bake until firm
to the touch and lightly browned, 10–12
minutes. • Transfer to racks to cool.

1¼ cups (180 g) all-
   purpose (plain) flour
1 teaspoon baking
   powder
⅛ teaspoon salt
⅓ cup (90 g) butter
¼ cup (50 g) granulated
   sugar
1 large egg yolk
1 tablespoon lavender
   flowers (heads only),
   rinsed and dried

Makes: about 20 cookies
Preparation: 20 minutes
Cooking: 10–12 minutes
Level: 1

ICED MACE COOKIES

60

Mix the flour, baking powder, and mace in a medium bowl. • Beat the butter, sugar, and vanilla in a large bowl with an electric mixer at high speed until pale and creamy. • With mixer at medium speed, add the eggs one at a time, beating until just combined after each addition. • With mixer at low speed, gradually beat in the mixed dry ingredients. • Wrap in plastic wrap (cling film) and refrigerate for at least 2 hours. • Preheat oven to 350°F (180°C/gas 4). • Grease and lightly flour a baking sheet. • Roll out the dough on a lightly floured work surface to ⅛-inch (3-mm) thick. Use variously shaped cookie cutters to cut out the cookies. Gather the dough scraps, re-roll, and continue cutting out cookies until all the dough is used. • Transfer the cookies to the prepared sheets. • Bake until golden, 10–12 minutes. Transfer to racks to cool. • Mix the confectioners' sugar with the water and spread over the cookies.

1¾ cups (275 g) all-purpose (plain) flour

2 teaspoons baking powder

½ teaspoon ground mace

½ cup (125 g) butter

1 cup (200 g) granulated sugar

1 teaspoon vanilla extract (essence)

2 large eggs

1½ cups (225 g) confectioners' (icing) sugar

2 tablespoons boiling water

Makes: about 36 cookies
Preparation: 30 minutes + 2 hours to chill
Cooking: 10–12 minutes
Level: 1

SHERRY CARAWAY CRISPS

Melt the butter with the cream in a small saucepan over low heat. • Transfer to a large bowl. • Mix in the flour, sugar, caraway seeds, nutmeg, and salt. • Beat the egg yolk and sherry in a small bowl until frothy. • Stir the egg mixture into the dry ingredients to form a stiff dough. • Press the dough into a disk, wrap in plastic wrap (cling film), and refrigerate for 1 hour. • Preheat the oven to 325°F (170°C/gas 3). • Butter two cookie sheets. • Roll out the dough on a lightly floured surface to $1/4$-inch (5-mm) thick. • Use a 2-inch (5-cm) cookie cutter to cut out the cookies. • Gather the dough scraps, re-roll, and continue cutting out cookies until all the dough is used. • Use a spatula to transfer the cookies to the cookie sheets, placing them 1 inch (2.5 cm) apart. • Bake until just golden, 10–15 minutes. • Transfer to racks to cool.

½ cup (125 g) butter, cut up

1 tablespoon half-and-half

1⅔ cups (250 g) all-purpose (plain) flour

¾ cup (150 g) granulated sugar

1½ teaspoon caraway seeds

½ teaspoon freshly grated nutmeg

⅛ teaspoon salt

1 large egg yolk

1 tablespoon sweet sherry

Makes: 18–22 cookies
Preparation: 40 minutes
    + 1 hour to chill
Cooking: 10–15 minutes
Level: 1

SUGAR AND CINNAMON SNAPS

Mix the flour, cinnamon, and salt in a medium bowl. • Use a wooden spoon to beat the butter and sugar in a medium bowl until creamy. • Mix in the dry ingredients to form a smooth dough. Press the dough into a disk, wrap in plastic wrap (cling film), and refrigerate for 30 minutes. • Preheat the oven to 400°F (200°C/gas 6). • Butter a cookie sheet. • Roll out the dough on a lightly floured surface to ¼-inch (5-mm) thick. • Use a 3-inch (8-cm) cookie cutter to cut out the cookies. Gather the dough scraps, re-roll, and continue cutting out cookies until all the dough is used. • Use a spatula to transfer the cookies to the prepared cookie sheet, placing them 2 inches (5 cm) apart. • Bake until just golden, about 10 minutes. • Transfer to racks to cool.

1⅓ cups (200 g) all-purpose (plain) flour

½ teaspoon ground cinnamon

⅛ teaspoon salt

½ cup (125 g) butter, melted

⅓ cup (50 g) confectioners' (icing) sugar

Makes: about 16 cookies
Preparation: 40 minutes + 30 minutes to chill
Cooking: 10 minutes
Level: 1

GOLDEN CRISPS

Mix the flour and arrowroot in a large bowl.
• Use a pastry blender to cut in the butter until the mixture resembles fine crumbs.
• Stir in the sugar. • Stir in the egg and egg yolk to form a stiff dough. • Press the dough into a disk, wrap in plastic wrap (cling film), and refrigerate for 30 minutes. • Preheat the oven to 400°F (200°C/gas 6). • Butter two cookie sheets. • Roll out the dough on a lightly floured surface to ¼-inch (5-mm) thick.
• Use a 2-inch (5-cm) cookie cutter to cut out the cookies. • Gather the dough scraps, re-roll, and continue cutting out cookies until all the dough is used. • Use a spatula to transfer the cookies to the cookie sheets, placing them 1 inch (2.5 cm) apart. Sprinkle with the extra sugar. • Bake until pale golden brown, 10–15 minutes. • Transfer to racks to cool.

66

1⅓ cups (200 g) all-purpose (plain) flour

2 tablespoons arrowroot starch

½ cup (125 g) butter, softened

¾ cup (150 g) granulated sugar + 2 tablespoons, to sprinkle

1 large egg + 1 large egg yolk, lightly beaten

Makes: 20–25 cookies
Preparation: 40 minutes + 30 minutes to chill
Cooking: 10–15 minutes
Level: 1

GINGER MOLASSES COOKIES

Mix the flour, ginger, baking powder, and salt in a medium bowl. • Melt the butter with the brown sugar and molasses in a medium saucepan over low heat. • Remove from the heat and mix in the dry ingredients to form a stiff dough. • Press the dough into a disk, wrap in plastic wrap (cling film), and refrigerate for 1 hour. • Preheat the oven to 350°F (180°C/gas 4). • Butter two cookie sheets. • Roll out the dough on a lightly floured surface to ¼-inch (5-mm) thick. • Use a 2-inch (5-cm) cookie cutter to cut out the cookies. • Gather the dough scraps, re-roll, and continue cutting out cookies until all the dough is used. • Use a spatula to transfer the cookies to the prepared cookie sheets, placing them 1 inch (2.5 cm) apart. • Bake until firm to the touch and just golden, 10–15 minutes. • Transfer to racks to cool.

1¼ cups (180 g) all-purpose (plain) flour

1 teaspoon ground ginger

½ teaspoon baking powder

⅛ teaspoon salt

¼ cup (60 g) butter, cut up

¼ cup (50 g) firmly packed light brown sugar

¼ cup (50 g) light molasses (treacle)

Makes: 25–30 cookies
Preparation: 40 minutes + 1 hour to chill
Cooking: 10–15 minutes
Level: 1

HONEY AND CREAM COOKIES

Mix the flour and salt in a medium bowl.
• Use a pastry blender to cut in the butter until the mixture resembles fine crumbs.
• Mix in the cream and honey to form a stiff dough. • Press the dough into a disk, wrap in plastic wrap (cling film), and refrigerate for 30 minutes. • Preheat the oven to 300°F (150°C/gas 2). • Butter two cookie sheets.
• Roll out the dough on a lightly floured surface to $\frac{1}{8}$-inch (3-mm) thick. Use a 2-inch (5-cm) cookie cutter to cut out the cookies.
• Gather the dough scraps, re-roll, and continue cutting out cookies until all the dough is used. • Use a spatula to transfer the cookies to the prepared cookie sheets, placing them 2 inches (5 cm) apart. • Bake until golden, 15–20 minutes. • Transfer to racks to cool.

$1\frac{2}{3}$ cups (250 g) all-purpose (plain) flour

$\frac{1}{8}$ teaspoon salt

$\frac{1}{2}$ cup (125 g butter, cut up

2 tablespoons heavy (double) cream

2 tablespoons honey

Makes: 20–24 cookies
Preparation: 40 minutes
+ 30 minutes to chill
Cooking: 15–20 minutes
Level: 1

NORTHERN LIGHTS COOKIES

Mix the flour, baking powder, ginger, cinnamon, and salt in a medium bowl.
• Dissolve the baking soda in the water.
• Melt the butter with the corn syrup and sugar in a small saucepan over medium heat.
• Mix in the baking soda mixture. • Stir the butter mixture into the dry ingredients.
• Shape into a disk, wrap in plastic wrap (cling film) and refrigerate for 12 hours.
• Preheat the oven to 300°F (150°C/gas 2).
• Butter two cookie sheets. • Roll out the dough on a lightly floured surface to ¼-inch (5-mm) thick. • Use 1-inch (2.5-cm) cookie cutters to cut out the cookies. • Gather the dough scraps, re-roll, and continue cutting out the cookies until all the dough is used.
• Use a spatula to transfer the cookies to the prepared cookie sheets, placing them 1 inch (2.5 cm) apart. • Bake until lightly browned, 15–20 minutes. • Transfer to racks to cool.

⅔ cup (100 g) all-purpose (plain) flour
1 teaspoon baking powder
½ teaspoon ground ginger
¼ teaspoon ground cinnamon
⅛ teaspoon salt
¼ teaspoon baking soda (bicarbonate of soda)
1 tablespoon warm water
3 tablespoons butter
¼ cup light corn syrup (golden syrup)
2 tablespoons granulated sugar

Makes: about 20 cookies
Preparation: 40 minutes + 12 hours to chill
Cooking: 15–20 minutes
Level: 1

OAT BRAN COOKIES

Mix the whole-wheat flour, baking soda, and salt in a medium bowl. • Cut in the butter until the mixture resembles fine crumbs. • Stir in the oat bran and sugar. • Mix in the beaten egg. • Press the dough into a disk, wrap in plastic wrap (cling film), and refrigerate for 30 minutes. • Preheat the oven to 375°F (190°C/gas 5). • Butter a cookie sheet. • Roll out the dough on a surface lightly dusted with oat bran to 1/4-inch (5-mm) thick. • Use a 2-inch (5-cm) cookie cutter to cut out the cookies. Gather the dough scraps, re-roll, and continue cutting out cookies until all the dough is used. • Transfer the cookies to the prepared cookie sheet, placing them 1 inch (2.5 cm) apart. • Bake until golden brown, 10–15 minutes. • Transfer to racks and let cool.

74

1 cup (150 g) whole-wheat (wholemeal) flour

1/2 teaspoon baking soda (bicarbonate of soda)

1/4 teaspoon salt

3/4 cup (180 g) butter, cut up

1 cup (150 g) oat bran

1/2 cup (100 g) granulated sugar

1 large egg, lightly beaten

Makes: about 20 cookies
Preparation: 40 minutes
 + 30 minutes to chill
Cooking: 10–15 minutes
Level: 1

ANISE COOKIES

Mix the flour, sugar, and salt in a large bowl.
• Gradually stir in the oil and wine. • Add the
anisette and aniseeds and knead until smooth.
• Press into a disk, wrap in plastic wrap (cling
film) and refrigerate for 30 minutes. • Preheat
the oven to 350°F (180°C/gas 4). • Butter
and flour two cookie sheets. • Roll out the
dough to ⅛-inch (3 mm) thick. • Use a 2-inch
(5-cm) cookie cutter to cut out the cookies.
Continue cutting out cookies until all the
dough is used. • Transfer the cookies to the
prepared cookie sheets. Prick all over with
a fork. • Brush the cookies with the beaten
egg and sprinkle with the vanilla sugar.
• Bake until just golden, 12–15 minutes.
• Transfer to racks and let cool.

2 cups (300 g) all-purpose (plain) flour

1 cup (200 g) granulated sugar

⅛ teaspoon salt

¼ cup (60 ml) extra-virgin olive oil

¼ cup (60 ml) Muscatel wine

2 tablespoons anisette

1 tablespoon aniseeds

1 large egg, lightly beaten

1 tablespoon vanilla sugar (see page 696)

Makes: about 25 cookies
Preparation: 40 minutes
 + 30 minutes to chill
Cooking: 12–15 minutes
Level: 1

BRAN FLAKE COOKIES

Mix both flours, the bran, baking powder, and salt in a large bowl. • Beat the butter and sugar in a large bowl with an electric mixer at high speed until creamy. • Add the egg, beating until just blended. • Mix in the dry ingredients. • Press the dough into a disk, wrap in plastic wrap (cling film), and refrigerate for 30 minutes. • Preheat the oven to 350°F (180°C/gas 4). • Set out two cookie sheets. • Roll out the dough on a lightly floured surface. Use a 2-inch (5-cm) cookie cutter to cut out the cookies. Gather the dough scraps, re-roll, and continue cutting out cookies until all the dough is used. • Use a spatula to transfer the cookies to the cookie sheets, placing them 1 inch (2.5 cm) apart.
• Bake until lightly browned, 12–15 minutes.
• Transfer to racks to cool.

1 cup (150 g) all-purpose (plain) flour
1 cup (150 g) whole-wheat (wholemeal) flour
1 cup (150 g) bran flakes
1 teaspoon baking powder
⅛ teaspoon salt
½ cup (125 g) butter, softened
½ cup (100 g) granulated sugar
1 large egg

Makes: 30–35 cookies
Preparation: 20 minutes + 30 minutes to chill
Cooking: 12–15 minutes
Level: 1

AFTERNOON TEA COOKIES

Mix the flour, cornstarch, and salt in a large bowl. Stir in the sugar and vanilla. • Dot the butter and marzipan evenly over the dry ingredients. Use a pastry blender to cut in the ingredients until the mixture resembles coarse crumbs. • Make a well in the center and add the egg. • Work the dough until combined and knead briefly on a lightly floured surface until smooth. • Wrap in plastic wrap (cling film) and refrigerate for 30 minutes. • Preheat the oven to 350°F (180°C/gas 4). • Butter two cookie sheets. • Roll out the dough on a lightly floured surface to ⅛-inch (3-mm) thick. Use variously shaped cookie cutters to cut out the cookies. • Gather the dough scraps, re-roll, and continue cutting out cookies until all the dough is used. • Arrange on the prepared cookie sheets, spacing 1 inch (2.5 cm) apart. • Brush with the egg glaze. • Bake until golden brown, 10–15 minutes. • Cool on the cookie sheets for 2 minutes. Transfer to racks to cool completely.

2⅔ cups (400 g) all-purpose (plain) flour

⅔ cup (100 g) cornstarch (cornflour)

⅛ teaspoon salt

¾ cup (150 g) granulated sugar

1 teaspoon vanilla extract (essence)

3 oz (90 g) marzipan, softened and cut up

1 cup (250 g) cold butter, cut up

1 large egg, lightly beaten + 1 egg yolk, mixed with ½ cup (125 ml) water, to glaze

Makes: 80–90 cookies
Preparation: 30 minutes + 30 minutes to chill
Cooking: 10–15 minutes
Level: 2

POLENTA COOKIES

Preheat the oven to 375°F (190°C/gas 5).
• Butter two cookie sheets. • Mix the polenta, flour, confectioners' sugar, baking powder, and salt in a large bowl. • Make a well in the center and add the egg and egg yolk, butter, lard, and lemon zest. • Use your hands to knead the mixture into a smooth dough.
• Roll out the dough on a lightly floured surface to ⅛-inch (3-mm) thick. • Use a 2-inch (5-cm) cookie cutter to cut out the cookies. Gather the dough scraps, re-roll, and continue cutting out cookies until all the dough is used. • Use a spatula to transfer the cookies to the prepared cookie sheets. • Bake until just golden, 12–15 minutes. • Transfer to racks and let cool completely.

2 cups (300 g) polenta (yellow cornmeal)

1 cup (150 g) all-purpose (plain) flour

1 cup (150 g) confectioners' (icing) sugar

1 teaspoon baking powder

⅛ teaspoon salt

1 large egg + 1 large egg yolk

⅔ cup (150 g) butter, cut up

¼ cup (60 g) lard or vegetable shortening

Finely grated zest of 1 lemon

Makes: about 25 cookies
Preparation: 40 minutes
Cooking: 12–15 minutes
Level: 1

BUTTER COOKIES WITH CHOCOLATE FLECKS

84

Mix the flour and salt in a large bowl.
• Use a wooden spoon to mix in the sugar,
butter, egg and egg yolks, and chocolate to
form a smooth dough. • Press the dough into
a disk, wrap in plastic wrap (cling film), and
refrigerate for 30 minutes. • Preheat the oven
to 350°F (180°C/gas 4). • Butter three cookie
sheets. • Roll out the dough on a lightly
floured surface to ¼-inch (5-mm) thick. • Use
a 2-inch (5-cm) cookie cutter to cut out the
cookies. Gather the dough scraps, re-roll, and
continue cutting out cookies until all the
dough is used. • Use a spatula to transfer the
cookies to the prepared cookie sheets, placing
them 1 inch (2.5 cm) apart. • Bake until just
golden, 10–15 minutes. • Transfer the cookies
to racks to cool.

2⅔ cups (400 g) all-
    purpose (plain) flour

⅛ teaspoon salt

1¼ cups (250 g)
    granulated sugar

¾ cup (180 g) butter,
    softened

1 large egg + 2 large egg
    yolks

3 oz (90 g) semisweet
    (dark) chocolate,
    coarsely grated

Makes: about 40 cookies
Preparation: 40 minutes
    + 30 minutes to chill
Cooking: 10–15 minutes
Level: 1

DUTCH SHORTBREAD

Mix the flour, cocoa, and salt in a medium
bowl. • Beat the butter, confectioners' sugar,
and vanilla in a large bowl until creamy.
• Gradually beat in the dry ingredients.
• Spread out a large sheet of plastic wrap
(cling film) and turn the dough onto it.
• Place a sheet of plastic wrap on top and roll
out the dough to about $2/3$-inch (1.5-cm) thick.
• Refrigerate for 2 hours. • Preheat the oven
to 325°F (170°C/gas 3). • Butter two cookie
sheets and line with parchment paper.
• Remove the dough from the refrigerator
and peel off the top sheet of plastic wrap.
• Use a 2-inch (5-cm) cookie cutter to cut out
cookies. Gather the dough scraps, re-roll, and
continue cutting out cookies until all the
dough is used. • Transfer to the prepared
baking sheets, spacing well. • Bake until
firm to the touch, 10–15 minutes.
• Let cool completely.

$1^2/_3$ cups (250 g) all-purpose (plain) flour

2 tablespoons unsweetened cocoa powder

¼ teaspoon salt

1 cup (250 g) butter, softened

1 cup (150 g) confectioners' (icing) sugar

1 teaspoon vanilla extract (essence)

Makes: about 30 cookies
Preparation: 40 minutes + 2 hours to chill
Cooking: 15–20 minutes
Level: 2

HAZELNUT COOKIES

88

Process the raw sugar, hazelnuts, flour, and salt in a food processor until well blended. • Add the butter and process briefly until the mixture resembles fine crumbs. • Add the egg and process briefly to mix. • Gather the dough together and press into a disk. Wrap in plastic wrap (cling film) and refrigerate for 30 minutes. • Preheat the oven to 350°F (180°C/gas 4). • Line two cookie sheets with parchment paper. • Roll out the dough on a lightly floured surface to $\frac{1}{8}$-inch (3-mm) thick. • Use a $2\frac{1}{2}$-inch (6-cm) cookie cutter to cut out the cookies. Gather the dough scraps, re-roll, and continue cutting out cookies until all the dough is used.
• Use a spatula to transfer the cookies to the prepared cookie sheets, spacing them 1 inch (2.5 cm) apart. • Bake until lightly browned, 12–15 minutes. • Transfer to racks to cool.

½ cup (100 g) raw sugar (Demerara or Barbados)

1⅔ cups (250 g) finely ground hazelnuts

1½ cups (225 g) all-purpose (plain) flour

⅛ teaspoon salt

⅔ cup (150 g) butter, cut up

1 large egg yolk, lightly beaten

Makes: 32–36 cookies
Preparation: 40 minutes + 30 minutes to chill
Cooking: 12–15 minutes
Level: 1

SUGAR SNAPS

Beat the egg yolk and milk in a small bowl until frothy. • Mix the flour, sugar, butter, and salt in a medium bowl. • Use a wooden spoon to stir in the beaten egg mixture until well blended. • Press the dough into a disk, wrap in plastic wrap (cling film), and refrigerate for 30 minutes. • Preheat the oven to 400°F (200°C/gas 6). • Butter a cookie sheet. • Roll out the dough on a lightly floured surface to ⅛-inch (3-mm) thick. • Use a 2-inch (5-cm) cookie cutter to cut out the cookies. Gather the dough scraps, re-roll, and continue cutting out cookies until all the dough is used. • Use a spatula to transfer the cookies to the prepared cookie sheet, placing them 1 inch (2.5 cm) apart. • Bake until lightly browned, 5–8 minutes. • Cool on the sheet until the cookies firm slightly. Transfer to a rack and let cool completely.

1 large egg yolk
2 tablespoons milk
1¼ cups (180 g) all-purpose (plain) flour
⅓ cup (70 g) granulated sugar
2 tablespoons butter, melted
⅛ teaspoon salt

Makes: about 16 cookies
Preparation: 40 minutes + 30 minutes to chill
Cooking: 5–8 minutes
Level: 1

SICILIAN CRISPS

Mix the flour, cornmeal, and salt in a large
bowl. • Use a pastry blender to cut in the
butter until the mixture resembles fine
crumbs. • Stir in the sugar, egg yolks,
Marsala, and orange zest to form a stiff
dough. • Press the dough into a disk, wrap
in plastic wrap (cling film), and refrigerate
for 30 minutes. • Preheat the oven to 350°F
(180°C/gas 4). • Butter two cookie sheets.
• Roll out the dough on a lightly floured
surface to ¼-inch (5-mm) thick. • Use a fluted
2-inch (5-cm) cookie cutter to cut out the
cookies. Gather the dough scraps, re-roll,
and continue cutting out cookies until all the
dough is used. • Use a spatula to transfer the
cookies to the prepared cookie sheets, placing
them 1 inch (2.5 cm) apart. • Bake until just
golden, 15–20 minutes. • Transfer to racks
to cool.

1   cup (150 g) all-purpose
    (plain) flour
1   cup (150 g) finely
    ground polenta
    (yellow cornmeal)
⅛   teaspoon salt
⅔   cup (150 g) butter,
    cut up
¾   cup (150 g) granulated
    sugar
3   large egg yolks,
    lightly beaten
1   tablespoon Marsala
    wine
    Finely grated zest
    of 1 orange

Makes: 25–30 cookies
Preparation: 40 minutes
  + 30 minutes to chill
Cooking: 10–15 minutes
Level: 1

92

VANILLA CRISPS

Mix the flour, cornstarch, baking powder, and salt in a large bowl. • Use a pastry blender to cut in the butter until the mixture resembles fine crumbs. • Mix in the sugar, eggs, and vanilla to form a smooth dough. • Press into a disk, wrap in plastic wrap (cling film) and refrigerate for 30 minutes. • Preheat the oven to 375°F (190°C/gas 5). • Butter two cookie sheets. • Roll out the dough on a lightly floured surface to ¼-inch (5-mm) thick.
• Use a 2-inch (5-cm) cookie cutter to cut out the cookies. Gather the dough scraps, re-roll, and continue cutting out cookies until all the dough is used. • Use a spatula to transfer the cookies to the cookie sheets, placing them 1 inch (2.5 cm) apart. • Prick the cookies all over with a fork. • Bake until just golden at the edges, 10–15 minutes. • Transfer to racks and let cool completely.

1²⁄₃ cups (250 g) all-purpose (plain) flour

¾ cup (125 g) cornstarch (cornflour)

1 teaspoon baking powder

½ cup (125 g) butter, cut up

⅛ teaspoon salt

¾ cup (150 g) granulated sugar

2 large eggs, lightly beaten

1 teaspoon vanilla extract (essence)

Makes: about 30 cookies
Preparation: 40 minutes
 + 30 minutes to chill
Cooking: 10–15 minutes
Level: 1

CITRUS MOONS

Cookies: Mix the flour and salt in a medium bowl. • Beat the butter and confectioners' sugar in a large bowl with an electric mixer at high speed until creamy. • Add the egg, egg yolk, and vanilla, beating until just blended. • Mix in the dry ingredients. • Divide the dough in half. Knead the orange zest into one half and lemon zest into the other. • Press each dough into a disk, wrap in plastic wrap (cling film), and refrigerate for 30 minutes. • Preheat the oven to 350°F (180°C/gas 4). • Set out three cookie sheets. • Roll out the dough on a lightly floured surface to ¼-inch (5-mm) thick. • Use 2-inch (5-cm) crescent-shaped cookie cutters to cut out the cookies. Gather the dough scraps, re-roll, and continue cutting out cookies until all the dough is used. • Transfer to the cookie sheets, spacing well. Topping: Beat the egg yolk and water in a small bowl. Brush over the cookies and decorate with almonds. • Bake until the edges are lightly golden, 8–10 minutes. • Transfer to racks to cool.

Cookies

- 1⅔ cups (250 g) all-purpose (plain) flour
- ⅛ teaspoon salt
- ½ cup (125 g) butter, softened
- ¾ cup (125 g) confectioners' (icing) sugar
- 1 large egg + 1 large egg yolk
- 1 teaspoon vanilla extract (essence)
- Finely grated zest of 1 orange
- Finely grated zest of ½ lemon

Topping

- 1 large egg yolk
- 1 tablespoon water
- 2 tablespoons flaked almonds

Makes: 20–25 cookies
Preparation: 45 minutes + 30 minutes to chill
Cooking: 8–10 minutes
Level: 1

GLAZED ORANGE CRISPS

98

Cookies: Beat the butter and sugar in a large bowl until creamy. • Add the egg yolk and orange zest. • Mix in the flour to form a stiff dough. Refrigerate for 30 minutes. • Preheat the oven to 350°F (180°C/gas 4). • Butter and flour a cookie sheet. • Roll out the dough to ⅛-inch (3-mm) thick. • Use a fluted cutter to stamp out small rounds. Continue cutting out cookies until all the dough is used. • Use a spatula to transfer the cookies to the prepared cookie sheet. • Bake until golden around the edges, 8–10 minutes. • Cool the cookies on the sheet for 2 minutes. Transfer to racks to cool. • Glaze: Mix the confectioners' sugar with enough orange juice to make a pourable glaze. • Drizzle the glaze in a zigzag pattern over the cookies.

Cookies
⅓ cup (90 g) butter, softened
5 tablespoons granulated sugar
1 large egg yolk
Finely grated zest of 1 orange
1¼ cups (180 g) all-purpose (plain) flour

Glaze
⅔ cup (100 g) confectioners' (icing) sugar
1 tablespoon freshly squeezed orange juice + more as needed

Makes: 20 cookies
Preparation: 40 minutes + 30 minutes to chill
Cooking: 8–10 minutes
Level: 1

SPIDER'S WEB COOKIES

Prepare the cookies and let cool completely. <u>Fondant:</u> Bring the sugar, water, and cream of tartar to a boil in a medium saucepan. Wash down the sides of the pan with a pastry brush dipped in cold water to prevent sugar crystals from forming. Cook, without stirring, until the mixture reaches 238°F (114°C), or the soft-ball stage. • Sprinkle a lightly oiled baking sheet with cold water. Pour the fondant syrup onto the sheet and let cool until warm, 10–15 minutes. When ready, the fondant should hold an indentation made with a fingertip. • Work the fondant, lifting from the edges toward the center, folding it until it begins to thicken, lose its gloss, and turn pure white. • Dust your hands with confectioners' sugar and knead the fondant until smooth. Place in a bowl and cover with a clean cloth. Let stand overnight. • Knead the fondant until malleable. Roll out on a surface lightly dusted with confectioners' sugar to ¼-inch (5-mm) thick. • Drape the fondant over the cookies and cut out rounds of fondant to fit the tops of the cookies. • Warm the preserves in a small saucepan over low heat until liquid. • Spread the

2 recipes Sugar and Cinnamon Snaps (see page 64)

Fondant

2 cups (400 g) granulated sugar

¾ cup (180 ml) cold water

¼ teaspoon cream of tartar

2 tablespoons confectioners' (icing) sugar, to dust

½ cup (160 g) apricot preserves (jam)

4 oz (125 g) bittersweet (dark) chocolate, coarsely chopped

Makes: about 30 cookies
Preparation: 1 hour + overnight to stand
Cooking: 8–10 minutes
Level: 3

preserves over the cookies and place the fondant layers on top. • Melt the chocolate in a double boiler over barely simmering water. • Spoon the chocolate into a freezer bag and cut off a tiny corner. • Pipe over the cookies in concentric circles. • Let stand for 5 minutes until set. • Draw through the lines from the center outward to create a spider's web effect.

CINNAMON SPICE COOKIES

Mix the flour, cinnamon, cloves, and salt in a medium bowl. • Beat the butter and sugar in a large bowl until creamy. • Add the egg yolk, beating until just blended. • Mix in the dry ingredients and enough milk to form a soft dough. • Press the dough into a disk, wrap in plastic wrap (cling film), and refrigerate for 30 minutes. • Preheat the oven to 350°F (180°C/gas 4). • Butter a cookie sheet. • Roll out the dough on a lightly floured surface to 1/2-inch (1-cm) thick. • Use a 2-inch (5-cm) cookie cutter to cut out the cookies. Gather the dough scraps, re-roll, and continue cutting out cookies until all the dough is used. • Use a sharp knife to mark a cross on top of each cookie. • Use a spatula to transfer the cookies to the prepared cookie sheet. • Bake until deep golden, 10–15 minutes. • Transfer to racks to cool.

3/4 cup (125 g) all-purpose (plain) flour
1/2 teaspoon ground cinnamon
1/4 teaspoon ground cloves
1/8 teaspoon salt
1/3 cup (90 g) butter, softened
1/3 cup (70 g) granulated sugar
1 large egg yolk
2 tablespoons milk + more as needed

Makes: 12–16 cookies
Preparation: 40 minutes + 30 minutes to chill
Cooking: 10–15 minutes
Level: 1

CINNAMON CRISPS

Mix the flour, cinnamon, cloves, ginger, and baking powder in a large bowl.
• Melt the butter with the sugar and corn syrup in a medium saucepan. • Let cool for 10 minutes. • Stir in the almonds, lemon zest, and candied peel. • Mix in the dry ingredients. • Refrigerate for 1 hour, or until firm. • Preheat the oven to 375°F (190°C/gas 5). • Butter two cookie sheets. • Roll out the dough a 1/4-inch (5-mm) thick. • Use a 2-inch (5-cm) cookie cutter to cut out the cookies. Continue cutting out cookies until all the dough is used. • Transfer the cookies to the prepared cookie sheets, placing them 1 inch (2.5 cm) apart. • Place a flaked almond piece on each cookie. • Bake until just golden, 8–10 minutes. • Transfer to racks to cool.

2 cups (300 g) all-purpose (plain) flour
2 tablespoons ground cinnamon
2 teaspoons ground cloves
1½ teaspoons ground ginger
1 teaspoon baking powder
¼ teaspoon salt
⅔ cup (150 g) butter, cut up
¾ cup (150 g) granulated sugar
½ cup (125 ml) light corn syrup (golden syrup)
⅓ cup (30 g) coarsely chopped almonds
1 tablespoon finely grated lemon zest
1 tablespoon finely chopped mixed candied peel
1 tablespoon flaked almonds

Makes: 28–32 cookies
Preparation: 40 minutes + 1 hour to chill
Cooking: 8–10 minutes
Level: 1

DRIED CURRANT COOKIES

108

Preheat the oven to 325°F (170°C/gas 3).
• Butter a cookie sheet. • Mix the flour, baking powder, and salt in a medium bowl.
• Beat the butter and sugar in a large bowl with an electric mixer at high speed until creamy. • Add the egg, beating until just blended. • Mix in the flour to form a smooth dough. • Knead in the currants. • Transfer the dough to a lightly floured surface and roll out to ¼-inch (5-mm) thick. • Use a 3-inch (8-cm) cookie cutter to cut out the cookies.
• Gather the dough scraps, re-roll, and continue cutting out the cookies until all the dough is used. • Arrange on the prepared cookie sheets, placing them 1 inch (2.5 cm) apart. • Bake until lightly browned, 10–15 minutes. • Transfer to racks to cool.

1⅓ cups (200 g) all-purpose (plain) flour

1 teaspoon baking powder

⅛ teaspoon salt

⅓ cup (90 g) butter, softened

1 cup (200 g) granulated sugar

1 large egg, lightly beaten

1 tablespoon dried currants

Makes: about 16 cookies
Preparation: 40 minutes
Cooking: 10–15 minutes
Level: 1

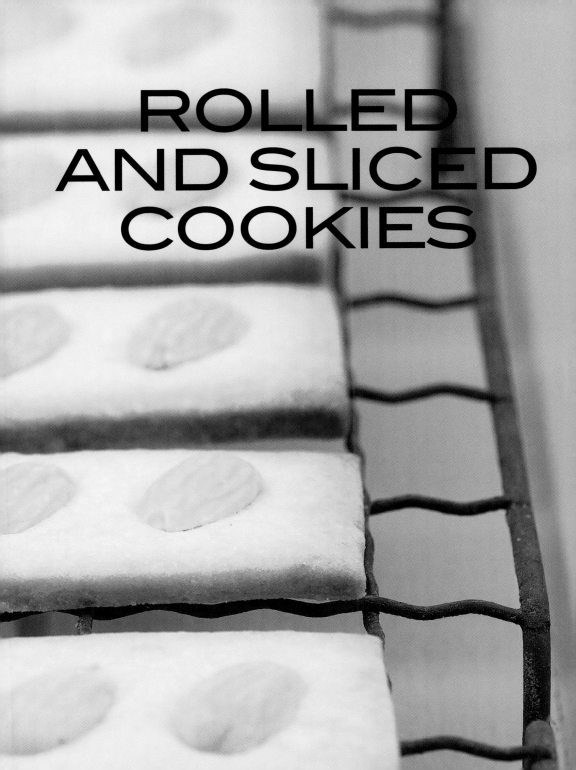

ROLLED AND SLICED COOKIES

SUNFLOWER AND GINGER COOKIES

<u>Cookies</u>: Mix the flour, baking powder, cinnamon, and salt in a medium bowl.
• Beat the butter and brown sugar in a large bowl with an electric mixer at high speed until creamy. • Add the egg, beating until just blended. • Mix in the raisins, apricots, almonds, and sunflower seeds. • Mix in the dry ingredients to form a soft dough. • Form the dough into a 14-inch (35-cm) log, wrap in plastic wrap (cling film), and refrigerate for 30 minutes. • Preheat the oven to 350°F (180°C/gas 4). • Line two cookie sheets with parchment paper. • Slice the dough ½-inch (1-cm) thick and place 1 inch (2.5 cm) apart on the prepared cookie sheets. • Bake until just golden, 10–15 minutes. • Transfer to racks and let cool completely. • <u>Glaze</u>: Heat the preserves and butter in a small saucepan over low heat and simmer for 2 minutes.
• Drizzle the glaze over the cookies.

Cookies

⅔ cup (100 g) all-purpose (plain) flour

½ teaspoon baking powder

¼ teaspoon ground cinnamon

⅛ teaspoon salt

¼ cup (60 g) butter, softened

¼ cup (50 g) firmly packed light brown sugar

1 large egg

½ cup (90 g) finely chopped raisins

¼ cup (50 g) finely chopped dried apricots

½ cup (50 g) finely chopped almonds

¼ cup (50 g) finely chopped sunflower seeds

Glaze

½ cup (160 g) ginger preserves

2 tablespoons butter

Makes: about 28 cookies
Preparation: 40 minutes
+ 30 minutes to chill
Cooking: 10–15 minutes
Level: 2

SESAME COOKIES

114

Plump the raisins in the brandy in a small bowl for 15 minutes. Drain and pat dry with paper towels. • Mix the flour, cornstarch, sugar, baking powder, cinnamon, and salt in a large bowl. • Stir in the oil, butter, sesame seeds, and raisins. • Add enough water to form a smooth dough. • Form the dough into a log 1 inch (2.5 cm) in diameter, wrap in plastic wrap (cling film), and refrigerate for at least 30 minutes. • Preheat the oven to 350°F (180°C/gas 4). • Butter two cookie sheets. • Slice the dough ½ inch (1 cm) thick and place 1 inch (2.5 cm) apart on the prepared cookie sheets. • Bake until golden, 15–20 minutes. • Transfer to racks and let cool completely.

■■■ Be sure to use only the freshest, extra-virgin olive oil in this Italian recipe. If the olive oil is old or not top quality it will spoil the flavor of the cookies. Replace with another vegetable oil, if preferred.

- ⅓ cup (60 g) golden raisins
- ½ cup (125 ml) brandy
- 1 cup (150 g) all-purpose (plain) flour
- 1 cup (150 g) cornstarch (cornflour
- ⅔ cup (140 g) granulated sugar
- 1 teaspoon baking powder
- ¼ teaspoon ground cinnamon
- ⅛ teaspoon salt
- 2 tablespoons extra-virgin olive oil
- ⅔ cup (150 g) butter, softened
- 1¼ cups (125 g) sesame seeds, toasted
- ½ cup (125 ml) water, + more, as needed

Makes: about 35 cookies
Preparation: 55 minutes
    + 30 minutes to chill
Cooking: 15–20 minutes
Level: 1

DATE CHOCOLATE CHIP COOKIES

Mix the flour, baking soda, and salt in a large bowl. • Beat the shortening and brown and granulated sugars in a large bowl with an electric mixer at high speed until creamy. • Add the eggs, beating until just blended. • Mix in the dry ingredients, oats, corn flakes, dates, and chocolate chips to form a stiff dough. • Divide the dough in half. Form into two 8-inch (20-cm) long logs, wrap in plastic wrap (cling film), and refrigerate for at least 30 minutes. • Preheat the oven to 375°F (190°C/gas 5). • Butter two cookie sheets. • Slice the dough ¼-inch (5-mm) thick and place 2 inches (5 cm) apart on the prepared cookie sheets. • Bake until lightly golden, 10–12 minutes. • Cool on the sheets until the cookies firm slightly. Transfer to racks to cool completely.

1 cup (150 g) all-purpose (plain) flour
½ teaspoon baking soda (bicarbonate of soda)
¼ teaspoon salt
½ cup (125 g) vegetable shortening
½ cup (100 g) firmly packed light brown sugar
½ cup (100 g) granulated sugar
2 large eggs
1 cup (150 g) old-fashioned rolled oats
½ cup (50 g) corn flakes
½ cup (50 g) finely chopped dates
½ cup (90 g) semisweet (dark) chocolate chips

Makes: about 50 cookies
Preparation: 45 minutes
 + 30 minutes to chill
Cooking: 10–12 minutes
Level: 2

CHERRY COOKIES

Mix the flour, baking powder, and salt in a large bowl. • Use a pastry blender to cut in the butter until the mixture resembles fine crumbs. • Add the egg, beating until just blended. • Stir in the sugar, cherries, and vanilla to form a soft dough. • Turn the dough out onto a lightly floured surface and knead until smooth. • Form the dough into a long log 2 inches (5 cm) in diameter, wrap in plastic wrap (cling film), and refrigerate for at least 30 minutes. • Preheat the oven to 375°F (190°C/gas 5). • Butter three cookie sheets. • Slice the dough ½-inch (1-cm) thick and place 1 inch (2.5 cm) apart on the prepared cookie sheets. • Bake until just golden, 8–10 minutes. • Transfer to racks to cool.

$1^2/_3$ cups (250 g) all-purpose (plain) flour

1 teaspoon baking powder

⅛ teaspoon salt

½ cup (125 g) butter, cut up

1 large egg, lightly beaten

¾ cup (150 g) granulated sugar

½ cup (50 g) finely chopped candied cherries

1 teaspoon vanilla extract (essence)

Makes: about 35 cookies
Preparation: 40 minutes
 + 30 minutes to chill
Cooking: 8–10 minutes
Level: 1

SPICED ALMOND COOKIES

Mix the flour, baking powder, cinnamon, allspice, cloves, and salt in a medium bowl. • Beat the eggs and sugar in a large bowl with an electric mixer at high speed until pale and thick. • Mix in the dry ingredients, almonds, chocolate, candied peel, and lemon zest to form a smooth dough. • Press the dough into a disk, wrap in plastic wrap (cling film), and refrigerate for 30 minutes. • Preheat the oven to 325°F (170°C/gas 3). • Line three cookie sheets with parchment paper. • Roll out the dough on a lightly floured surface to ¼-inch (5-mm) thick. • Cut into 2-inch (5 cm) squares and triangles. Gather the dough scraps, re-roll, and continue cutting out cookies until all the dough is used. • Use a spatula to transfer the cookies to the prepared cookie sheets, placing them 1 inch (2.5 cm) apart. • Bake until the edges are firm, 12–15 minutes. • Transfer to racks to cool. • Drizzle the glaze over the cookies and let stand until set.

2 cups (300 g) all-purpose (plain) flour

1 teaspoon baking powder

1 teaspoon ground cinnamon

½ teaspoon allspice

¼ teaspoon ground cloves

⅛ teaspoon salt

3 large eggs

1½ cups (300 g) granulated sugar

2½ cups (350 g) ground almonds

4 oz (125 g) semisweet (dark) chocolate, grated

½ cup (50 g) each finely chopped candied lemon and orange peel

1 teaspoon finely grated lemon zest

½ recipe chocolate glaze (see page 697)

Makes: 35–40 cookies
Preparation: 50 minutes
  + 1 hour to chill and set
Cooking: 12–15 minutes
Level: 2

POLENTA COOKIES WITH POPPY SEEDS

122

Place the polenta, flour, baking powder, and salt in a large bowl. • Stir in the sugar, butter, and 2 eggs. • Add the wine and mix to form a smooth dough. • Press the dough into a disk, wrap in plastic wrap (cling film), and refrigerate for 30 minutes. • Preheat the oven to 400°F (200°C/gas 6). • Butter two cookie sheets. • Roll out the dough on a lightly floured surface to ¼-inch (5-mm) thick. • Cut into 2-inch (5-cm) triangles and place 1 inch (2.5 cm) apart on the prepared cookie sheets. • Beat the remaining egg with the milk in a small bowl. Brush over the cookies. • Sprinkle with the poppy seeds and confectioners sugar. • Bake until just golden, 10–15 minutes. • Transfer to racks to cool.

1⅓ cups (200 g) finely ground polenta (yellow cornmeal)

1⅓ cups (200 g) all-purpose (plain) flour

2 teaspoons baking powder

⅛ teaspoon salt

¾ cup (150 g) granulated sugar

⅔ cup (150 g) butter, softened

3 large eggs, lightly beaten

2 teaspoons dry white wine

1 tablespoon milk

⅓ cup (40 g) poppy seeds

⅓ cup (50 g) confectioners' (icing) sugar

Makes: about 36 cookies
Preparation: 40 minutes
  + 30 minutes to chill
Cooking: 10–15 minutes
Level: 1

PASSIONFRUIT BUTTER DIAMONDS

Butter Cookie Base: Mix both flours and salt in a medium bowl. • Beat the butter and sugar in a large bowl with an electric mixer at high speed until creamy. • Mix in the dry ingredients. • Turn the dough out onto a lightly floured surface and knead until smooth. • Press the dough into a disk, wrap in plastic wrap (cling film), and refrigerate for 30 minutes. • Preheat the oven to 300°F (150°C/gas 2). • Line four cookie sheets with parchment paper. • Roll out the dough on a lightly floured surface to ¼-inch (5-mm) thick. • Cut into 1½-inch (4-cm) diamonds. • Transfer to the prepared cookie sheets, spacing well. • Bake until just golden at the edges, 12–15 minutes. • Transfer to racks to cool. • Passionfruit Drizzle: Mix the confectioners' sugar, passionfruit pulp, butter, and water in a double boiler over barely simmering water until smooth. • Drizzle over the cookies. • Melt the white chocolate in a double boiler over barely simmering water and drizzle over the cookies. Let stand for 30 minutes.

Butter Cookie Base
2¼cups (330 g) all-purpose (plain) flour
2 tablespoons rice flour
⅛ teaspoon salt
1 cup (250 g) butter, softened
⅓ cup (70 g) granulated sugar

Passionfruit Drizzle
1 cup (150 g) confectioners' (icing) sugar
2 tablespoons passionfruit pulp
1 tablespoon butter, softened
1 tablespoon cold water
2 oz (60 g) white chocolate, coarsely chopped

Makes: 35–40 cookies
Preparation: 40 minutes + 1 hour to chill and set
Cooking: 12–15 minutes
Level: 2

GLAZED NUT COOKIES

Cookies: Beat the egg white and salt in a large bowl with an electric mixer at medium speed until frothy. • With mixer at high speed, gradually add the sugar, beating until stiff peaks form. • Fold in the hazelnuts, almonds, pistachios, and candied peel to form a stiff dough. • Press the dough into a disk, wrap in plastic wrap (cling film), and refrigerate for 30 minutes. • Preheat the oven to 300°F (150°C/gas 2). • Line three cookie sheets with parchment paper. • Roll out the dough between sheets of waxed paper dusted with confectioners' sugar to 1/4-inch (5-mm) thick. • Cut into 2 x 3/4-inch (5 x 4-cm) strips. • Transfer to the prepared cookie sheets, spacing well. • Bake until golden brown, 12–15 minutes. • Transfer to racks to cool.
Orange Glaze: Mix the confectioners' sugar, orange juice, and orange zest in a small bowl. • Dip the cookies halfway into the glaze and let stand until set.

Cookies
- 1 large egg white
- 1/8 teaspoon salt
- 1/2 cup (100 g) superfine (caster) sugar
- 1 cup (150 g) finely ground hazelnuts + more as needed
- 1 cup (150 g) finely ground almonds + more as needed
- 1/2 cup (50 g) coarsely chopped pistachios
- 2 teaspoons finely chopped candied peel

Orange Glaze
- 2/3 cup (100 g) confectioners' (icing) sugar
- 1 tablespoon freshly squeezed orange juice
- Finely grated zest of 1/2 orange

Makes: 35–40 cookies
Preparation: 45 minutes + 1 hour to chill and set
Cooking: 12–15 minutes
Level: 2

ORTHODOX COOKIES

Mix the flour, baking powder, and salt in a medium bowl. • Beat the butter and sugar in a large bowl with an electric mixer at high speed until creamy. • Add the aniseeds and lemon zest. • With mixer at high speed, beat the egg, egg yolk, and 2 tablespoons milk in a large bowl until frothy. • Beat the egg mixture into the batter. • Mix in the dry ingredients to form a smooth dough. • Divide the dough in half. • Form into 3-inch (8-cm) thick logs, wrap in plastic wrap (cling film), and refrigerate for at least 30 minutes. • Preheat the oven to 375°F (190°C/gas 5). • Line two cookie sheets with parchment paper. • Discard the plastic wrap. • Cut the logs into $\frac{1}{2}$-inch (1-cm) thick slices. • Place the cookies 1 inch (2.5 cm) apart on the prepared cookie sheets. • Mix the egg white and remaining milk in a small bowl. • Brush over the cookies and sprinkle with sesame seeds. • Bake until just golden at the edges, 8–10 minutes. • Transfer to racks and let cool.

$1\frac{1}{3}$ cups (200 g) all-purpose (plain) flour

1 teaspoon baking powder

$\frac{1}{8}$ teaspoon salt

$\frac{1}{2}$ cup (125 g) butter, softened

$\frac{1}{2}$ cup (100 g) granulated sugar

1 teaspoon ground aniseeds

1 teaspoon finely grated lemon zest

1 large egg + 1 large egg yolk + 1 large egg white

2 tablespoons + 1 teaspoon milk

4 tablespoons sesame seeds

Makes: about 32 cookies
Preparation: 40 minutes
+ 30 minutes to chill
Cooking: 8–10 minutes
Level: 2

COCONUT LIME COOKIES

Mix the flour and salt in a medium bowl.
• Beat the butter and sugar in a large bowl
with an electric mixer at high speed until
creamy. • Add the eggs, beating until just
blended. • Add the lime zest, lime juice, and
vanilla and almond extracts. • Mix in the dry
ingredients and ¾ cup (90 g) of coconut to
form a stiff dough. • Divide the dough in half.
Form the dough into two logs 2 inches (5 cm)
in diameter, wrap each in plastic wrap (cling
film), and flatten slightly to form oblongs.
• Refrigerate for at least 30 minutes.
• Preheat the oven to 375°F (190°C/gas 5).
• Butter three cookie sheets. • Discard the
plastic wrap. • Slice the dough ¼ inch (5 mm)
thick and place 1 inch (2.5 cm) apart on the
prepared cookie sheets. • Sprinkle with the
remaining coconut. • Bake until just golden,
10–12 minutes. • Transfer to racks and
let cool completely.

2¼ cups (330 g) all-
    purpose (plain) flour
½ teaspoon salt
1 cup (250 g) butter,
    softened
1 cup (200 g) granulated
    sugar
2 large eggs, lightly
    beaten
    Finely grated zest
    of 1 lime
1 tablespoon freshly
    squeezed lime juice
½ teaspoon vanilla extract
    (essence)
½ teaspoon almond
    extract (essence)
1 cup (125 g) shredded
    (desiccated) coconut

Makes: about 36 cookies
Preparation: 40 minutes
    + 30 minutes to chill
Cooking: 10–12 minutes
Level: 1

RISORGIMENTO COOKIES

Mix the flour, baking powder, cinnamon, and salt in a medium bowl. • Beat the butter, vegetable shortening, ½ cup (100 g) of granulated sugar, and brown sugar in a large bowl with an electric mixer at high speed until creamy. • Dissolve 1 tablespoon of the coffee granules in the hot water. • Add the coffee mixture and egg, beating until just blended. • Mix in the dry ingredients to form a stiff dough. • Divide the dough in half. Form into two 7-inch (18-cm) long logs, wrap in plastic wrap (cling film), and refrigerate for 1 hour. • Preheat the oven to 375°F (190°C/gas 5). • Butter four cookie sheets. • Slice the dough ¼-inch (5-mm) thick and place 1 inch (2.5 cm) apart on the prepared cookie sheets. • Mix the remaining granulated sugar and 1 teaspoon coffee granules in a small bowl. Sprinkle over the tops of the cookies and decorate with the coffee beans. • Bake until pale gold, 8–10 minutes. • Cool on the sheets until the cookies firm slightly. Transfer to racks to finish cooling.

1 cup (150 g) all-purpose (plain) flour

½ teaspoon baking powder

½ teaspoon ground cinnamon

⅛ teaspoon salt

½ cup (125 g) butter, softened

2 tablespoons vegetable shortening

½ cup (100 g) + 2 tablespoons granulated sugar

¼ cup (50 g) firmly packed light brown sugar

1 tablespoon + 1 teaspoon instant coffee granules

1 large egg

2 teaspoon hot water

Coffee beans, to decorate

Makes: about 56 cookies
Preparation: 40 minutes + 1 hour to chill
Cooking: 8–10 minutes
Level: 1

WHITE CHOCOLATE CHIP COOKIES

134

Mix the flour, baking powder, and salt in a medium bowl. • Beat the butter, oil, and brown sugar in a large bowl with an electric mixer at high speed until creamy. • Add the egg and vanilla, beating until just blended. • Mix in the dry ingredients, chocolate chips, and walnuts. • Form the dough into a 7-inch (18-cm) long log, wrap in plastic wrap (cling film), and refrigerate for at least 30 minutes. • Preheat the oven to 375°F (190°C/gas 5). • Butter two cookie sheets. • Slice the dough ¼ inch (5-mm) thick and place 2 inches (5 cm) apart on the prepared cookie sheets. • Bake until just golden at the edges, 8–10 minutes. • Transfer to racks to cool.

1²/₃ cups (250 g) all-purpose (plain) flour

1½ teaspoons baking powder

¼ teaspoon salt

½ cup (125 g) butter, softened

¼ cup (60 ml) sunflower or peanut oil

¾ cup (150 g) firmly packed light brown sugar

1 large egg, lightly beaten

½ teaspoon vanilla extract (essence)

1 cup (180 g) white chocolate chips

1 cup (100 g) chopped walnuts

Makes: about 28 cookies
Preparation: 40 minutes
 + 30 minutes to chill
Cooking: 8–10 minutes
Level: 1

■■■*If liked, substitute the white chocolate chips with milk or semisweet (dark) chocolate chips.*

CHECKERBOARD COOKIES

Mix the flour, baking powder, and salt in a bowl. • Beat the butter, sugar, and vanilla with an electric mixer at high speed until creamy. • Mix in the dry ingredients to form a stiff dough. • Divide the dough in half. Knead the cocoa powder into one half. Wrap both pieces of dough in plastic wrap (cling film) and refrigerate for at least 30 minutes. • Cut each portion in three and form into logs 1 inch (2.5 cm) in diameter. Press the edges of the logs to make them into even-sided oblongs. • Arrange the chocolate logs and plain logs on top of each other in a checkerboard pattern. • Seal the sections together by brushing them with a little egg white. The dough will now be rectangular in shape. • Wrap in plastic wrap and refrigerate for at least 1 hour. • Preheat the oven to 375°F (190°C/gas 5). • Butter two large cookie sheets. • Slice the dough ¼-inch (5-mm) thick and place 1½ inches (4 cm) apart on the prepared cookie sheets. • Bake until lightly browned and the edges are firm, 10–15 minutes. • Transfer to racks to cool.

1⅓ cups (200 g) all-purpose (plain) flour
½ teaspoon baking powder
⅛ teaspoon salt
⅔ cup (150 g) butter, softened
½ cup (100 g) granulated sugar
½ teaspoon vanilla extract (essence)
2 tablespoons unsweetened cocoa powder
1 large egg white, lightly beaten

Makes: about 20 cookies
Preparation: 50 minutes + 90 minutes to chill
Cooking: 10–15 minutes
Level: 2

FIJIAN COOKIES

Beat the butter and cream cheese in a large bowl with an electric mixer at medium speed for 1 minute. • Beat in the confectioners' sugar, baking soda, and salt. • Add the egg, beating until just blended. • Beat in the orange zest, juice, and vanilla. • Mix in the flour to form a soft dough. • Turn the dough out on a lightly floured surface and knead until smooth. • Divide the dough in half. Form into two 8-inch (20-cm) long logs and roll each in the coconut. Wrap in plastic wrap (cling film), and refrigerate for at least 30 minutes. • Preheat the oven to 375°F (190°C/gas 5). • Set out three cookie sheets. • Slice the dough ¼ inch (5 mm) thick and place 1 inch (2.5 cm) apart on the cookie sheets. • Bake until just golden, 8–10 minutes. • Cool on the sheet until the cookies firm slightly. Transfer to racks to finish cooling.

½ cup (125 g) butter, softened

½ cup (125 g) cream cheese, softened

1¼ cups (180 g) confectioners' (icing) sugar

¼ teaspoon baking soda (bicarbonate of soda)

¼ teaspoon salt

1 large egg, lightly beaten

1 tablespoon finely grated orange zest

1 tablespoon freshly squeezed orange juice

½ teaspoon vanilla extract (essence)

2¼ cups (330 g) all-purpose (plain) flour

½ cup (60 g) shredded (desiccated) coconut

Makes: about 64 cookies
Preparation: 40 minutes
 + 30 minutes to chill
Cooking: 8–10 minutes
Level: 2

LEMON ZEST COOKIES

Mix the flour, baking powder, baking soda, and salt in a medium bowl. • Beat the butter, and both sugars in a large bowl with an electric mixer at high speed until creamy. • Add the eggs, beating until just blended. • Stir in the vanilla and lemon zest and juice. • Mix in the dry ingredients until well blended. • Add enough milk to form a soft, but not sticky dough. • Turn the cookie dough onto a lightly floured surface and knead until smooth. • Divide the dough in half. Form each half into a 12-inch (30-cm) long log, wrap in plastic wrap (cling film), and refrigerate for 30 minutes. • Preheat the oven to 400°F (200°C/gas 6). • Butter two cookie sheets • Slice the dough ¼-inch (5-mm) thick and place 1 inch (2.5 cm) apart on the prepared cookie sheets. • Bake until lightly browned and firm around the edges, 8–10 minutes. • Transfer to racks to cool.

3   cups (450 g) all-purpose (plain) flour
1   teaspoon baking powder
½   teaspoon baking soda (bicarbonate of soda)
½   teaspoon salt
1   cup (250 g) butter, softened
¾   cup (150 g) granulated sugar
¾   cup (150 g) firmly packed light brown sugar
2   large eggs, lightly beaten
1   teaspoon vanilla extract (essence)
1   teaspoon finely grated lemon zest
1   teaspoon freshly squeezed lemon juice
2   tablespoons milk, + more, as needed

Makes: about 40 cookies
Preparation: 40 minutes
    + 30 minutes to chill
Cooking: 8–10 minutes
Level: 1

CHERRY FINGERS

Preheat oven to 350°F (180°C/gas 4).
• Line a baking sheet with parchment paper.
• Beat the margarine and sugar in an electric
mixer on medium speed until pale and
creamy. • With mixer on low, gradually beat in
the flour. • Turn out onto a floured surface
and roll into a rectangle about ¼-inch (5-mm)
thick. Cut into 2½ x 1-inch (6 x 2.5-cm)
fingers. • Prick all over with a fork and
decorate with the cherries and almonds.
Transfer to the prepared baking sheet.
• Bake until just firm, but not browned,
about 15 minutes. • Remove carefully
to a wire rack and let cool completely.

½ cup (125 g) margarine

¼ cup (60 g) superfine
(caster) sugar

1¼ cups (175 g) all-
purpose (plain) flour

Candied cherries,
halved

Split blanched almonds

Makes: about 20 cookies
Preparation: 15 minutes
Cooking: 15 minutes
Level: 1

ALMOND BISCOTTI WITH CANDIED CHERRIES

Soak the cherries in the cherry brandy in a small bowl for 15 minutes. Drain and pat dry with paper towels. • Preheat the oven to 375°F (190°C/gas 5). • Butter two cookie sheets. • Mix the flour, baking powder, and salt in a large bowl. • Beat the butter and sugar in a large bowl with an electric mixer at high speed until creamy. • Add the eggs and vanilla, beating until just blended. • Mix in the dry ingredients, almonds, and cherries to form a stiff dough. • Divide the dough in half. Form the dough into two 12-inch (30-cm) logs and place 2 inches (5-cm) apart on the prepared cookie sheets, flattening them slightly. • Bake until firm to the touch, 20–25 minutes. • Transfer to a cutting board to cool for 15 minutes. • Reduce the oven temperature to 325°F (170°C/gas 3). • Cut the cookies on the diagonal into 1-inch (2.5-cm) slices. • Arrange the slices cut-side up on two cookie sheets and bake for 10–15 minutes, or until golden and toasted. • Transfer to racks to cool.

¼ cup (30 g) candied cherries

1 tablespoon cherry brandy

1½ cups (225 g) all-purpose (plain) flour

½ teaspoon baking powder

⅛ teaspoon salt

¼ cup (60 g) butter, softened

½ cup (100 g) granulated sugar

2 large eggs

½ teaspoon vanilla extract (essence)

½ cup (50 g) coarsely chopped almonds

Makes: about 30 cookies
Preparation: 25 minutes
Cooking: 35–45 minutes
Level: 2

POLISH BREAKFAST COOKIES

Preheat the oven to 400°F (200°C/gas 6).
• Butter two cookie sheets. • Mix the flour
and salt in a large bowl. • Use a pastry
blender to cut in the butter until the mixture
resembles fine crumbs. • Stir in ⅓ cup (70 g)
of sugar and make a well in the center. • Mix
in the cream, egg, 2 tablespoons of the wine,
and the candied peel to form a smooth
dough. • Press the dough into a disk, wrap
in plastic wrap (cling film), and refrigerate for
30 minutes. • Roll out the dough on a lightly
floured surface to a large ¼-inch (5-mm) thick
rectangle. • Use a rolling pin to transfer the
dough to the prepared cookie sheets. • Brush
the remaining 1 tablespoon of wine over the
dough. Sprinkle with the remaining sugar
and almonds. • Bake until just golden, 12–15
minutes. • Cut into 2-inch (5-cm) triangles.
• Bake for 3–5 minutes more, or until firm
to the touch and golden brown. • Cool
completely on the cookie sheet.

1 cup (150 g) all-purpose (plain) flour
⅛ teaspoon salt
½ cup (125 g) butter, softened
⅓ cup (70 g) + 1 tablespoon granulated sugar
½ cup (125 ml) heavy (double) cream
1 large egg, lightly beaten
3 tablespoons sweet white wine
1 teaspoon finely chopped mixed candied peel
⅓ cup (40 g) finely chopped almonds

Makes: 30–35 cookies
Preparation: 30 minutes + 30 minutes to chill
Cooking: 15–18 minutes
Level: 1

ALMOND AND COFFEE BISCOTTI

Preheat the oven to 350°F (180°C/gas 4).
• Line three cookie sheets with parchment paper. • Spread the almonds and pistachios on separate large baking sheets. Toast until lightly golden, 7 minutes. • Chop in a food processor until finely chopped. • Coarsely grind 2 tablespoons of the coffee beans in a food processor. • Grind the remaining beans until very fine. • Mix the flour, baking powder, and salt in a large bowl. • Cut in the butter until the mixture resembles coarse crumbs.
• Mix in the almonds, pistachios, coffee beans, sugar, eggs, and coffee to form a stiff dough.
• Divide the dough in three. Form into logs about 2 inches (5 cm) in diameter and place 2 inches (5 cm) apart on the prepared cookie sheets, flattening slightly. Dust each log with cocoa powder and cinnamon. • Bake until firm to the touch, 25–30 minutes. • Transfer to a cutting board to cool for 15 minutes. • Lower the oven temperature to 300°F (150°C/gas 2).
• Cut the cookies on the diagonal into 1-inch (2.5-cm) slices. • Arrange the slices cut-side up on the cookie sheets and bake until golden and toasted, 15–20 minutes. • Transfer to racks to cool.

1 cup (150 g) almonds
½ cup (50 g) coarsely chopped pistachios
5 tablespoons coffee beans
2⅓ cups (500 g) all-purpose (plain) flour
2 teaspoons baking powder
½ teaspoon salt
½ cup (125 g) butter, cut up
1 cup (200 g) granulated sugar
3 large eggs, lightly beaten
½ cup (125 ml) strong black coffee
1 tablespoon unsweetened cocoa powder
½ teaspoon ground cinnamon

Makes: about 40 cookies
Preparation: 40 minutes
Cooking: 40–50 minutes
Level: 2

HAZELNUT CLOVE BISCOTTI

Preheat the oven to 325°F (170°C/gas 4).
• Spread the hazelnuts on a large baking sheet. Toast for 7 minutes, or until lightly golden. • Transfer to a large cotton kitchen towel. Fold the towel over the nuts and rub to remove the thin inner skins. • Discard the skins and coarsely chop the nuts. • Butter a cookie sheet. • Mix the flour, cinnamon, cloves, and salt in a medium bowl. • Beat the eggs and egg yolk and sugar in a large bowl with an electric mixer at high speed until very pale and thick. • Mix in the dry ingredients, hazelnuts, lemon zest, and vanilla to form a smooth dough. • Divide the dough in half. Form the dough into two 12-inch (30-cm) long logs about 1½ inches (4 cm) in diameter and place them 2 inches (5 cm) apart on the prepared sheet. • Bake until firm to the touch, 25–30 minutes. • Cool on the cookie sheet for 15 minutes. • Cut on the diagonal into 1½-inch (4-cm) slices. Arrange the slices cut-side up on the cookie sheets and bake until golden and toasted, 10–15 minutes. • Transfer to racks to cool.

1¼ cups (175 g) whole hazelnuts

1⅔ cups (250 g) all-purpose (plain) flour

1 teaspoon ground cinnamon

½ teaspoon ground cloves

⅛ teaspoon salt

2 large eggs + 1 egg yolk

1 cup (200 g) granulated sugar

Finely grated zest of 1 lemon

½ teaspoon vanilla extract (essence)

Makes: about 25 cookies
Preparation: 35 minutes
Cooking: 40–50 minutes
Level: 2

ALMOND SHORTBREAD

Mix the flour and salt in a medium bowl.
• Beat the butter and sugar in a large bowl
with an electric mixer at high speed until
creamy. • Add the egg and lemon zest,
beating until just blended. • Mix in the dry
ingredients to form a stiff dough. • Press the
dough into a disk, wrap in plastic wrap (cling
film), and refrigerate for 30 minutes. • Preheat
the oven to 350°F (180°C/gas 4). • Set out
two cookie sheets. • Roll out the dough on a
lightly floured surface to ¼ inch (5 mm) thick.
• Use a sharp knife to cut into 2 x 3-inch
(4 x 8-cm) rectangles. • Sprinkle the cookies
lightly with the water. • Arrange the almond
halves on top of the cookies in a diagonal line.
• Use a spatula to transfer the cookies to the
cookie sheets, placing them 1 inch (2.5 cm)
apart. • Bake until pale gold and firm to the
touch, 20–25 minutes. • Cool completely
on the sheets.

1⅓ cups (200 g) all-
purpose (plain) flour

⅛ teaspoon salt

⅔ cup (150 g) butter,
softened

½ cup (100 g) granulated
sugar

1 large egg

1 tablespoon finely grated
lemon zest

1 teaspoon iced water

¾ cup (125 g) almond
halves

Makes: 20–25 cookies
Preparation: 40 minutes
+ 30 minutes to chill
Cooking: 20–25 minutes
Level: 1

CASHEW NUT COOKIES

154

Mix the flour and salt in a large bowl.
• Use a pastry blender to cut in the butter until the mixture resembles coarse crumbs.
• Add the egg yolks, granulated sugar, cashew nuts, lemon zest, and milk to form a stiff dough. • Press the dough into a disk, wrap in plastic wrap (cling film), and refrigerate for 30 minutes. • Preheat the oven to 325°F (170°C/ gas 3). • Butter two cookie sheets.
• Roll out the dough on a lightly floured surface to ¼-inch (5-mm) thick. • Cut into 1½-inch (4-cm) wide strips, then cut the strips into 2½-inch (6-cm) rectangles. • Use a spatula to transfer the cookies to the prepared cookie sheets, placing them 1 inch (2.5 cm) apart. • Bake until just golden, 12–15 minutes.
• Transfer to racks to cool.

1⅔ cups (250 g) all-purpose (plain flour
½ teaspoon salt
¼ cup (60 g) butter, cut up
3 large egg yolks, lightly beaten
¾ cup (150 g) granulated sugar
¼ cup (25 g) coarsely chopped cashew nuts
Finely grated zest of ½ lemon
⅓ cup (90 ml) milk

Makes: about 30 cookies
Preparation: 40 minutes + 30 minutes to chill
Cooking: 12–15 minutes
Level: 1

LEMON BISCOTTI

Preheat the oven to 375°F (190°C/gas 5).
• Set out a cookie sheet. • Mix the flour,
baking powder, and salt in a medium bowl.
Stir in the aniseeds. • Beat the butter and
sugar in a large bowl with an electric mixer
at high speed until creamy. • Add the lemon
zest and eggs, beating until just blended.
• Mix in the dry ingredients to form a stiff
dough. • Divide the dough in half. Form into
two 11-inch (28-cm) long logs and place
3 inches (8 cm) apart on the cookie sheet.
• Bake until firm to the touch, 25–35 minutes.
• Transfer to a cutting board to cool for 15
minutes. • Cut on the diagonal into 1-inch
(2.5-cm) slices. • Arrange the slices cut-side
up on two cookie sheets and bake until golden
and toasted, 5–7 minutes more.
• Transfer to racks to cool.

3 cups (450 g) all-purpose (plain flour

2 teaspoons baking powder

⅛ teaspoon salt

2 teaspoons ground aniseeds

⅔ cup (150 g) butter, softened

1 cup (200 g) granulated sugar

Finely grated zest of 2 lemons

3 large eggs

Makes: 30–35 cookies
Preparation: 40 minutes
Cooking: 30–40 minutes
Level: 2

CARDAMOM BISCOTTI

<u>Cookies</u>: Preheat the oven to 350°F (180°C/gas 4). • Butter two cookie sheets. • Mix the flour, baking powder, cardamom, allspice, and salt in a medium bowl. • Stir in the sugar, candied peel, and lemon and orange zests. • Beat the eggs, egg white, and lemon extract until frothy. • Mix in the dry ingredients. • Form into three 10-inch (25-cm) logs and place 4 inches (10 cm) apart on the prepared cookie sheets. • <u>Glaze</u>: Mix the egg yolk and milk and brush over the logs. Sprinkle with sugar and cardamom.
• Bake until firm, 25–30 minutes. • Transfer to a cutting board. • Reduce the oven temperature to 300°F (150°C/gas 2).
• Cut on the diagonal into 1-inch (2.5-cm) slices. • Arrange the slices cut-side up on two cookie sheets and bake until golden and toasted, 8–10 minutes. • Transfer to racks to cool.

Cookies

2½ cups (375 g) all-purpose (plain) flour

1 teaspoon baking powder

1 teaspoon ground cardamom

¼ teaspoon ground allspice

¼ teaspoon salt

1¼ cups (250 g) raw sugar (Barbados or Demerara)

2 large eggs + 1 large egg white

1 teaspoon lemon extract (essence)

2 tablespoons finely chopped candied mixed peel

1 tablespoon finely grated lemon zest

1 tablespoon finely grated orange peel

Glaze

1 large egg yolk

1 tablespoon milk

1 teaspoon sugar

¼ teaspoon ground cardamom

Makes: about 35 cookies
Preparation: 40 minutes
Cooking: 33–40 minutes
Level: 2

DRIED FRUIT BISCOTTI

Preheat the oven to 325°F (170°C/gas 3).
• Spread the blanched almonds on a large
baking sheet. Toast until lightly golden, about
7 minutes. • Let cool completely then cut
the almonds in half. • Increase the oven
temperature to 350°F (180°C/gas 4). • Line
a cookie sheet with parchment paper. • Toast
the pine nuts in a frying pan over medium heat
until lightly golden, 5–7 minutes. • Mix the flour,
baking powder, and salt in a large bowl. Stir in
the sugar, dates, apricots, prunes, halved and
whole almonds, pine nuts, and the orange and
lemon zests. • Beat the eggs with an electric
mixer at high speed until frothy. • Add the
beaten egg to the dry ingredients, reserving
1 tablespoon. • Divide the dough in half. Form
the dough into two long logs about 1¼ inches
(3 cm) in diameter. • Transfer the logs to the
prepared cookie sheets, flattening slightly.
• Bake until firm to the touch, 15–20 minutes.
• Transfer to a cutting board to cool for 10
minutes. • Lower the oven temperature to 300°F
(150°C/gas 2). • Cut the cookies on the diagonal
into ½-inch (1-cm) slices. • Arrange the slices
cut-side up on the cookie sheet and bake until
golden, 7–10 minutes. • Transfer to racks
to cool.

¼ cup (40 g) blanched almonds

½ cup (90 g) pine nuts

2 cups (300 g) all-purpose (plain) flour

1 teaspoon baking powder

¼ teaspoon salt

1¼ cups (250 g) granulated sugar

½ cup (50 g) finely chopped pitted dates

¼ cup (25 g) finely chopped dried apricots

¼ cup (50 g) finely chopped pitted prunes

¼ cup (40 g) whole almonds with skins

Finely grated zest of 1 orange

1 teaspoon finely grated lemon zest

3 large eggs, lightly beaten

Makes: about 40 biscotti
Preparation: 40 minutes
Cooking: 22–30 minutes
Level: 2

SPICE SQUARES

Mix the flour, ginger, cinnamon, cloves, baking soda, and salt in a medium bowl. • Mix the butter, brown sugar, and molasses in a medium saucepan over low heat. • Cook, stirring constantly, until the sugar has dissolved completely. • Remove from the heat and mix in the dry ingredients and lemon zest to form a stiff dough. • Divide the dough in half. Press the dough into two disks, wrap in plastic wrap (cling film), and refrigerate for 1 hour. • Preheat the oven to 350°F (180°C/gas 4). • Butter two cookie sheets. • Roll half the dough out on a lightly floured surface to 10-inch (25-cm) square. • Cut into 2-inch (5-cm) squares. • Use a spatula to transfer the cookies to the prepared cookie sheets, placing them 1 inch (2.5 cm) apart. • Prick all over with a fork. • Repeat with the remaining dough. • Sprinkle with the granulated sugar. • Bake until lightly browned, 5–7 minutes. • Transfer to racks and let cool completely.

1¼ cups (180 g) all-purpose (plain flour

1 teaspoon ground ginger

1 teaspoon ground cinnamon

¼ teaspoon ground cloves

¼ teaspoon baking soda (bicarbonate of soda)

⅛ teaspoon salt

¼ cup (60 g) butter, cut up

¼ cup (50 g) firmly packed dark brown sugar

2 tablespoons dark molasses (treacle)

Finely grated zest of 1 lemon

¼ cup (50 g) granulated sugar

Makes: about 30 cookies
Preparation: 40 minutes + 1 hour to chill
Cooking: 5–7 minutes
Level: 1

VANILLA HONEY COOKIES

Use a wooden spoon to mix the flour, sugar, egg, butter, water, baking soda, honey, vanilla, and salt in a large bowl to form a smooth dough. • Press the dough into a disk, wrap in plastic wrap (cling film), and refrigerate for 30 minutes. • Preheat the oven to 350°F (180°C/gas 4). • Butter two cookie sheets. • Roll out the dough on a lightly floured surface to ¼-inch (5-mm) thick. • Use a knife to cut out squares. • Use a spatula to transfer the cookies to the prepared cookie sheets, placing them 1 inch (2.5 cm) apart. • Brush with the milk. • Bake until just golden at the edges, 10–15 minutes. • Transfer to racks to cool.

2⅓ cups (350 g) all-purpose (plain flour

½ cup (100 g) granulated sugar

1 large egg

⅓ cup (90 g) butter, softened

2 tablespoons water

1 teaspoon baking soda (bicarbonate of soda)

2 tablespoons honey

1 teaspoon vanilla extract (essence)

¼ teaspoon salt

1 tablespoon milk

Makes: about 25 cookies
Preparation: 35 minutes
  + 30 minutes to chill
Cooking: 10–15 minutes
Level: 1

PECAN BISCOTTI

Preheat the oven to 350°F (180°C/gas 4).
• Butter two cookie sheets. • Mix the flour, cornmeal, baking powder, and salt in a medium bowl. • Beat the eggs, egg yolk, and vanilla in a large bowl until frothy.
• Mix in the dry ingredients, pecans, and maple syrup until stiff. • Form into four logs about 1 inch (2.5 cm) in diameter and place 2 inches (5 cm) apart on the prepared cookie sheets, flattening them slightly. • Bake until firm to the touch, 25–30 minutes. • Transfer to a cutting board to cool for 15 minutes.
• Reduce the oven temperature to 300°F (150°C/gas 2). • Cut the cookies on the diagonal into 1-inch (2.5-cm) slices. • Arrange the slices cut-side down on the cookie sheets and bake until golden and toasted, 15–20 minutes. • Transfer to racks to cool.

1²/₃ cups (250 g) all-purpose (plain) flour
²/₃ cup (100 g) polenta (finely ground cornmeal)
1 teaspoon baking powder
¼ teaspoon salt
2 large eggs + 1 large egg yolk
½ teaspoon vanilla extract (essence)
1 cup (100 g) coarsely chopped pecans
½ cup (125 ml) maple syrup

Makes: about 35 cookies
Preparation: 40 minutes
Cooking: 40–50 minutes
Level: 2

POLENTA BISCOTTI

Biscotti: Preheat the oven to 300°F (150°C/ gas 2). • Line two cookie sheets with parchment paper. • Mix the flour, baking soda, and salt in a medium bowl. • Beat the eggs and sugar in a large bowl with an electric mixer at high speed until thick and creamy. • Beat in the anisette, polenta flour, lemon zest, and coriander seed. • Mix in the dry ingredients and nuts to form a sticky dough. • Form the dough into 3 flat logs, about 2½ inches (6 cm) wide. • Transfer the logs to the prepared cookie sheets. • Glaze: Mix the egg yolk and milk in a small bowl and brush it over the logs. Sprinkle with the sugar. • Bake until firm to the touch, 25–30 minutes. • Transfer to a cutting board to cool for 10 minutes. • Cut on the diagonal into ½-inch (1-cm) slices. • Arrange the slices cut-side up on three cookie sheets and bake until golden and toasted 7–10 minutes.
• Transfer to racks to cool.

Biscotti
- 1½ cups (225 g) all-purpose (plain) flour
- 1 teaspoon baking soda (bicarbonate of soda)
- ⅛ teaspoon salt
- 2 large eggs
- 1 cup (200 g) granulated sugar
- 2 tablespoons anisette
- ⅓ cup (50 g) polenta (finely ground yellow cornmeal)
- Finely grated zest of 1 lemon
- 1 teaspoon coriander seeds
- ¼ cup (45 g) almonds

Glaze
- 1 large egg yolk
- 2 tablespoons milk
- 4 tablespoons granulated sugar

Makes: about 40 biscotti
Preparation: 15 minutes
Cooking: 32–40 minutes
Level: 2

DROP
COOKIES

MOCHA COOKIES WITH BLACK PEPPER

Preheat the oven to 350°F (180°C/gas 4).
• Butter two cookie sheets. • Mix the flour, baking powder, pepper, and salt in a small bowl. • Heat the raisins with the coffee liqueur in a small saucepan over low heat. • Melt the chocolate with the butter in a double boiler over barely simmering water. Set aside to cool. • Beat the eggs and sugar in a large bowl until creamy. • Beat in the melted chocolate and vanilla. • Beat in the dry ingredients, followed by the raisin mixture and the chocolate chips. • Drop tablespoons of the dough 2 inches (5 cm) apart onto the prepared cookie sheets. • Bake until set but still slightly soft, 10–12 minutes. • Cool until the cookies firm slightly. Transfer to racks to finish cooling.

2 cups (300 g) all-purpose (plain) flour

½ teaspoon baking powder

½ teaspoon freshly ground black pepper

¼ teaspoon salt

½ cup (90 g) raisins

2 tablespoons coffee liqueur

8 oz (250 g) bittersweet (plain) chocolate, coarsely chopped

¼ cup (60 g) butter

2 large eggs

¾ cup (150 g) granulated sugar

2 teaspoons vanilla extract (essence)

1 cup (180) semisweet (dark) chocolate chips

Makes: 25–30 cookies
Preparation: 20 minutes
Cooking: 10–12 minutes
Level: 1

HAZELNUT ROUNDS

174

Preheat the oven to 350°F (180°C/gas 4).
• Butter a cookie sheet. • Beat the butter and brown sugar in a large bowl with an electric mixer at high speed until creamy. • Add the egg, beating until just blended. • Mix in the flour, oats, cocoa, baking powder, and salt. • Stir in the white and milk chocolates and hazelnuts. • Drop teaspoons of the mixture ½ inch (1 cm) apart on the prepared baking sheet. • Bake until risen and craggy, 10–15 minutes. • Cool on the sheet until the cookies firm slightly. Transfer to racks and let cool completely.

½ cup (125 g) butter, softened

½ cup (150 g) firmly packed dark brown sugar

1 large egg, lightly beaten

⅔ cup (100 g) all-purpose (plain) flour

⅓ cup (50 g) old-fashioned rolled oats

1½ tablespoons unsweetened cocoa powder

½ teaspoon baking powder

⅛ teaspoon salt

3 oz (90 g) white chocolate, coarsely chopped

3 oz (90 g) milk chocolate, coarsely chopped

1 cup (100 g) coarsely chopped hazelnuts

Makes: 16–20 cookies
Preparation: 30 minutes
Cooking: 10–15 minutes
Level: 1

HOT CHOCOLATE COOKIES

Preheat the oven to 350°F (180°C/gas 4).
• Butter two cookie sheets. • Mix the flour, paprika, baking powder, and salt in a medium bowl. • Beat the butter and both sugars in a large bowl with an electric mixer at high speed until creamy. • Add the egg and vanilla, beating until just blended. • Mix in the dry ingredients and chopped chocolate. • Drop teaspoons of the dough 1 inch (2.5 cm) apart onto the prepared cookie sheets. • Bake until firm to the touch, 12–15 minutes. • Transfer to racks to cool.

3/4 cup (125 g) all-purpose (plain) flour

1 teaspoon spicy paprika

½ teaspoon baking powder

⅛ teaspoon salt

½ cup (125 g) butter, softened

2 tablespoons granulated sugar

¼ cup (50 g) firmly packed dark brown sugar

1 large egg

½ teaspoon vanilla extract (essence)

3 oz (90 g) semisweet (dark) chocolate, finely chopped

Makes: 20–25 cookies
Preparation: 20 minutes
Cooking: 12–15 minutes
Level: 1

CHOCOLATE VANILLA COOKIES

Preheat the oven to 375°F (190°C/gas 5).
• Butter two cookie sheets. • Mix the flour, cocoa, baking powder, and salt in a medium bowl. • Beat the butter and sugar in a large bowl with an electric mixer at high speed until creamy. • Mix in the vanilla and dry ingredients. • Drop tablespoons of the dough 2 inches (5 cm) apart onto the prepared cookie sheets. • Bake until firm to the touch, 15–18 minutes. • Cool on the sheets until the cookies firm slightly. Transfer to racks to finish cooling.

1   cup (150 g) all-purpose (plain) flour
2   tablespoons unsweetened cocoa powder
1   teaspoon baking powder
⅛   teaspoon salt
⅔   cup (175 g) butter, softened
½   cup (100 g) granulated sugar
½   teaspoon vanilla extract (essence)

Makes: 15–20 cookies
Preparation: 20 minutes
Cooking: 15–18 minutes
Level: 1

DUSTED COOKIES

180

Preheat the oven to 350°F (180°C/gas 4).
• Butter two cookie sheets. • Mix the flour,
baking powder, and salt in a large bowl
and make a well in the center. • Add the
butter, sugar, eggs, and milk. • Use your
hands to knead the mixture into a smooth
dough. • Form the dough into balls the size
of walnuts and place 1 inch (2.5 cm) apart on
the prepared cookie sheets. • Bake until just
golden, 15–20 minutes. • Transfer to racks and
let cool completely. • Dust half of each cookie
with the confectioners' sugar and the other
half with the cocoa.

$1^2/_3$ cups (250 g) all-purpose (plain) flour

1 teaspoon baking powder

⅛ teaspoon salt

⅓ cup (90 g) butter, softened

¼ cup (50 g) granulated sugar

2 large eggs

1 tablespoon milk

4 tablespoons confectioners' (icing) sugar

4 tablespoons unsweetened cocoa powder

Makes: 20–25 cookies
Preparation: 35 minutes
Cooking: 15–20 minutes
Level: 1

PECAN TORTOISES

182

Preheat the oven to 350°F (180°C/gas 4).
• Line two cookie sheets with parchment paper. • Mix the flour, coffee granules, baking powder, and salt in a large bowl. • Melt the chocolate and butter in a double boiler over barely simmering water. • Stir in the sugar until completely dissolved. • Remove from the heat and mix in the vanilla and eggs. • Mix in the dry ingredients, finely chopped pecans, and chocolate chips. • Drop tablespoons of the dough 3 inches (8 cm) apart onto the prepared cookie sheets. • Press four pecan halves into each corner of the cookies to resemble the legs of a turtle and an additional one to resemble a head. • Bake until just set, 8–10 minutes. • Let cool on wire racks.

1¼ cups (175 g) all-purpose (plain) flour

1 tablespoon instant coffee granules

1 teaspoon baking powder

⅛ teaspoon salt

14 oz (400 g) semisweet (dark) chocolate, coarsely chopped

¼ cup (60 g) butter

1½ cups (300 g) granulated sugar

1 teaspoon vanilla extract (essence)

4 large eggs

2 cups (200 g) finely chopped pecans + 1 cup (100 g) pecan halves

1 cup (180 g) semisweet (dark) chocolate chips

Makes: about 24 cookies
Preparation: 20 minutes
Cooking: 8–10 minutes
Level: 1

WHITE CHOCOLATE AND WALNUT COOKIES

Preheat the oven to 350°F (180°C/gas 4).
• Butter a cookie sheet. • Mix the flour, baking soda, and salt in a medium bowl. • Beat the butter and raw sugar in a large bowl with an electric mixer at high speed until creamy.
• Add the vanilla and egg, beating until just blended. • Mix in the dry ingredients, white chocolate, and walnuts. • Form the dough into balls the size of walnuts and place 2 inches (5 cm) apart on the prepared cookie sheet.
• Bake until just golden, 10–12 minutes.
• Cool on the sheet until the cookies firm slightly. Transfer to racks and let cool completely.

1⅓ cups (200 g) all-purpose (plain) flour

½ teaspoon baking soda (bicarbonate of soda)

⅛ teaspoon salt

½ cup (125 g) butter, softened

½ cup (150 g) raw sugar (Demerara or Barbados)

1 teaspoon vanilla extract (essence)

1 large egg

4 oz (125 g) white chocolate, coarsely chopped

½ cup (50 g) finely chopped walnuts

Makes: about 20 cookies
Preparation: 20 minutes
Cooking: 10–12 minutes
Level: 1

CHOCOLATE MUNCHIES

Preheat the oven to 350°F (180°C/gas 4).
• Butter two cookie sheets. • Mix the flour, cocoa, baking powder, cinnamon, and salt in a medium bowl. • Beat the butter and sugar in a large bowl with an electric mixer at high speed until creamy. • Add the egg yolk, beating until just blended. • Mix in the dry ingredients. • Drop teaspoons of the dough 1 inch (2.5 cm) apart onto the prepared cookie sheets. • Bake until firm around the edges, 12–15 minutes. • Transfer to racks to cool. • Melt the chocolate in a double boiler over barely simmering water. Drizzle the tops with the melted chocolate.

1 cup (150 g) all-purpose (plain) flour

2 tablespoons unsweetened cocoa powder

1 teaspoon baking powder

¼ teaspoon ground cinnamon

⅛ teaspoon salt

½ cup (125 g) butter, softened

½ cup (100 g) granulated sugar

1 large egg yolk

2 oz (60 g) semisweet (dark) chocolate, coarsely chopped

Makes: 25–30 cookies
Preparation: 20 minutes
Cooking: 12–15 minutes
Level: 1

DOUBLE CHOCOLATE CHERRY COOKIES

Preheat the oven to 350°F (180°C/gas 4).
• Line three cookie sheets with parchment paper. • Soak the cherries in the kirsch in a medium bowl for 15 minutes. • Drain well. • Mix the flour, baking soda, and salt in a medium bowl. • Beat the butter and both sugars in a large bowl with an electric mixer at high speed until creamy. • Add the vanilla and almond extracts and egg, beating until just blended. • Mix in the dry ingredients, followed by the cherries, white and semisweet chocolates, and the macadamia nuts. • Drop heaped tablespoons of the dough 2 inches (5 cm) apart onto the prepared cookie sheets. • Bake until lightly browned, 12–15 minutes. • Cool the cookies on the sheets for 15 minutes. Transfer to racks and let cool completely.

188

1 (7-oz/200-g) can pitted sour cherries, drained
½ cup (125 ml) kirsch
1½ cups (225 g) all-purpose (plain) flour
½ teaspoon baking soda (bicarbonate of soda)
¼ teaspoon salt
½ cup (125 g) butter, softened
½ cup (100 g) granulated sugar
½ cup (100 g) raw sugar (Demerara or Barbados)
1½ teaspoons vanilla extract (essence)
¼ teaspoon almond extract (essence)
1 large egg
5 oz (150 g) white chocolate, chopped
5 oz (150 g) semisweet (dark) chocolate, coarsely chopped
½ cup (50 g) finely chopped macadamia nuts

Makes: about 36 cookies
Preparation: 20 minutes + 15 minutes to soak the cherries
Cooking: 12–15 minutes
Level: 1

CANDIED FRUIT COOKIES

Preheat the oven to 400°F (200°C/gas 6).
• Line two cookie sheets with parchment paper. • Mix the flour, baking powder, and salt in a large bowl. • Use a pastry blender to cut in the butter until the mixture resembles coarse crumbs. • Stir in the granulated sugar, apricots, pineapple, and cherries. • Beat the egg and orange juice and zest in a small bowl until pale. • Add the egg mixture to the dry ingredients and mix until well blended. • Drop teaspoons of the mixture 2 inches (5 cm) apart onto the prepared cookie sheets. • Sprinkle with the brown sugar. • Bake until golden brown, 15–20 minutes. • Cool the cookies on the cookie sheets for 5 minutes. • Transfer to racks and let cool completely.

$1\frac{1}{3}$ cups (200 g) all-purpose (plain) flour

2 teaspoons baking powder

½ teaspoon salt

½ cup (125 g) cold butter, cut up

¼ cup (50 g) granulated sugar

3 tablespoons coarsely chopped dried apricots

1 tablespoon coarsely chopped candied pineapple

1 tablespoon coarsely chopped candied cherries

1 large egg

1 tablespoon freshly squeezed orange juice

1 teaspoon finely grated orange zest

2 tablespoons firmly packed light brown sugar, to sprinkle

Makes: 15–18 cookies
Preparation: 20 minutes
Cooking: 15–20 minutes
Level: 1

CHEWY RAISIN COOKIES

Preheat the oven to 350°F (180°C/gas 4).
• Butter two baking sheets. • Stir together the shortening and sugar in a medium bowl until well blended. • Beat in the egg and add the raisins. Gradually stir in the water, salt, cinnamon, nutmeg, and walnuts until well mixed. Mix in the flour and baking soda.
• Drop tablespoons of the dough onto the prepared baking sheets. • Bake until golden brown, about 10 minutes. • Let cool on wire racks.

½ cup (125 g) vegetable shortening

½ cup (150 g) firmly packed brown sugar

1 large egg

1 cup (180 g) raisins

½ cup (125 ml) water

2 cups (300 g) all-purpose (plain) flour

½ teaspoon baking soda (bicarbonate of soda)

¼ teaspoon salt

½ teaspoon ground cinnamon

½ teaspoon ground nutmeg

½ cup (50 g) chopped walnuts

Makes: about 36 cookies
Preparation: 15 minutes
Cooking: 10–12 minutes
Level: 1

APPLESAUCE COOKIES

Preheat the oven to 350°F (180°C/gas 4).
• Butter three cookie sheets. • Mix the flour, cinnamon, ginger, cloves, baking soda, and salt in a medium bowl. • Beat the butter and both sugars in a large bowl with an electric mixer at high speed until creamy. • Add the vanilla and egg, beating until just blended.
• Stir in the applesauce. • Mix in the dry ingredients, followed by the raisins and walnuts. • Drop tablespoons of the dough 2 inches (5 cm) apart onto the prepared cookie sheets. • Bake until just golden, 8–10 minutes. • Transfer to racks and let cool.

2 cups (300 g) all-purpose (plain) flour

1 teaspoon ground cinnamon

1 teaspoon ground ginger

½ teaspoon ground cloves

½ teaspoon baking soda (bicarbonate of soda)

½ teaspoon salt

½ cup (125 g) butter, softened

½ cup (100 g) firmly packed light brown sugar

⅓ cup (70 g) granulated sugar

1 teaspoon vanilla extract (essence)

1 large egg

1 cup (250 ml) applesauce

1 cup (180 g) golden raisins (sultanas)

¾ cup (75 g) finely chopped walnuts

Makes: about 36 cookies
Preparation: 20 minutes
Cooking: 8–10 minutes
Level: 1

SOFT COCONUT COOKIES

Preheat the oven to 400°F (200°C/gas 6).
• Butter a cookie sheet. • Mix the flour, baking powder, and salt in a medium bowl.
• Beat the butter and sugar in a large bowl with an electric mixer at high speed until creamy. • Add the egg, beating until just blended. • Mix in the dry ingredients and coconut until well blended. • Drop tablespoons of the dough 2 inches (5 cm) apart onto the prepared cookie sheet, pressing down lightly with a fork. • Bake until golden brown, 10–15 minutes.
• Cool on the cookie sheets for 15 minutes.
• Transfer to racks to cool.

1 cup (150 g) all-purpose (plain) flour

1 teaspoon baking powder

⅛ teaspoon salt

½ cup (125 g) butter, softened

½ cup (100 g) granulated sugar

1 large egg

1 cup (125 g) shredded (desiccated) coconut

Makes: about 15 cookies
Preparation: 20 minutes
Cooking: 10–15 minutes
Level: 1

CHEWY FRUIT COOKIES

Preheat the oven to 400°F (200°C/gas 6).
• Butter three cookie sheets. • Soak the raisins and cranberries in the water in a large bowl for 15 minutes. • Drain well, reserving 6 tablespoons of the liquid, and set aside.
• Mix the flour, cinnamon, baking soda, ginger, baking powder, allspice, and salt in a medium bowl. • Beat the butter and brown sugar in a large bowl with an electric mixer at high speed until creamy. • Add the vanilla and eggs, beating until just blended. • Mix in the dry ingredients and reserved liquid. • Stir in the oats, walnuts, prunes, dates, raisins, and cranberries until well blended. • Drop tablespoons of the dough 3 inches (8 cm) apart onto the prepared cookie sheets, flattening them slightly. • Bake until just golden at the edges, 8–10 minutes. • Transfer to racks and let cool completely.

2   cups (360 g) raisins

1   cup (180 g) dried cranberries

1   cup (250 ml) hot water

2½ cups (375 g) all-purpose (plain) flour

2   teaspoons ground cinnamon

1½ teaspoons baking soda (bicarbonate of soda)

1   teaspoon ground ginger

½   teaspoon baking powder

½   teaspoon allspice

½   teaspoon salt

3/4 cup (180 g) butter, softened

1½ cups (300 g) light brown sugar

1½ teaspoons vanilla extract (essence)

2   large eggs

2   cups (300 g) old-fashioned rolled oats

2   cups (200 g) coarsely chopped walnuts

1¼ cups (280 g) coarsely chopped pitted prunes

1¼ cups (280 g) coarsely chopped pitted dates

Makes: about 75 cookies
Preparation: 20 minutes
    + 15 minutes to soak
Cooking: 8–10 minutes
Level: 1

FRUITY RAISIN MOMENTS

Preheat the oven to 400°F (200°C/gas 6).
• Butter two cookie sheets. • Mix the flour, baking powder, nutmeg, and salt in a large bowl. • Use a pastry blender to cut in the butter until the mixture resembles coarse crumbs. • Stir in the brown sugar, candied peel, raisins, and egg. • Drop tablespoons of the dough 2 inches (5 cm) apart onto the prepared cookie sheets. • Bake until golden brown 20–25 minutes. • Transfer the cookies to racks to cool.

2 cups (300 g) all-purpose (plain) flour
1 teaspoon baking powder
¼ teaspoon freshly grated nutmeg
⅛ teaspoon salt
½ cup (125 g) butter, cut up
½ cup (100 g) firmly packed light brown sugar
⅔ cup (70 g) finely chopped candied peel
⅓ cup (45 g) raisins
1 large egg, lightly beaten

Makes: 20–25 cookies
Preparation: 30 minutes
Cooking: 20–25 minutes
Level: 1

HAZELNUT AND OAT COOKIES

Preheat the oven to 350°F (180°C/gas 4).
• Line three cookie sheets with parchment paper. • Beat the egg whites and 1 tablespoon of raw sugar in a large bowl with an electric mixer at medium speed until soft peaks form. • With mixer at high speed, gradually add the remaining raw sugar, beating until stiff peaks form. • Use a large rubber spatula to fold in the vanilla, oats, hazelnuts, and figs.
• Drizzle with the lemon juice and sprinkle with the zest. • Drop teaspoons of the mixture 1 inch (2.5 cm) apart onto the prepared cookie sheets. Sprinkle with the sunflower seeds. • Bake until lightly browned, 12–15 minutes. • Cool the cookies on the cookie sheet for 15 minutes. • Transfer to racks and let cool completely.

2 large egg whites

½ cup (100 g) raw sugar (Demerara or Barbados)

1 teaspoon vanilla extract (essence)

½ cup (75 g) old-fashioned rolled oats

½ cup (50 g) finely ground hazelnuts

1 tablespoon very finely chopped dried figs

1 tablespoon freshly squeezed lemon juice

Finely grated zest of 1 lemon

2 tablespoons sunflower seeds

Makes: about 45 cookies
Preparation: 20 minutes
Cooking: 12–15 minutes
Level: 1

SOFT DATE COOKIES

Preheat the oven to 375°F (190°C/gas 5).
• Butter two cookie sheets. • Beat the butter, sugar, and vanilla in a large bowl with an electric mixer at high speed until creamy.
• Mix in the flour and dates. • Drop rounded teaspoons of the dough 1 inch (2.5 cm) apart onto the prepared cookie sheets. • Bake until just golden, 15–20 minutes. • Cool on the sheets until the cookies firm slightly.
• Transfer to racks to finish cooling.

½ cup (125 g) butter, softened

¼ cup (50 g) granulated sugar

½ teaspoon vanilla extract (essence)

¼ cup (60 g) finely chopped dates

¾ cup (125 g) all-purpose (plain) flour

Makes: 18–20 cookies
Preparation: 20 minutes
Cooking: 15–20 minutes
Level: 1

LEMON, RAISIN, AND OAT COOKIES

Preheat the oven to 375°F (190°C/gas 5).
• Butter a cookie sheet. • Mix the flour, baking powder, and salt in a large bowl. • Beat the butter, sugar, and lemon zest in a large bowl with an electric mixer at high speed until creamy. • Add the egg, beating until just blended. • Mix in the dry ingredients, oats, and raisins. • Drop tablespoons of the dough 3 inches (8 cm) apart onto the prepared cookie sheet. • Bake until just golden at the edges, 10–15 minutes. • Transfer to racks to cool.

1½ cups (225 g) all-purpose (plain) flour

1 teaspoon baking powder

⅛ teaspoon salt

½ cup (125 g) butter, softened

½ cup (100 g) granulated sugar

Finely grated zest of 1 lemon

1 large egg

2 tablespoons old-fashioned rolled oats

1 cup (180 g) raisins

Makes: about 16 cookies
Preparation: 20 minutes
Cooking: 15–20 minutes
Level: 1

FRUIT AND NUT COOKIES

Preheat the oven to 400°F (200°C/gas 6).
• Butter two cookie sheets. • Mix the flour
and cinnamon in a medium bowl. • Mix the
baking soda and water in a small bowl. Add
the dates and raisins. • Beat the butter and
sugar in a large bowl with an electric mixer
at high speed until creamy. • Add the egg,
beating until just blended. • Stir in the date
and raisin mixture. • Mix in the dry
ingredients and walnuts. • Drop tablespoons
of the dough 1 inch (2.5 cm) apart onto the
prepared cookie sheets. • Bake until lightly
browned, 8–10 minutes. • Cool on the sheets
until the cookies firm slightly. Transfer to
racks and let cool completely.

1 cup (150 g) all-purpose (plain) flour
½ teaspoon ground cinnamon
¼ teaspoon baking soda (bicarbonate of soda)
2 tablespoons water
¾ cup (75 g) finely chopped dates
¾ cup (135 g) golden raisins (sultanas)
⅓ cup (90 g) butter, softened
½ cup (100 g) granulated sugar
1 large egg
½ cup (50 g) finely chopped walnuts

Makes: about 26 cookies
Preparation: 20 minutes
Cooking: 8–10 minutes
Level: 1

CHEWY BROWN COOKIES

Preheat the oven to 325°F (170°C/gas 3).
• Butter two cookie sheets. • Chop the dates very finely and place in a large bowl. Add the almonds. • Stir in the egg whites, confectioners' sugar, cocoa, and lemon juice and mix until well blended. • Drop teaspoons of the dough 1 inch (2.5 cm) apart onto the prepared cookie sheets. • Bake until just golden at the edges, 25–30 minutes.

$1^3/_4$ cups (175 g) finely chopped pitted dates

$1^3/_4$ cups (175 g) finely chopped almonds

2 large egg whites

1 cup (150 g) confectioners' (icing) sugar

1 tablespoon unsweetened cocoa powder

Freshly squeezed juice of 1 lemon

Makes: about 25 cookies
Preparation: 20 minutes
Cooking: 25–30 minutes
Level: 1

SPICY RAISIN COOKIES

Mix the flour, cinnamon, baking powder, cloves, nutmeg, and salt in a medium bowl. • Beat the butter, brown sugar, and eggs in a large bowl with an electric mixer at medium speed until well combined. • Mix in the dry ingredients, followed by the raisins and almonds. • Cover the bowl with plastic wrap (cling film) and refrigerate for 30 minutes. • Preheat the oven to 375°F (190°C/gas 5). • Butter two cookie sheets. • Drop heaped teaspoons of the cookie dough 2 inches (5 cm) apart onto the prepared cookie sheets. • Bake until golden brown, 8–10 minutes. • Transfer to racks and let cool.

2⅓ cups (350 g) all-purpose (plain) flour

2 teaspoon ground cinnamon

1 teaspoon baking powder

½ teaspoon ground cloves

½ teaspoon freshly grated nutmeg

¼ teaspoon salt

½ cup (125 g) butter, softened

¾ cup (150 g) firmly packed dark brown sugar

2 large eggs

½ cup (90 g) raisins

½ cup (50 g) flaked almonds

Makes: 24–30 cookies
Preparation: 20 minutes
    + 30 minutes to chill
Cooking: 8–10 minutes
Level: 1

LIGHT CRANBERRY COOKIES

Preheat the oven to 375°F (190°C/gas 5).
• Line two cookie sheets with parchment paper. • Mix the flour, baking soda, and salt in a medium bowl. • Beat the butter, shortening, and both sugars in a large bowl with an electric mixer at high speed until creamy. • Add the vanilla and egg, beating until just blended. • Mix in the dry ingredients, cranberries, candied peel, and pecans. • Drop tablespoons of the dough 1½ inches (4 cm) apart onto the prepared cookie sheets. • Bake until golden at the edges, 8–10 minutes. • Cool on the sheets until the cookies firm slightly. Transfer to racks to finish cooling.

1 cup (150 g) all-purpose (plain) flour

¼ teaspoon baking soda (bicarbonate of soda)

⅛ teaspoon salt

2 tablespoons butter, softened

2 tablespoons vegetable shortening

¼ cup (50 g) granulated sugar

¼ cup (50 g) firmly packed light brown sugar

1/24 teaspoon vanilla extract (essence)

1 large egg

½ cup (50 g) coarsely chopped dried cranberries

¼ cup (30 g) finely chopped mixed candied peel

¼ cup (30 g) finely chopped pecans

Makes: 25–30 cookies
Preparation: 20 minutes
Cooking: 8–10 minutes
Level: 1

RAISIN COOKIES WITH ORANGE

216

Preheat the oven to 375°F (190°C/gas 5).
• Butter two cookie sheets. • Mix the flour,
baking powder, and salt in a medium bowl.
• Beat the butter and sugar in a large bowl
with an electric mixer at high speed until
creamy. • Add the egg and vanilla, beating
until just blended. • Mix in the dry
ingredients, followed by the raisins and
orange zest. • Drop tablespoons of the
dough 2 inches (5 cm) apart onto the
prepared cookie sheets. • Bake until just
golden, 12–15 minutes. • Cool on the sheets
until the cookies firm slightly. Transfer to
racks to finish cooling

1⅓ cups (200 g) all-purpose flour

½ teaspoon baking powder

½ teaspoon salt

½ cup (125 g) butter, softened

¾ cup (150 g) granulated sugar

1 large egg, lightly beaten

½ teaspoon vanilla extract (essence)

⅔ cup (120 g) raisins

1 tablespoon finely grated orange zest

Makes: about 25 cookies
Preparation: 25 minutes
Cooking: 12–15 minutes
Level: 1

CANDIED GINGER COOKIES

Preheat the oven to 350°F (180°C/gas 4).
• Butter two cookie sheets. • Mix the flour, baking powder, and salt in a medium bowl.
• Beat the butter and brown sugar in a large bowl with an electric mixer at high speed until creamy. • Add the egg, beating until just blended. • Mix in the dry ingredients, almond extract, and crushed cardamom, followed by the cherries, apricots, and ginger. • Drop rounded teaspoons of the dough 1 inch (2.5 cm) apart onto the prepared cookie sheets. • Bake until lightly browned, 20–25 minutes. • Transfer to racks and let cool.

1¼ cups (180 g) all-purpose (plain) flour

1 teaspoon baking powder

⅛ teaspoon salt

⅓ cup (90 g) butter, softened

⅓ cup (70 g) firmly packed light brown sugar

1 large egg, lightly beaten

1 teaspoon almond extract (essence)

Seeds of 8 cardamom pods, crushed

½ cup (50 g) finely chopped candied cherries

½ cup (50 g) finely chopped dried apricots

½ cup (50 g) finely chopped crystallized ginger

Makes: about 24 cookies
Preparation: 20 minutes
Cooking: 20–25 minutes
Level: 1

RUSTIC COOKIES

Preheat the oven to 425°F (220°C/gas 7).
• Butter a cookie sheet. • Mix the flour and salt in a large bowl. Stir in the coconut, sugar, and lemon zest. • Use a pastry blender to cut in the butter until the mixture resembles coarse crumbs. • Add the lemon juice and eggs, mixing until a smooth dough has formed. • Drop heaped tablespoons of the dough 2 inches (5 cm) apart onto the prepared cookie sheet. • Bake until lightly browned, 8–10 minutes. • Transfer to racks to cool.

3/4 cup (125 g) whole-wheat (wholemeal) flour

1/8 teaspoon salt

1 cup (125 g) shredded (desiccated) coconut

1/4 cup (50 g) granulated sugar

Finely grated zest and juice of 1/2 lemon

1/4 cup (60 g) butter, cut up

2 large eggs, lightly beaten

Makes: about 12 cookies
Preparation: 20 minutes
Cooking: 8–10 minutes
Level: 1

SWEET MINCEMEAT COOKIES

Preheat the oven to 375°F (190°C/gas 5).
• Butter three cookie sheets. • Mix the flour, baking soda, and salt in a medium bowl.
• Beat the butter and both sugars in a large bowl with an electric mixer at high speed until creamy. • Add the egg, beating until just blended. • Mix in the dry ingredients, mincemeat, and brandy. • Drop heaped teaspoons of the dough 2 inches (5 cm) apart onto the prepared cookie sheets. • Bake until golden brown, 10–12 minutes. Transfer to racks to cool

1¼ cups (180 g) all-purpose (plain) flour

¼ teaspoon baking soda (bicarbonate of soda)

⅛ teaspoon salt

⅓ cup (90 g) butter, softened

¼ cup (50 g) granulated sugar

¼ cup (50 g) firmly packed light brown sugar

1 large egg

¾ cup (180 g) sweet mincemeat

2 teaspoons brandy

Makes: 40–50 cookies
Preparation: 40 minutes
Cooking: 10–12 minutes
Level: 1

DATE AND NUT BITES

Preheat the oven to 325°F (170°C/gas 3).
• Butter two cookie sheets. • Chop the dates very finely and place in a large bowl. Add the walnuts. • Stir in the egg whites, confectioners' sugar, cocoa, and lemon juice and mix until well blended. • Drop teaspoons of the dough 1 inch (2.5 cm) apart onto the prepared cookie sheets. • Bake until just golden at the edges, 25–30 minutes.
• Transfer to racks and let cool.

1³/₄ cups (175 g) finely chopped pitted dates

1³/₄ cups (175 g) finely chopped walnuts

2 large egg whites

1 cup (150 g) confectioners' (icing) sugar

1 tablespoon unsweetened cocoa powder

Freshly squeezed juice of 1 lemon

Makes: about 25 cookies
Preparation: 20 minutes
Cooking: 25–30 minutes
Level: 1

CANDIED FRUIT DELIGHTS

Preheat the oven to 350°F (180°C/gas 4).
• Line three cookie sheets with parchment
paper. • Mix the flour and salt in a medium
bowl. • Beat the egg whites in a large bowl
with an electric mixer at medium speed until
frothy. • With mixer at high speed, gradually
add the granulated sugar, beating until stiff,
glossy peaks form. • Use a large rubber
spatula to fold in the candied peel and dry
ingredients. • With mixer at high speed, beat
the egg yolks in a small bowl until frothy.
• Fold the beaten egg yolks into the batter.
• Drop teaspoons of the dough 2 inches
(5 cm) apart onto the prepared cookie sheets.
• Sprinkle with confectioners' sugar. • Bake
until pale gold, 10–12 minutes. • Cool on the
sheets until the cookies firm slightly.
• Transfer to racks to finish cooling.

1½ cups (225 g) all-purpose (plain) flour

⅛ teaspoon salt

3 large eggs, separated

1 cup (200 g) granulated sugar

½ cup (50 g) very finely chopped mixed candied peel

2 tablespoons confectioners' (icing) sugar, to dust

Makes: 35–40 cookies
Preparation: 25 minutes
Cooking: 10–12 minutes
Level: 1

RAW SUGAR RAISIN COOKIES

228

Preheat the oven to 350°F (180°C/gas 4).
• Butter two cookie sheets. • Plump the
raisins in hot water in a small bowl for
10 minutes. • Drain well and pat dry with
paper towels. • Mix the flour, baking powder,
cinnamon, nutmeg, and salt in a medium
bowl. • Mix the milk and lemon juice in a
small bowl. • Beat the butter and both sugars
in a large bowl with an electric mixer at high
speed until creamy. • Add the eggs, beating
until just blended. • Mix in the dry
ingredients, milk mixture, and raisins.
• Drop teaspoons of the dough 1 inch
(2.5 cm) apart onto the prepared cookie
sheets. • Bake until just golden, 12–15
minutes. • Transfer to racks to cool.

1 cup (180 g) golden raisins (sultanas)
2 cups (300 g) all-purpose (plain) flour
1 teaspoon baking powder
1 teaspoon ground cinnamon
⅛ teaspoon freshly grated nutmeg
⅛ teaspoon salt
¼ cup (60 ml) milk
1 teaspoon fresh lemon juice
½ cup (125 g) butter, softened
1 cup (200 g) raw sugar (Demerara or Barbados)
½ cup (50 g) granulated sugar
2 large eggs

Makes: about 32 cookies
Preparation: 25 minutes
Cooking: 12–15 minutes
Level: 1

NUTTY ELEVENSES

Preheat the oven to 350°F (180°C/gas 4).
• Butter three cookie sheets. • Mix the flour, cinnamon, and salt in a large bowl. • Beat the butter and brown sugar in a large bowl with an electric mixer on high speed until creamy. • Add the eggs one at a time, beating until just blended after each addition. • Stir in the baking soda mixture. • Mix in the dry ingredients, walnuts, and raisins. • Drop tablespoons of the dough 3 inches (8 cm) apart onto the prepared cookie sheets. • Bake until just golden at the edges, 8–10 minutes. • Place on wire racks to cool.

3¼ cups (480 g) all-purpose (plain) flour

½ teaspoon ground cinnamon

⅛ teaspoon salt

1 cup (250 g) butter, softened

1½ cups (300 g) firmly packed light brown sugar

3 large eggs

1 teaspoon baking soda dissolved in 1½ tablespoons hot water

1 cup (100 g) coarsely chopped walnuts

1 cup (180 g) raisins

Makes: about 50 cookies
Preparation: 20 minutes
Cooking: 8–10 minutes
Level: 1

DATE AND LEMON SPECIALS

232

Mix the flour, cornstarch, and salt in a medium bowl. • Beat the butter and sugar in a large bowl with an electric mixer at high speed until creamy. • Add the lemon zest. • With mixer at high speed, beat the egg whites in a large bowl until soft peaks form. • Fold into the butter mixture. • Mix in the dry ingredients, dates, lemon juice, and rum extract. Refrigerate for 30 minutes. • Preheat the oven to 375°F (190°C/gas 5). • Butter two cookie sheets. • Drop teaspoons of the mixture 1½ inches (4 cm) apart onto the prepared cookie sheets. • Bake until golden brown, 8–10 minutes. • Transfer to racks to cool.

½ cup (75 g) all-purpose (plain) flour

2 tablespoons cornstarch (cornflour)

¼ teaspoon salt

⅓ cup (90 g) butter, softened

½ cup (100 g) granulated sugar

1 tablespoon finely grated lemon zest

3 large egg whites

½ cup (50 g) finely chopped pitted dates

1 tablespoon freshly squeezed lemon juice

1 teaspoon rum extract (essence)

Makes: 30 cookies
Preparation: 20 minutes + 30 minutes to chill
Cooking: 10 minutes
Level: 2

WHOLE-WHEAT DATE COOKIES

Preheat the oven to 400°F (200°C/gas 6).
• Butter two cookie sheets. • Mix the all-purpose and whole-wheat flours, baking powder, and salt in a large bowl. • Beat the butter and granulated sugar in a large bowl with an electric mixer at high speed until creamy. • Add the egg, beating until just blended. • Mix in the dry ingredients and dates to make a stiff dough. • Form the dough into balls the size of walnuts and place 2 inches (5 cm) apart on the prepared cookie sheets, flattening slightly with a fork.
• Bake until lightly browned, 15–20 minutes.
• Transfer to racks and let cool.

1 cup (150 g) all-purpose (plain) flour
2/3 cup (100 g) whole-wheat flour
1 teaspoon baking powder
1/8 teaspoon salt
3/4 cup (180 g) butter, softened
3/4 cup (150 g) granulated sugar
1 large egg
1 cup (200 g) finely chopped pitted dates

Makes: 20–25 cookies
Preparation: 20 minutes
Cooking: 15–20 minutes
Level: 1

PECAN DATE COOKIES

Preheat the oven to 400°F (200°C/gas 6).
• Butter two cookie sheets. • Mix the flour
and cinnamon in a medium bowl. • Mix the
baking soda and water in a small bowl. Add
the dates and currants. • Beat the butter and
sugar in a large bowl with an electric mixer at
high speed until creamy. • Add the egg,
beating until just blended. • Stir in the date
and currant mixture. • Mix in the dry
ingredients and pecans. • Drop tablespoons
of the dough 1 inch (2.5 cm) apart onto the
prepared cookie sheets. • Bake until lightly
browned, 8–10 minutes. • Cool on the sheets
until the cookies firm slightly. Transfer to
racks and let cool completely.

1 cup (150 g) all-purpose (plain) flour
½ teaspoon ground cinnamon
¼ teaspoon baking soda (bicarbonate of soda)
2 tablespoons water
¾ cup (75 g) finely chopped dates
¾ cup (150 g) dried currants
⅓ cup (90 g) butter, softened
½ cup (100 g) granulated sugar
1 large egg
½ cup (50 g) finely chopped pecans

Makes: about 26 cookies
Preparation: 20 minutes
Cooking: 8–10 minutes
Level: 1

MOCHA NUT COOKIES

238

Preheat the oven to 325°F (170°C/gas 3).
• Set out two cookie sheets. • Mix the flour, baking powder, and salt in a large bowl.
• Melt the chocolate and butter in a double boiler over barely simmering water. • Beat the eggs and sugar in a large bowl with an electric mixer at high speed until pale and thick. • Beat in the chocolate mixture, coffee granules, and vanilla. • Mix in the dry ingredients, pecans, hazelnuts, and chocolate chips. • Drop tablespoons of the dough 3 inches (8 cm) apart onto the cookie sheets.
• Bake until lightly cracked on top, 20–25 minutes. Transfer to racks to cool.

²/₃ cup (100 g) all-purpose (plain) flour

½ teaspoon baking powder

⅛ teaspoon salt

12 oz (350 g) bittersweet (dark) chocolate, coarsely chopped

½ cup (125 g) butter, cut up

3 large eggs

1 cup (200 g) granulated sugar

1 tablespoon instant coffee granules

1 teaspoon vanilla extract (essence)

1½ cups (150 g) coarsely chopped pecans

1½ cups (150 g) coarsely chopped hazelnuts

1 cup (180 g) semisweet (dark) chocolate chips

Makes: about 20 cookies
Preparation: 20 minutes
Cooking: 20–25 minutes
Level: 1

MOCHA HAZELNUT COOKIES

Preheat the oven to 325°F (170°C/gas 3).
• Butter two cookie sheets. • Mix the flour, baking powder, and salt in a large bowl.
• Beat the butter and sugar in a large bowl with an electric mixer at high speed until creamy. • Add the coffee extract and vanilla.
• Mix in the dry ingredients to form a smooth dough. • Roll into balls the size of walnuts and place 1½ inches (4 cm) apart on the prepared baking sheets, pressing down lightly.
• Press three hazelnuts into the top of each cookie. • Bake until firm to the touch, 15–20 minutes. • Transfer to racks to cool.

1¼ cups (180 g) all-purpose (plain) flour

1 teaspoon baking powder

⅛ teaspoon salt

½ cup (125 g) butter, softened

⅔ cup (140 g) granulated sugar

2 teaspoons coffee extract or 2 teaspoons instant coffee granules dissolved in 1 tablespoon boiling water

1 teaspoon vanilla extract (essence)

½ cup (75 g) toasted hazelnuts

Makes: about 30 cookies
Preparation: 15 minutes
Cooking: 15–20 minutes
Level: 1

COFFEE DROPS

Preheat the oven to 325°F (170°C/gas 3).
• Butter three cookie sheets. • Mix the flour, cocoa, and salt in a medium bowl. • Beat the butter, sugar, and vanilla in a large bowl with an electric mixer at high speed until creamy. • Mix in the dry ingredients, coffee granules, pecans, and cherries until well blended. • Form the dough into balls the size of walnuts and place 1 inch (2.5 cm) apart on the prepared cookie sheets. • Bake until firm to the touch, 15–18 minutes. • Transfer to racks and let cool completely. • Dust with the confectioners' sugar.

1 cup (150 g) all-purpose (plain) flour
1 tablespoon unsweetened cocoa powder
⅛ teaspoon salt
½ cup (125 g) butter, softened
¼ cup (50 g) granulated sugar
1 teaspoon vanilla extract (essence)
2 teaspoons instant coffee granules
½ cup (50 g) finely chopped pecans
2 tablespoons finely chopped candied cherries
⅓ cup (50 g) confectioners' (icing) sugar

Makes: about 36 cookies
Preparation: 20 minutes
Cooking: 15–18 minutes
Level: 1

COFFEE CRUNCH COOKIES

244

Preheat the oven to 375°F (190°C/gas 5).
• Butter a cookie sheets. • Mix the flour,
baking powder, and salt in a large bowl.
• Beat the butter and sugar in a large bowl
with an electric mixer at high speed until
creamy. • Mix in the dry ingredients, walnuts,
and coffee granules until well blended.
• Drop tablespoons of the dough 1 inch
(2.5 cm) apart onto the prepared cookie
sheet. • Bake until just golden, 15–20 minutes.
• Cool on the sheets until the cookies firm
slightly. • Transfer to wire racks and
let cool completely.

3/4 cup (125 g) all-purpose (plain) flour
½ teaspoon baking powder
⅛ teaspoon salt
½ cup (125 g) butter, softened
¼ cup (50 g) granulated sugar
⅔ cup (70 g) finely chopped walnuts
2 teaspoons instant coffee granules

Makes: about 16 cookies
Preparation: 20 minutes
Cooking: 15–20 minutes
Level: 1

ESPRESSO COOKIES

Preheat the oven to 375°F (190°C/gas 5).
• Butter two cookie sheets. • Mix the flour, baking powder, and salt in a medium bowl.
• Beat the butter and sugar in a large bowl with an electric mixer at high speed until creamy. • Mix in the dry ingredients, pecans, and coffee until well blended. • Drop tablespoons of the dough 1 inch (2.5 cm) apart onto the prepared cookie sheets.
• Bake until just golden, 15–20 minutes.
• Cool on the sheets until the cookies firm slightly. Transfer to racks to finish cooling.

1   cup (150 g) all-purpose (plain) flour
½   teaspoon baking powder
⅛   teaspoon salt
½   cup (125 g) butter, softened
¼   cup (50 g) granulated sugar
⅔   cup (60 g) finely chopped pecans
2   tablespoons strong black coffee

Makes: 20–25 cookies
Preparation: 20 minutes
Cooking: 15–20 minutes
Level: 1

HAZELNUT SNAPS

Stir together the hazelnuts, sugar, flour, cornstarch, and salt in a large bowl.
• Add the butter, vanilla, and cinnamon.
• Stir in the egg whites. • Refrigerate for 30 minutes. • Preheat the oven to 400°F (200°C/gas 6). • Line two cookie sheets with aluminum foil. • Drop spoonfuls of the dough 2 inches (5 cm) apart onto the prepared cookie sheets. • Bake until golden brown, 5–7 minutes. • Transfer to racks to cool.

1¼ cups (125 g) coarsely chopped hazelnuts

¾ cup (140 g) granulated sugar

3 tablespoons all-purpose (plain) flour

1 tablespoon cornstarch (cornflour)

⅛ teaspoon salt

3 tablespoons butter, melted

1 teaspoon vanilla extract (essence)

1 teaspoon ground cinnamon

3 large egg whites, lightly beaten

Makes: about 25 cookies
Preparation: 20 minutes
Cooking: 5–7 minutes
Level: 1

HAZELNUT COOKIES

Preheat the oven to 350°F (180°C/gas 4).
• Line two cookie sheets with parchment paper. • Use a wooden spoon to mix the hazelnuts, egg, sugar, orange liqueur, lemon juice, vanilla, and salt until a stiff dough has formed. • Form the dough into balls the size of walnuts and place 1 inch (2.5 cm) apart on the prepared cookie sheets. • Decorate with cherry halves. • Bake until just golden at the edges, 15–20 minutes. • Transfer to racks and let cool completely.

2½ cups (250 g) finely chopped hazelnuts

1 large egg, lightly beaten

¾ cup (150 g) granulated sugar

1 teaspoon orange liqueur

½ teaspoon freshly squeezed lemon juice

½ teaspoon vanilla extract (essence)

⅛ teaspoon salt

13 candied cherries, cut in half

Makes: about 26 cookies
Preparation: 25 minutes
Cooking: 15–20 minutes
Level: 1

FROSTED WALNUT BITES

252

Cookies: Preheat the oven to 375°F (190°C/gas 5). • Butter two cookie sheets. • Mix the flour, baking powder, cinnamon, ginger, and salt in a large bowl. • Beat the butter, shortening, and brown sugar in a large bowl with an electric mixer at high speed until creamy. • Add the eggs one at a time, beating until just blended after each addition. • Mix in the dry ingredients, raisins, and walnuts. • Drop teaspoons of the dough 1 inch (2.5 cm) apart onto the prepared cookie sheets. • Bake until just lightly browned at the edges, 8–10 minutes. • Transfer the cookies to racks to cool.
Frosting: Mix the confectioners' sugar and enough milk in a small bowl to make a drizzling consistency. Drizzle the frosting over the cookies.

Cookies

2½ cups (375 g) all-purpose (plain) flour
1½ teaspoons baking powder
½ teaspoon ground cinnamon
¼ teaspoon ground ginger
¼ teaspoon salt
½ cup (125 g) butter, softened
½ cup (125 g) vegetable shortening
2 large eggs
1 cup (200 g) firmly packed light brown sugar
½ cup (90 g) raisins
½ cup (50 g) finely chopped walnuts

Frosting

1½ cups (225 g) confectioners' (icing) sugar
½ cup (125 ml) milk + more, as needed

Makes: about 40 cookies
Preparation: 25 minutes
Cooking: 8–10 minutes
Level 1

WALNUT GINGER COOKIES

Preheat the oven to 375°F (190°C/gas 5).
• Butter two cookie sheets. • Mix the flour, baking soda, ginger, and salt in a medium bowl. • Beat the brown sugar, corn syrup, water, and egg in a large bowl with an electric mixer at high speed until well blended. • Stir in the dry ingredients, cherries, and walnuts.
• Drop teaspoons of the dough 2 inches (5 cm) apart onto the prepared cookie sheets. • Bake until just golden at the edges, 10–12 minutes. • Transfer to racks to cool.

2   cups (300 g) all-purpose (plain) flour

1   teaspoon baking soda (bicarbonate of soda)

1   tablespoon ground ginger

¼   teaspoon salt

1   cup (200 g) firmly packed light brown sugar

3   tablespoons light corn syrup (golden syrup)

3   tablespoons water

1   large egg

½   cup (50 g) finely chopped candied cherries

½   cup (50 g) finely chopped walnuts

Makes: about 30 cookies
Preparation: 20 minutes
Cooking: 10–12 minutes
Level: 1

MIXED CHOCOLATE COOKIES

Preheat the oven to 325°F (170°C/gas 3).
• Set out two cookie sheets. • Mix the flour, baking powder, and salt in a large bowl.
• Melt the semisweet and white chocolates and butter in a double boiler over barely simmering water. • Beat the eggs and sugar in a large bowl with an electric mixer at high speed until pale and thick. • Beat in the chocolate mixture, coffee granules, and almond extract. • Mix in the dry ingredients, almonds, and white chocolate chips. • Drop tablespoons of the dough 3 inches (8 cm) apart onto the cookie sheets. • Bake until lightly cracked on top, 20–25 minutes.
• Transfer to racks and let cool.

2/3 cup (100 g) all-purpose (plain) flour

½ teaspoon baking powder

⅛ teaspoon salt

6 oz (180 g) semisweet (dark) chocolate, coarsely chopped

6 oz (180 g) white chocolate, coarsely chopped

½ cup (125 g) butter, cut up

3 large eggs

1 cup (200 g) granulated sugar

1 tablespoon instant coffee granules

1 teaspoon almond extract (essence)

3 cups (300 g) coarsely chopped almonds

1 cup (180 g) white chocolate chips

Makes: about 40 cookies
Preparation: 20 minutes
Cooking: 20–25 minutes
Level: 1

ORANGE SPICE COOKIES

Preheat the oven to 350°F (180°C/gas 4).
• Butter two cookie sheets. • Plump the raisins in the brandy in a small bowl for 15 minutes. • Mix the flour, cinnamon, nutmeg, baking soda, and salt in a medium bowl. • Beat the butter and both sugars in a large bowl with an electric mixer at high speed until creamy. • Mix in the milk, raisin mixture, dry ingredients, and orange zest. • Drop teaspoons of the dough 1 inch (2.5 cm) apart onto the prepared cookie sheets. • Bake until just golden, 10–15 minutes. • Cool on the sheets until the cookies firm slightly. Transfer to racks to finish cooling.

⅓ cup (60 g) raisins

2 tablespoons brandy

1½ cups (225 g) all-purpose (plain) flour

1 teaspoon ground cinnamon

1 teaspoon freshly grated nutmeg

½ teaspoon baking soda (bicarbonate of soda)

⅛ teaspoon salt

¾ cup (180 g) butter, softened

¾ cup (150 g) granulated sugar

¼ cup (50 g) firmly packed dark brown sugar

¼ cup (60 ml) milk

Finely grated zest of 1 orange

Makes: 24–30 cookies
Preparation: 20 minutes
+ 15 minutes to plump the raisins
Cooking: 10–15 minutes
Level: 1

PECAN CINNAMON COOKIES

Preheat the oven to 375°F (190°C/gas 5).
• Butter two cookie sheets. • Mix the flour, baking powder, and salt in a medium bowl.
• Beat the butter and sugar in a large bowl with an electric mixer at high speed until creamy. • Add the egg, beating until just blended. • Mix in the dry ingredients to form a smooth dough. • Mix the pecans and cinnamon in a small bowl. • Form the dough into balls the size of walnuts and roll them in the nut mixture until well coated. • Place the cookies 2 inches (5 cm) apart on the prepared cookie sheets. • Bake until golden, 10–15 minutes. • Transfer to racks to cool.

1¼ cups (180 g) all-purpose (plain)) flour
1 teaspoon baking powder
⅛ teaspoon salt
½ cup (125 g) butter, softened
¾ cup (150 g) granulated sugar
1 large egg
¾ cup (75 g) finely chopped pecans
2 teaspoons ground cinnamon

Makes: 20–25 cookies
Preparation: 20 minutes
Cooking: 10–15 minutes
Level: 1

PEANUT BUTTER COOKIES

262

Preheat the oven to 375°F (190°C/gas 5).
• Line two cookie sheets with parchment paper. • Mix the flour, baking powder, cinnamon, nutmeg, cloves, and salt in a large bowl. • Beat the oil, honey, and peanut butter in a large bowl with an electric mixer at high speed until well blended. • Mix in the dry ingredients, oats, and raisins. • Drop tablespoons of the dough 1 inch (2.5 cm) apart onto the prepared cookie sheets.
• Bake until golden brown, 8–10 minutes.
• Cool on the sheets until the cookies firm slightly. Transfer to racks to finish cooling.

1²⁄₃ cups (250 g) all-purpose (plain) flour

1 teaspoon baking powder

½ teaspoon ground cinnamon

½ teaspoon ground nutmeg

¼ teaspoon ground cloves

¼ teaspoon salt

⅓ cup (90 ml) sunflower or canola oil

⅓ cup (90 ml) honey

1 cup (250 g) smooth peanut butter

½ cup (75 g) old-fashioned rolled oats

½ cup (90 g) raisins

Makes: about 30 cookies
Preparation: 20 minutes
Cooking: 8–10 minutes
Level: 1

GINGER CRUNCHIES

264

Preheat the oven to 350°F (180°C/gas 4).
• Butter two cookie sheets. • Mix the flour,
ginger, baking powder, baking soda, and salt
in a large bowl. • Stir in the brown sugar.
• Melt the butter with the corn syrup in a
small saucepan over low heat. • Remove from
the heat and let cool.• Stir the butter mixture
into the dry ingredients. • Add the egg and
mix to make a stiff dough. • Form the dough
into balls the size of walnuts and place 2
inches (5 cm) apart on the prepared cookie
sheets. • Bake until just golden and firm to
the touch, 12–15 minutes. • Cool the cookies
on the sheets for 5 minutes. Transfer to racks
and let cool completely.

1¼ cups (180 g) all-
   purpose (plain) flour

2 teaspoons ground
   ginger

1 teaspoon baking
   powder

½ teaspoon baking soda
   (bicarbonate of soda)

⅛ teaspoon salt

⅓ cup (70 g) firmly
   packed light brown
   sugar

¼ cup (60 g) butter,
   softened

3 tablespoons light corn
   syrup (golden syrup

1 large egg

Makes: about 20 cookies
Preparation: 20 minutes
Cooking: 12–15 minutes
Level: 1

ANISEED CORIANDER COOKIES

266

Preheat the oven to 350°F (180°C/gas 4).
• Butter two cookie sheets. • Mix the flour, coriander, aniseeds, and salt in a large bowl.
• Beat the eggs and sugar in a medium bowl with an electric mixer at high speed until pale and thick. • Mix in the dry ingredients until well blended. • Drop teaspoons of the cookie dough 3 inches (8 cm) apart onto the prepared cookie sheets. • Bake until faintly tinged with brown on top and slightly darker at the edges, 8–12 minutes. • Use a spatula to turn the cookies over. • Bake until firm to the touch, 3–5 minutes more. • Transfer to racks and let cool completely.

¾ cup (125 g) all-purpose (plain) flour
1 teaspoon ground coriander
½ teaspoon ground aniseeds
⅛ teaspoon salt
2 large eggs
¾ cup (150 g) granulated sugar

Makes: 20–25 cookies
Preparation: 20 minutes
Cooking: 11–17 minutes
Level: 1

GOLDEN GINGER CRISPS

Preheat the oven to 400°F (200°C/gas 6).
• Butter two cookie sheets. • Mix the flour, ginger, baking powder, baking soda, allspice, cinnamon, and salt in a large bowl. • Use a pastry blender to cut in the butter until the mixture resembles fine crumbs. • Stir in the sugar and corn syrup until well blended. • Form the dough into balls the size of walnuts and place 2 inches (5 cm) apart on the prepared cookie sheets. • Bake until just golden, 10–15 minutes. Watch them closely toward the end of the baking time as they darken very quickly. • Cool on the sheets until the cookies firm slightly. Transfer to racks and let cool completely.

1½ cups (225 g) all-purpose (plain) flour

1 tablespoon ground ginger

2 teaspoons baking powder

1 teaspoon baking soda (bicarbonate of soda)

1 teaspoon ground allspice

1 teaspoon ground cinnamon

⅛ teaspoon salt

½ cup (125 g) butter, cut up

½ cup (100 g) granulated sugar

¼ cup (60 ml) light corn syrup (golden syrup)

Makes: 20–24 cookies
Preparation: 25 minutes
Cooking: 10–15 minutes
Level: 1

LEBKUCHEN

Cookies: Preheat the oven to 325°F
(170°C/gas 3). • Pound the cloves, cinnamon,
cardamom seeds, mace, and nutmeg in
a pestle and mortar until finely ground.
• Spread the almonds on a large baking
sheet. Toast for 7 minutes, or until lightly
golden. • Finely chop the almonds. • Increase
the oven temperature to 350°F (180°C/gas 4).
• Line three cookie sheets with rice paper.
• Let the almonds cool completely and
transfer to a medium bowl. • Stir in the
candied lemon and orange peel, lemon zest,
and ground spices. • Mix the flour, baking
powder, and salt in a medium bowl. • Beat
the eggs and sugar in a large bowl with an
electric mixer at high speed until pale and
thick. • Beat in the honey and almond
mixture. • Add the kirsch. • Mix in the dry
ingredients. • Drop rounded tablespoons of
the mixture 2 inches (5 cm) apart onto the
prepared cookie sheets. • Bake until lightly
browned, 15–20 minutes. • Cool on the sheets
until the cookies firm slightly. • Transfer the
cookies still on the rice paper to racks and let
cool completely. • Tear away the excess rice
paper from around the cookies.

Cookies

- 10 cloves
- 1 (3-inch/8-cm) piece cinnamon stick
- Seeds from 5 cardamom pods
- 1 blade mace
- ½ teaspoon freshly grated nutmeg
- 2 cups (300 g) whole almonds
- ½ cup (50 g) finely chopped candied lemon peel
- ½ cup (50 g) finely chopped candied orange peel
- Finely grated zest of ½ lemon
- 2⅓ cups (350 g) all-purpose (plain) flour
- 1 teaspoon baking powder
- ⅛ teaspoon salt
- 3 large eggs
- 1 cup (200 g) granulated sugar
- 2 tablespoons honey
- 1 teaspoon kirsch

<u>Rum Glaze</u>: Mix the confectioners' sugar, water, and rum in a small bowl until smooth. • Spread the glaze over the cookies and let stand for 30 minutes until set.

Rum Glaze

1   **cup (150 g) confectioners' (icing) sugar**

1   **tablespoon warm water**

½   **teaspoon white rum**

Makes: 35–40 cookies
Preparation: 50 minutes
   + 30 minutes to set
Cooking: 15–20 minutes
Level: 2

ALMOND CRISPS

274

Stir the almonds, sugar, flour, cornstarch, and salt in a large bowl. • Add the butter, almond extract, and cinnamon. • Stir in the egg whites. • Refrigerate for 30 minutes.
• Preheat the oven to 400°F (200°C/gas 6).
• Line two cookie sheets with aluminum foil.
• Drop spoonfuls of the dough 2 inches (5 cm) apart onto the prepared cookie sheets.
• Bake until golden brown, 5–7 minutes.
• Transfer to racks to cool.

1⅓ cups (150 g) coarsely chopped almonds

¾ cup (150 g) granulated sugar

5 tablespoons all-purpose (plain) flour

1 tablespoon cornstarch (cornflour)

⅛ teaspoon salt

3 tablespoons butter, melted

½ teaspoon almond extract (essence)

1 teaspoon ground cinnamon

3 large egg whites, lightly beaten

Makes: about 25 cookies
Preparation: 20 minutes
Cooking: 5–7 minutes
Level: 1

HIGHLAND COOKIES

Preheat the oven to 350°F (180°C/gas 4).
• Line two cookie sheets with parchment
paper. • Mix the flour, baking soda, and salt
in a large bowl. • Beat the butter and brown
sugar in a large bowl with an electric mixer at
high speed until creamy. • Add the egg,
beating until just blended. Add the vanilla.
• Mix in the dry ingredients, oats, and water.
• Roll teaspoons of the mixture into balls and
place on the prepared cookie sheets, about
$1\frac{1}{2}$ inches (4 cm) apart, flattening them
slightly. • Bake until golden brown, 12–15
minutes. • Transfer to racks to cool.

1 cup (150 g) all-purpose (plain) flour

$\frac{1}{2}$ teaspoon baking soda (bicarbonate of soda)

$\frac{1}{8}$ teaspoon salt

$\frac{2}{3}$ cup (150 g) butter, softened

$1\frac{1}{4}$ cups (250 g) firmly packed dark brown sugar

1 large egg

1 teaspoon vanilla extract (essence)

1 cup (150 g) old-fashioned rolled oats

1 tablespoon water + more, as needed

Makes: 35–40 cookies
Preparation: 30 minutes
Cooking: 12–15 minutes
Level: 1

GEORDIE COOKIES

Preheat the oven to 350°F (180°C/gas 4).
• Butter three cookie sheets. • Mix the flour,
baking soda, and salt in a large bowl.
• Beat the butter and both sugars in a large
bowl with an electric mixer at high speed until
creamy. • Add the vanilla and egg, beating
until just blended. • Mix in the dry
ingredients, oats, raisins, and peanuts.
• Drop heaping teaspoons of the dough
2 inches (5 cm) apart onto the prepared
cookie sheets. • Bake until lightly browned,
12–15 minutes. • Transfer to racks and let
cool completely.

1¼ cups (180 g) all-purpose (plain) flour

½ teaspoon baking soda (bicarbonate of soda)

¼ teaspoon salt

½ cup (125 g) butter, softened

½ cup (100 g) granulated sugar

½ cup (100 g) firmly packed dark brown sugar

½ teaspoon vanilla extract (essence)

1 large egg, lightly beaten

⅓ cup (50 g) old-fashioned rolled oats

½ cup (90 g) raisins

⅔ cup (60 g) coarsely chopped walnuts

Makes: about 45 cookies
Preparation: 20 minutes
Cooking: 12–15 minutes
Level: 1

OAT AND DATE COOKIES

Preheat the oven to 350°F (180°C/gas 4).
• Butter two cookie sheets. • Mix the flour,
baking powder, and salt in a large bowl.
• Use a pastry blender to cut in the butter
until the mixture resembles fine crumbs.
• Add the egg, beating until just blended.
• Mix in the sugar, oats, and dates. • Drop
tablespoons of the dough 2 inches (5 cm)
apart onto the prepared cookie sheets.
• Bake until lightly browned, 12–15 minutes.
• Cool on the sheets until the cookies firm
slightly. Transfer to racks to cool.

1½ cups (225 g) all-purpose (plain) flour
½ teaspoon baking powder
⅛ teaspoon salt
½ cup (125 g) butter, cut up
1 large egg, lightly beaten
1 cup (200 g) granulated sugar
½ cup (75 g) old-fashioned rolled oats
½ cup (50 g) coarsely chopped dates

Makes: about 20 cookies
Preparation: 20 minutes
Cooking: 12–15 minutes
Level: 1

CORNFLAKE AND APRICOT COOKIES

Preheat the oven to 350°F (180°C/gas 4).
• Line two cookie sheets with parchment paper. • Mix the flour and baking powder in a large bowl. • Beat the butter and brown sugar in a large bowl with an electric mixer at high speed until creamy. • Add the eggs one at a time, beating until just blended after each addition. • Mix in the dry ingredients, followed by the corn flakes, apricots, and coconut. • Drop heaping teaspoons of the mixture 1½ inches (4 cm) apart onto the prepared cookie sheets. • Bake until lightly browned, 10–12 minutes. • Transfer the cookies, still on the parchment paper, to racks to cool.

²/₃ cup (100 g) all-purpose (plain) flour

1 teaspoon baking powder

⅓ cup (90 g) butter, softened

¾ cup (150 g) firmly packed light brown sugar

2 large eggs

2 tablespoons corn flakes

½ cup (50 g) finely chopped dried apricots

3 tablespoons shredded (desiccated) coconut

Makes: about 35 cookies
Preparation: 30 minutes
Cooking: 10–12 minutes
Level: 2

PEANUT MUNCHIES

Preheat the oven to 300°F (150°C/gas 2).
• Butter two cookie sheets. • Mix the flour, baking powder, and baking soda in a medium bowl. • Beat the butter and sugar in a large bowl with an electric mixer at high speed until creamy. • Add the egg, beating until just blended. • Mix in the dry ingredients, peanuts, corn flakes, and oats to make a stiff dough. • Drop teaspoons of the dough 1 inch (2.5 cm) apart onto the prepared cookie sheet. • Bake until lightly browned, 10–15 minutes. • Cool on the sheets until the cookies firm slightly. Transfer to racks and let cool completely.

1 cup (150 g) all-purpose (plain) flour

½ teaspoon baking powder

½ teaspoon baking soda (bicarbonate of soda)

½ cup (125 g) butter, softened

1 cup (200 g) granulated sugar

1 large egg, lightly beaten

½ cup (50 g) salted peanuts

1 cup (150 g) corn flakes

2¼ cups (330 g) old-fashioned rolled oats

Makes: about 25 cookies
Preparation: 20 minutes
Cooking: 10–15 minutes
Level: 1

WALNUT CRISPS

Preheat the oven to 375°F (190°C/gas 5).
• Butter three cookie sheets. • Mix the
flour, baking soda, and salt in a large bowl.
• Beat the butter and both sugars in a large
bowl with an electric mixer at high speed until
creamy. • Add the vanilla and egg, beating
until just blended. • Mix in the dry
ingredients, followed by the corn flakes and
walnuts. • Drop teaspoons of the dough
1 inch (2.5 cm) apart onto the prepared
cookie sheets. • Bake until lightly browned,
12–15 minutes: • Cool on the sheets until the
cookies firm slightly. Transfer to racks to
finish cooling.

$2/3$ cup (100 g) all-purpose (plain) flour

$1/2$ teaspoon baking soda (bicarbonate of soda)

$1/8$ teaspoon salt

$1/2$ cup (125 g) butter, softened

$1/4$ cup (50 g) granulated sugar

$2/3$ cup (70 g) firmly packed light brown sugar

$1/2$ teaspoon vanilla extract (essence)

1 large egg, lightly beaten

$1/3$ cup (50 g) corn flakes

$2/3$ cup (70 g) coarsely chopped walnuts

Makes: about 36 cookies
Preparation: 20 minutes
Cooking: 12–15 minutes
Level: 1

SUNFLOWER SEED DROPS

Preheat the oven to 350°F (180°C/gas 4).
• Butter three cookie sheets. • Mix the flour,
baking soda, and salt in a medium bowl.
• Beat the butter and both sugars in a large
bowl with an electric mixer at high speed until
creamy. • Add the eggs and vanilla, beating
until just blended. • Mix in the dry
ingredients, oats, and sunflower seeds.
• Drop tablespoons of the dough 2 inches
(5 cm) apart onto the prepared cookie sheets.
• Bake until golden brown, 10–15 minutes.
• Cool on the sheets until the cookies firm
slightly. Transfer to racks to finish cooling.

1½ cups (225 g) all-
purpose (plain) flour

1 teaspoon baking soda
(bicarbonate of soda)

¼ teaspoon salt

1 cup (250 g) butter,
softened

1 cup (200 g) firmly
packed light brown
sugar

1 cup (200 g) granulated
sugar

2 large eggs, lightly
beaten

½ teaspoon vanilla extract
(essence)

2 cups (300 g) old-
fashioned rolled oats

1 cup (100 g) sunflower
seeds

Makes: 36–40 cookies
Preparation: 20 minutes
Cooking: 10–15 minutes
Level: 1

MINSTREL COOKIES

Preheat the oven to 325°F (170°C/gas 3).
• Butter two cookie sheets. • Mix the flour, polenta, baking powder, and salt in a large bowl. • Use a pastry blender to cut in the butter until the mixture resembles coarse crumbs. • Mix in the eggs and brown sugar to form a soft dough. • Form the dough into balls the size of walnuts and place 1½ inches (4 cm) apart on the prepared cookie sheets. • Bake until lightly browned, 20–25 minutes. • Transfer to racks to cool.

1½ cups (225 g) all-purpose (plain) flour

1 cup (150 g) polenta (finely ground yellow cornmeal)

1 teaspoon baking powder

⅛ teaspoon salt

½ cup (125 g) butter, cut up

2 large eggs, lightly beaten

⅔ cup (140 g) firmly packed dark brown sugar

Makes: about 35 cookies
Preparation: 25 minutes
Cooking: 20–25 minutes
Level: 1

CARAWAY MOMENTS

Preheat the oven to 375°F (190°C/gas 5).
• Set out two cookie sheets. • Mix the flour, baking powder, and salt in a medium bowl.
• Beat the butter and ¼ cup (50 g) of sugar in a large bowl with an electric mixer at high speed until creamy. • Mix in the dry ingredients, followed by the milk to make a soft dough. • Form the dough into balls the size of walnuts and place 2 inches (5 cm) apart on the cookie sheets. • Sprinkle with the caraway seeds and remaining sugar.
• Bake until lightly browned, 12–15 minutes.
• Cool on the sheets until the cookies firm slightly. Transfer to racks to finish cooling.

1 cup (150 g) all-purpose (plain) flour

1 teaspoon baking powder

⅛ teaspoon salt

7 tablespoons butter, softened

¼ cup (50 g) + 1 teaspoon granulated sugar

1 teaspoon milk

1 teaspoon caraway seeds

Makes: about 20 cookies
Preparation: 30 minutes
Cooking: 12–15 minutes
Level: 1

WHEAT GERM CRISPS

Preheat the oven to 350°F (180°C/gas 4).
• Butter two cookie sheets. • Stir together the wheat germ, baking soda, cinnamon, nutmeg, and salt in a large bowl. Stir in the oats and sugar. • Melt the butter with the corn syrup and milk in a small saucepan over low heat. • Pour into the dry ingredients and mix until smooth. • Form into balls the size of walnuts and place 2 inches (5 cm) apart on the prepared cookie sheets, flattening them slightly. • Bake until golden brown, 12–15 minutes. • Cool the cookies completely on the cookie sheets.

294

- $3/4$ cup (125 g) wheat germ, toasted
- $1/2$ teaspoon baking soda (bicarbonate of soda)
- 1 teaspoon ground cinnamon
- $1/2$ teaspoon ground nutmeg
- $1/8$ teaspoon salt
- $1/2$ cup (75 g) old-fashioned rolled oats
- $1/3$ cup (70 g) granulated sugar
- $1/3$ cup (90 g) butter, cut up
- 1 tablespoon light corn syrup (golden syrup)
- 1 tablespoon milk

Makes: about 25 cookies
Preparation: 15 minutes
Cooking: 12–15 minutes
Level: 1

OATMEAL COCONUT COOKIES

296

Preheat the oven to 350°F (180°C/gas 4).
• Butter two cookie sheets. • Mix the flour, baking soda, and salt in a large bowl. Stir in the coconut and oats. • Melt the butter with the sugar and corn syrup in a small saucepan over medium heat. • Mix in the dry ingredients until well blended. • Roll into balls the size of walnuts and place 1 inch (2.5 cm) apart on the prepared cookie sheets, flattening them slightly with a fork. • Bake until golden brown, 15–20 minutes. • Cool on the sheets until the cookies firm slightly.
• Transfer to racks to cool.

1 cup (150 g) all-purpose (plain) flour
½ teaspoon baking soda (bicarbonate of soda)
⅛ teaspoon salt
1 cup (125 g) shredded (desiccated) coconut
1 cup (150 g) old-fashioned rolled oats
½ cup (125 g) butter, cut up
¾ cup (150 g) granulated sugar
2 tablespoons light corn syrup (golden syrup)

Makes: about 20 cookies
Preparation: 20 minutes
Cooking: 15–20 minutes
Level: 1

SESAME SNAPS

Preheat the oven to 400°F (200°C/gas 6).
• Butter and flour two cookie sheets. • Beat the butter, sugar, and lemon zest in a large bowl with an electric mixer at high speed until pale and creamy. • With mixer at low speed, gradually beat in the flour. • Place the egg white, honey, and sesame seeds in a small bowl and mix well. The mixture should be dense and dry. • Scoop out 1 heaped tablespoon of dough and shape into a ball about the size of a walnut. • Place over the sesame mixture and press down with your fingers until 3 inches (8 cm) in diameter. Repeat until all the dough and filling are used up. • Place the cookies, sesame seed-side up, on the sheet. • Bake until golden brown, 10–15 minutes. • Let cool completely.

1 cup (250 g) butter, softened

1 cup (200 g) granulated sugar

1 tablespoon finely grated lemon zest

2 cups (300 g) all-purpose (plain) flour

1 large egg white, lightly beaten

2 tablespoons honey

1⅓ cups (130 g) sesame seeds

Makes about 25 cookies
Preparation: 10 minutes
Cooking: 10–15 minutes
Level: 1

SUNFLOWER COOKIES

Preheat the oven to 350°F (180°C/gas 4).
• Butter two cookie sheets. • Mix the flour, baking soda, and salt in a medium bowl.
• Beat the butter and both sugars in a large bowl with an electric mixer at high speed until creamy. • Add the eggs and vanilla, beating until just blended. • Mix in the dry ingredients, corn flakes, and sunflower seeds.
• Drop tablespoons of the dough 2 inches (5 cm) apart onto the prepared cookie sheets.
• Bake until golden brown, 10–15 minutes.
• Cool on the sheets until the cookies firm slightly. Transfer to racks to cool.

1½ cups (225 g) all-purpose (plain) flour

1 teaspoon baking soda (bicarbonate of soda)

¼ teaspoon salt

1 cup (250 g) butter, softened

1 cup (200 g) firmly packed light brown sugar

1 cup (200 g) granulated sugar

2 large eggs, lightly beaten

½ teaspoon vanilla extract (essence)

2 cups (200 g) corn flakes

1 cup (100 g) sunflower seeds

Makes: 36–40 cookies
Preparation: 20 minutes
Cooking: 10–15 minutes
Level: 1

RICE COOKIES

Preheat the oven to 350°F (180°C/gas 4).
• Butter two cookie sheets. • Mix the flour,
baking powder, baking soda, and salt in a
large bowl. • Stir in the sugar. • Mix in the
olive oil and enough water to form a stiff
dough. • Form the dough into balls the size
of walnuts and place 1 inch (2.5 cm) apart
on the prepared cookie sheets, flattening
them slightly. • Bake until just golden,
20–25 minutes. • Transfer to racks and
let cool completely.

302

$1^2/_3$ cups (250 g) rice flour

½ teaspoon baking
powder

⅛ teaspoon baking soda
(bicarbonate of soda)

⅛ teaspoon salt

⅓ cup (70 g) granulated
sugar

¼ cup (60 ml) best-
quality extra-virgin
olive oil

½ cup (125 ml) water

Makes: about 24 cookies
Preparation: 20 minutes
Cooking: 20–25 minutes
Level: 1

POPPY SEED ALMOND COOKIES

Preheat the oven to 350°F (180°C/gas 4).
• Line two cookie sheets with parchment
paper. • Beat the egg whites in a large bowl
with an electric mixer at high speed until soft
peaks form. • Use a large rubber spatula to
fold in the flour, superfine sugar, almonds,
poppy seeds, and almond oil until smooth.
• Drop teaspoons of the cookie dough 1 inch
(2.5 cm) apart onto the prepared cookie
sheets. • Bake until golden brown around
the edges, 6–8 minutes. • Cool the cookies
on the cookie sheet for 1 minute. Transfer
to racks to finish cooling.

4 **large egg whites**
2 **tablespoons all-purpose (plain) flour**
¼ **cup (50 g) superfine (caster) sugar**
2 **cups (300 g) finely ground almonds**
2 **tablespoons poppy seeds**
1 **tablespoon almond oil**

Makes: about 24 cookies
Preparation: 20 minutes
Cooking: 6–8 minutes
Level: 1

COCONUT BUTTER THINS

Preheat the oven to 375°F (190°C/gas 5).
• Set out a cookie sheet. • Mix the flour and salt in a medium bowl. • Beat the butter, sugar, and vanilla in a large bowl with an electric mixer at high speed until creamy.
• Mix in the dry ingredients and coconut to form a smooth dough. • Form the dough into balls the size of walnuts and place 2 inches (5 cm) apart on the cookie sheet. • Press a half-cherry into each cookie. • Bake until just golden at the edges, 12–15 minutes.
• Transfer to racks to cool.

²/₃ cup (100 g) all-purpose (plain) flour

¹/₈ teaspoon salt

½ cup (125 g) butter, softened

¼ cup (50 g) granulated sugar

½ teaspoon vanilla extract (essence)

2 tablespoons shredded (desiccated) coconut

8 candied cherries, cut in half

Makes: 16–18 cookies
Preparation: 20 minutes
Cooking: 12–15 minutes
Level: 1

BROWN SUGAR DROPS

Preheat the oven to 375°F (190°C/gas 5).
• Butter three cookie sheets. • Mix the flour, baking soda, and salt in a medium bowl.
• Beat the butter and both sugars in a large bowl with an electric mixer at high speed until creamy. • Add the egg and vanilla extract, beating until just blended. • Mix in the dry ingredients. • Drop teaspoons of the dough 2 inches (5 cm) apart onto the prepared cookie sheets. • Bake until golden, 7–10 minutes. • Transfer to racks to cool.

1¼ cups (180 g) all-purpose (plain) flour

½ teaspoon baking soda (bicarbonate of soda)

⅛ teaspoon salt

½ cup (125 g) butter, softened

3 tablespoons firmly packed light brown sugar

3 tablespoons granulated sugar

1 large egg, lightly beaten

½ teaspoon vanilla extract (essence)

Makes: 40–45 cookies
Preparation: 20 minutes
Cooking: 7–10 minutes
Level: 1

FROSTED PINEAPPLE BITES

310

Cookies: Preheat the oven to 400°F (200°C/gas 6). • Butter three cookie sheets. • Mix the flour, baking powder, and salt in a medium bowl. • Beat the shortening and brown sugar in a large bowl with an electric mixer at high speed until creamy. • Add the egg and vanilla, beating until just blended. • Mix in the pineapple, reserving a few pieces for decoration, and the dry ingredients. • Drop teaspoons of the dough 2 inches (5 cm) apart onto the prepared cookie sheets. • Bake until just golden at the edges, 8–10 minutes. • Transfer to racks to cool. Pineapple Glaze: Mix the confectioners' sugar and pineapple juice in a small bowl. • Spread the glaze over the tops of the cookies and top with the reserved pineapple. Let set for 30 minutes.

Cookies

2   cups (300 g) all-purpose (plain) flour

1½ teaspoons baking powder

¼   teaspoon salt

½   cup (125 g) vegetable shortening

1   cup (200 g) firmly packed light brown sugar

1   large egg

½   teaspoon vanilla extract (essence)

1   (8-oz/250-g) can crushed pineapple, drained (juice reserved)

Pineapple Glaze

3   cups (450 g) confectioners' (icing) sugar

¼   cup (60 ml) pineapple juice (see above)

Makes: 32–36 cookies
Preparation: 25 minutes
  + 30 minutes to set
Cooking: 8–10 minutes
Level: 1

GREEN APPLE COOKIES

Preheat the oven to 375°F (170°C/gas 3).
• Butter three cookie sheets. • Mix the flour, baking powder, baking soda, cinnamon, and salt in a medium bowl. • Beat the butter and both sugars in a large bowl with an electric mixer at high speed until creamy. • Add the egg and applesauce, beating until just blended. • Mix in the dry ingredients, apple, and walnuts. • Drop tablespoons of the dough 2 inches (5 cm) apart onto the prepared cookie sheets. • Bake until just golden at the edges, 15–20 minutes. • Transfer to racks to cool.

2 cups (300 g) all-purpose (plain) flour

½ teaspoon baking powder

½ teaspoon baking soda (bicarbonate of soda)

½ teaspoon ground cinnamon

¼ teaspoon salt

½ cup (125 g) butter, softened

½ cup (100 g) granulated sugar

¼ cup (50 g) firmly packed dark brown sugar

1 large egg

1 cup (250 ml) applesauce

1 tart apple, such as Granny Smith, peeled, cored, and finely chopped

1 cup (100 g) finely chopped walnuts

Makes: 45–48 cookies
Preparation: 20 minutes
Cooking: 15–20 minutes
Level: 1

SWEET APPLE COOKIES

314

Cook the apples with 1 tablespoon of sugar in a small saucepan over low heat, stirring often, until softened. Remove from the heat and let cool completely. • Preheat the oven to 400°F (200°C/gas 6). • Butter three cookie sheets. • Mix the flour, baking powder, cinnamon, and salt in a medium bowl. • Beat the butter and remaining sugar in a large bowl with an electric mixer at high speed until creamy. • Add the egg, beating until just blended. • Mix in alternating tablespoons of the dry ingredients and the cooked apples until well blended. • Stir in the raisins and corn flakes. • Drop teaspoons of the dough 1 inch (2.5 cm) apart onto the prepared cookie sheets. • Bake until golden brown, 10–15 minutes. • Transfer to racks to cool.

2 medium sweet cooking apples, peeled, cored, and finely chopped
3/4 cup (150 g) granulated sugar
2 cups (300 g) all-purpose (plain) flour
1 teaspoon baking powder
1 teaspoon ground cinnamon
1/8 teaspoon salt
3/4 cup (180 g) butter, softened
1 large egg
3/4 cup (120 g) raisins
1 cup (100 g) corn flakes

Makes: 40–45 cookies
Preparation: 30 minutes
Cooking: 10–15 minutes
Level: 1

LIME COOKIES

Preheat the oven to 350°F (180°C/gas 4).
• Line three cookie sheets with parchment paper. • Mix the flour, baking soda, and salt in a medium bowl. • Stir in the sunflower seeds. • Beat the butter, 2 cups (400 g) of sugar, oil, and grated zest of 1 lime in a large bowl with an electric mixer at high speed until creamy. • Add the eggs, beating until just blended. • Mix in the dry ingredients and lime juice. • Mix the remaining sugar and lime zest in a small bowl. • Form the dough into balls the size of walnuts and roll in the lime sugar. • Place the cookies 2 inches (5 cm) apart on the prepared cookie sheets, flattening them slightly. • Bake until just golden at the edges, 10–12 minutes. • Transfer to racks and let cool completely.

3½ cups (535 g) all-purpose (plain) flour

1 teaspoon baking soda (bicarbonate of soda)

½ teaspoon salt

½ cup (50 g) sunflower seeds, toasted and finely ground

½ cup (125 g) butter, softened

2¼ cups (450 g) granulated sugar

2 tablespoons extra-virgin olive oil

Finely grated zest of 2 limes

2 large eggs

3 tablespoons freshly squeezed lime juice

Makes: about 60 cookies
Preparation: 25 minutes
Cooking: 10–12 minutes
Level: 1

CARROT AND ORANGE COOKIES

Preheat the oven to 375°F (190°C/gas 5).
• Oil four cookie sheets. • Mix the flour, baking soda, cinnamon, allspice, nutmeg, ginger, and salt in a medium bowl. • Beat the butter and brown sugar in a large bowl with an electric mixer at high speed until creamy.
• Add the orange zest and vanilla. • Add the eggs, carrots, raisins, coconut, and oats.
• Mix in the dry ingredients. • Drop teaspoons of the dough 2 inches (5 cm) apart on the prepared cookie sheets. • Bake until golden brown, 8–10 minutes. • Transfer to racks and let cool completely.

1⅓ cups (200 g) all purpose (plain) flour

1 teaspoon baking soda (bicarbonate of soda)

1 teaspoon ground cinnamon

½ teaspoon ground allspice

½ teaspoon freshly grated nutmeg

¼ teaspoon ground ginger

¼ teaspoon salt

1 cup (250 g) butter, softened

1 cup (200 g) firmly packed light brown sugar

1 teaspoon finely grated orange zest

1 teaspoon vanilla extract (essence)

2 large eggs

1½ cups (185 g) finely shredded carrots

½ cup (90 g) raisins

½ cup (60 g) shredded (desiccated) coconut

¼ cup (30 g) old-fashioned rolled oats

Makes: about 50 cookies
Preparation: 20 minutes
Cooking: 8–10 minutes
Level: 1

LEMON CARROT COOKIES

320

Preheat the oven to 350°F (180°C/gas 4).
• Butter a cookie sheet. • Mix the flour,
baking powder, and salt in a medium bowl.
• Reserve 2 teaspoons of the sugar. • Beat the
margarine and remaining sugar with the
lemon zest in a medium bowl with an electric
mixer at high speed until creamy. • Use a
wooden spoon to mix in the shredded carrot,
followed by the dry ingredients to make a soft
dough. • If the dough is stiff, add the water.
• Drop tablespoons of the dough 2 inches
(5 cm) apart onto the prepared cookie sheet.
Sprinkle the tops of the cookies with the
reserved sugar. • Bake until golden and firm
to the touch, 15–20 minutes.

½ cup (75 g) all-purpose
(plain) flour

1 teaspoon baking
powder

⅛ teaspoon salt

¼ cup (50 g) granulated
sugar

2 tablespoons finely
grated lemon zest

2 tablespoons margarine
or butter, softened

1⅔ cups (200 g) very
finely shredded carrots
or grated carrots

Makes: about 16 cookies
Preparation: 40 minutes
Cooking: 15–20 minutes
Level: 1

CRISP ORANGE COOKIES

322

Preheat the oven to 350°F (180°C/gas 4).
• Butter two cookie sheets. • Mix the flour, cornstarch, baking powder, and salt in a large bowl. • Beat the butter and $^2/_3$ cup (100 g) confectioners' sugar in a large bowl with an electric mixer at high speed until creamy.
• Mix in the dry ingredients and orange zest.
• Drop teaspoons of the mixture 2 inches (5 cm) apart onto the prepared cookie sheets.
• Bake until golden brown, 12–15 minutes.
• Cool completely on the sheets.

$1^{1/2}$ cups (225 g) all-purpose (plain) flour

1 tablespoon cornstarch (cornflour)

½ teaspoon baking powder

⅛ teaspoon salt

1 cup (250 g) butter, softened

$^2/_3$ cup (100 g) confectioners' (icing) sugar + extra, to dust

Finely grated zest of 2 oranges

Makes: about 25 cookies
Preparation: 25 minutes
Cooking: 12–15 minutes
Level: 1

SPICED DUTCH COOKIES

Preheat the oven to 375°F (190°C/gas 5).
• Butter two cookie sheets. • Mix the flour, cinnamon, cloves, mace, and salt in a large bowl. • Stir in the lemon zest, aniseeds, and black pepper. • Mix the honey, molasses, and granulated sugar in a medium saucepan over low heat. • Cook, stirring constantly, until the sugar has dissolved completely. • Add the butter and remove from the heat. • Add the egg, beating until just blended. • Mix in the dry ingredients to form a stiff dough. • Drop teaspoons of the dough 2 inches (5 cm) apart onto the prepared sheets. • Bake until firm and golden brown, 12–15 minutes. • Cool on the sheets until the cookies firm slightly.
• Transfer to racks and let cool completely.

3/4 cup (125 g) all-purpose (plain) flour

1 teaspoon ground cinnamon

1/2 teaspoon ground cloves

1/2 teaspoon ground mace

1/8 teaspoon salt

1/2 teaspoon finely grated lemon zest

1/8 teaspoon ground aniseeds

1/8 teaspoon ground black pepper

1/3 cup (90 ml) honey

1/3 cup (90 ml) light molasses (treacle)

1/4 cup (50 g) granulated sugar

2 tablespoons butter

1 large egg, lightly beaten

Makes: 30–35 cookies
Preparation: 20 minutes
Cooking: 12–15 minutes
Level of difficulty: 1

ZESTY COOKIES

Preheat the oven to 375°F (190°C/gas 5).
• Butter two cookie sheets. • Mix the all-purpose and rice flours, baking powder, and salt in a medium bowl. • Beat the butter and sugar in a large bowl with an electric mixer until creamy. • Add the egg and lemon zest, beating until just blended. • Mix in the dry ingredients. • Drop tablespoons of the dough 1 inch (2.5 cm) apart onto the prepared cookie sheets. • Bake until pale gold, 8–10 minutes. • Transfer to racks to cool.

1½ cups (275 g) all-purpose (plain) flour

⅓ cup (50 g) rice flour

1¼ teaspoons baking powder

⅛ teaspoon salt

¼ cup (60 g) butter, softened

¾ cup (150 g) granulated sugar

1 large egg

1 tablespoon finely grated lemon zest

Makes: 20–24 cookies
Preparation: 25 minutes
Cooking: 8–10 minutes
Level of difficulty: 1

CHOCOLATE CRISPS

Preheat oven to 325°F (160°C/gas 3).
• Line two baking sheets with parchment paper. • Place the butter, sugar, milk, and cocoa in a saucepan and melt over low heat. Stir until smooth and well-blended, then remove from the heat. • Add the vanilla, then gradually stir in the wheat flakes, coating well with the chocolate mixture. Stir in the raisins and walnuts. • Drop heaped teaspoons of the mixture on the prepared cookie sheets. • Bake until crisp, about 10 minutes. • Let cool until firm on the baking sheet, then transfer to wire racks to cool completely. • Serve in mini paper cases, if liked.

¼ cup (60 g) butter
¼ cup (60 g) superfine (caster) sugar
2 tablespoons milk
3 tablespoons unsweetened cocoa powder
1 teaspoon vanilla extract (essence)
3 cups (300 g) wheat flakes (or corn flakes)
½ cup (90 g) raisins
½ cup (50 g) chopped walnuts

Makes: about 40 cookies
Preparation: 15 minutes
Cooking: 10 minutes
Level: 1

BLUEBERRY CHOCOLATE SOFT-BAKE COOKIES

Preheat the oven to 375 (190°C/gas 5).
• Lightly grease a large baking sheet.
• Mix the flour, baking powder, and cinnamon in a medium bowl. • Rub in the butter or margarine, using your fingertips, until the mixture resembles rough bread crumbs. Stir in the sugar. • Stir in the milk, blueberries, and chocolate chips until just combined (the dough will be quite sticky). • Spoon 8 mounds, spaced well apart, onto the prepared baking sheet. • Bake until golden and springy to the touch, 15–20 minutes. • Cool on a wire rack for a few minutes to firm a little. Serve while still hot or warm.

¼ cup (60 g) butter or margarine, cubed
1 cup (150 g) all-purpose (plain) flour
1½ teaspoons baking powder
1 teaspoon ground cinnamon
½ cup (100 g) raw (demerara) sugar
⅓ cup (90 ml) milk
4 oz (125 g) fresh blueberries
⅓ cup (60 g) white chocolate chips

Makes: 8 large cookies
Preparation: 10 minutes
Cooking: 15–20 minutes
Level: 1

CRAZY COOKIES

Preheat oven to 350°F (180°C/gas 4).
• Line two baking sheets with parchment paper. • Melt the chocolate in a double boiler over barely simmering water until smooth. Set aside to cool slightly. • Mix the flour and baking powder in a medium bowl. • Beat the butter and sugar in an electric mixer on medium speed until pale and creamy. • With mixer on low, gradually beat in the flour and chocolate. • Roll tablespoons of the mixture into balls and place on the prepared baking sheets. Flatten slightly and press a freckle or caramel whirl into the center of each cookie.
• Bake until firm, about 12 minutes. • Cool on the baking sheets for 10 minutes, then transfer to a wire rack to cool completely.

4 oz (125 g) milk chocolate
1¼ cups (175 g) all-purpose (plain) flour
1½ teaspoons baking powder
1 cup (250 g) butter, softened
1½ cups (300 g) superfine (caster) sugar
½ cup freckles (hundreds-and-thousands-coated chocolates)
½ cup caramel whirls

Makes: about 36 cookies
Preparation: 15 minutes
Cooking: 12 minutes
Level: 1

CHOCKY ROAD COOKIES

334

Preheat oven to 350°F (180°C/gas 4).
• Butter two baking sheets. • Beat the butter and sugar in an electric mixer on medium speed until pale and creamy. • Add the eggs one at a time, beating until just combined after each addition. • With mixer on low, gradually beat in the flour and cocoa powder, alternating with the buttermilk or milk. Stir in the peanuts and chocolate chips, mixing well to combine. • Drop tablespoons of the mixture onto the prepared baking sheets. • Bake until firm to the touch, 10–12 minutes, spacing well. • Let cool on the baking sheets for 5 minutes then transfer to wire racks to cool completely.

1 cup (250 g) butter, softened

1 cup (200 g) firmly packed brown sugar

2 large eggs

2½ cups (375 g) all-purpose (plain) flour

½ cup (75 g) unsweetened cocoa powder

½ cup (125 ml) buttermilk or milk

1 cup (150 g) dry roasted peanuts

1 cup (180 g) white chocolate chips

1 cup (180 g) semisweet (dark) chocolate chips

Makes: about 36 cookies
Preparation: 15 minutes
Cooking: 10–12 minutes
Level: 1

JAFFA COOKIES

Preheat oven to 350°F (180°C/gas 4).
• Butter two baking sheets. • Melt the butter in a saucepan large enough to mix all the ingredients. Remove from the heat and mix in chocolate chips and confectioners' sugar. Mix until the chocolate just starts to melt. Add the orange zest, flour, baking powder, and custard powder. Mix to combine. • Roll tablespoons of the batter into balls. Place on the prepared baking sheets, spacing well. Flatten with a fork. • Bake until firm and starting to color.
• Let cool on the baking sheets for 5 minutes then transfer to wire racks to cool completely.

¾ cup (200 g) butter

½ cup (90 g) semisweet (dark) chocolate chips

½ cup (75 g) confectioners' (icing) sugar

2 teaspoons finely grated orange zest

1½ cups (225 g) all-purpose (plain) flour

1 teaspoon baking powder

½ cup (75 g) custard powder

Makes: about 30 cookies
Preparation: 15 minutes
Cooking: 15–20 minutes
Level: 1

CANDIED CHERRY COOKIES

Preheat oven to 350°F (180°C/gas 4).
• Line two baking sheets with parchment paper. • Melt the margarine, sugar, and corn syrup in a saucepan over low heat. • Mix the flour and baking powder in a medium bowl. • Pour in the melted margarine mixture while still hot and mix quickly. Add the vanilla and cherries. • Form the dough into small balls. Place on the prepared baking sheets, spacing well, and flatten the top of each one with a fork. • Bake until pale golden brown, 12–15 minutes. • Let cool on the baking sheets for 2 minutes then transfer to wire racks to cool completely.

½ cup (125 g) margarine

1 tablespoon granulated sugar

1 tablespoon corn (golden) syrup

1¼ cups (175 g) all-purpose (plain) flour

1 teaspoon baking powder

½ teaspoon vanilla extract (essence)

2 oz (60 g) candied (glacé) cherries, chopped

Makes: about 30 cookies
Preparation: 15 minutes
Cooking: 12–15 minutes
Level: 1

CHOCOLATE MACADAMIA SOUR CREAM COOKIES

Preheat oven to 350°F (180°C/gas 4).
• Line three baking sheets with parchment paper. • Mix the flour, baking soda, and salt in a medium bowl. • Beat the butter and both sugars in a large bowl with an electric mixer on medium speed until pale and creamy.
• Add the eggs one at a time, beating until just combined after each addition. • With mixer on low, gradually beat in the vanilla, mixed dry ingredients, and sour cream.
• Stir in the chocolate chips and nuts.
• Drop heaped teaspoons of the batter well spaced on the prepared cookie sheets.
• Bake until golden brown and the middle is soft to the touch, 15–17 minutes. • Cool on the baking sheets for 2–3 minutes, then transfer to a wire rack to cool completely.

2½ cups (375 g) all-purpose (plain) flour
1 teaspoon baking soda (bicarbonate of soda)
½ teaspoon salt
1 cup (250 g) butter, softened
1 cup (200 g) firmly packed light brown sugar
½ cup (100 g) granulated sugar
2 large eggs
2 cups (350 g) semisweet (dark) chocolate chips
1 cup (150 g) crushed macadamia nuts
½ cup (125 ml) sour cream
1 teaspoon vanilla extract (essence)

Makes: about 50 cookies
Preparation: 20 minutes
Cooking: 15–17 minutes
Level: 1

BANANA, OAT, AND NUT COOKIES

Preheat oven to 375°F (190°C/gas 5).
• Line two baking sheets with parchment paper. • Mix the flour, baking soda, salt, rolled oats, pecans, and almonds in a large bowl.
• Beat the butter and sugar in a medium bowl with an electric mixer on medium speed until pale and creamy. • Add eggs one at a time, beating until just combined after each addition. • With mixer on low speed, gradually beat in the mixed dry ingredients and then the mashed banana. • Scoop heaped tablespoons of the batter and drop them onto the prepared cookie sheets about 4 inches (10 cm) apart. Flatten slightly. Bake until golden brown, 10–12 minutes.
• Cool on the baking sheets for 2–3 minutes, then transfer to a wire rack to cool completely.

1²/₃ cups (250 g) all-purpose (plain) flour
1 teaspoon baking soda (bicarbonate of soda)
¼ teaspoon salt
3 cups (300 g) rolled oats
1 cup (150 g) chopped pecan nuts
1 cup (150 g) chopped almonds
1 cup (250 g) butter, softened
1 cup (200 g) firmly packed brown sugar
1 cup (200 g) granulated sugar
2 large eggs
½ banana, mashed

Makes: about 35 cookies
Preparation: 15 minutes
Cooking: 10–12 minutes
Level: 1

MILK CHOCOLATE NUT COOKIES

Preheat oven to 400°F (200°C/gas 6).
• Line two baking sheets with parchment
paper. • Place the peanut butter, sugar, flour,
baking soda, and egg in a large bowl and mix
thoroughly. Stir in the chocolate chips. • Roll
heaped tablespoons of the mixture into balls
and place, well spaced, on the prepared
baking sheets. Press lightly with the back of a
folk. • Bake until golden brown, 10–12
minutes. • Cool on the baking sheets for 2–3
minutes, then transfer to a wire rack to cool
completely.

1 cup (250 g) crunchy peanut butter
1 cup (200 g) firmly packed brown sugar
1 teaspoon baking soda (bicarbonate of soda)
1 large egg, lightly beaten
1 cup (180 g) milk chocolate chips
2 cups (300 g) all-purpose (plain) flour
1 tablespoon vanilla extract (essence)
1 cup (200 g) granulated sugar
3/4 cup (200 g) butter
1½ cups (225 g) pecans, coarsely chopped

Makes: about 30 large cookies
Preparation: 15 minutes
Cooking: 10–12 minutes
Level: 1

SUPER CHOCOLATE RAISIN COOKIES

Beat the butter, both sugars, vanilla, and water in a large bowl with an electric mixer on medium speed until pale and creamy. Beat in the egg. • With mixer on low, gradually beat in the flour, baking soda, and salt. Stir in the raisins and chocolate chips by hand. • Place the dough lengthways in the center of a 15-inch (40-cm) long piece of parchment paper and roll into a plump log, about 3 inches (7 cm thick) and 8 inches (20 cm) long, twist the ends to tighten the dough and place in the refrigerator for 1 hour. Preheat oven to 350°F (180°C/gas 4). • Line two baking sheets with parchment paper. • Remove the cookie dough from the parchment paper and cut into ½-inch (1-cm) thick disks. • Place the cookies on the prepared cookie sheets, spacing 10 cm apart. Chill in the refrigerator for 10 minutes before cooking. • Bake until golden brown, 10 minutes. • Cool on the baking sheets for 2–3 minutes, then transfer to a wire rack to cool completely.

⅔ cup (180 g) butter, softened

½ cup (100 g) firmly packed dark brown sugar

½ cup (100 g) superfine (caster) sugar

½ teaspoon vanilla extract (essence)

½ teaspoon water

1 large egg

1¼ cups (175 g) all-purpose (plain) flour

½ teaspoon baking soda (bicarbonate of soda)

¼ teaspoon salt

½ cup (75 g) raisins

1 cup (180 g) semisweet (dark) chocolate chips

1 cup (180 g) white chocolate chips

Makes: about 16 huge cookies
Preparation: 15 minutes
Cooking: 10–12 minutes
Level: 1

TOFFEE OATMEAL COOKIES

Preheat oven to 350°F (180°C/gas 4).
• Line two baking sheets with parchment paper. • Beat the butter and sugar in a medium bowl with an electric mixer on medium speed until pale and creamy. Beat in the egg and vanilla. • With mixer on low speed, gradually beat in the flour, baking soda, and salt. Stir in the rolled oats and chopped toffee pieces by hand. • Scoop up heaped tablespoons of the batter and drop onto the prepared cookie sheets. Flatten slightly. • Bake until golden brown, 10 minutes. • Cool on the baking sheets for 2–3 minutes, then transfer to a wire rack to cool completely.

¾ cup (180 g) butter, softened

½ cup (100 g) firmly packed light brown sugar

1 large egg

1 teaspoon vanilla extract (essence)

1 cup (150 g) all-purpose (plain) flour

¼ teaspoon baking soda (bicarbonate of soda)

¼ teaspoon salt

1½ cups (150 g) rolled oats

½ cup (75 g) chopped almonds

2 cups (200 g) toffee baking bits

Makes: about 30 cookies
Preparation: 15 minutes
Cooking: 10 minutes
Level: 1

PRESSED AND PIPED COOKIES

APRICOT PRETZELS

Preheat the oven to 350°F (180°C/gas 4).
• Line three cookie sheets with parchment paper. • Mix the apricots, orange juice, and 1 tablespoon of butter in a small saucepan. Simmer over low heat until the apricots have softened, 5 minutes. Let cool completely.
• Mix the flour, baking powder, and salt in a large bowl. Stir in the sugar. • Use a pastry blender to cut in the remaining butter until the mixture resembles fine crumbs. • Add the egg yolks, chocolate, and apricot mixture to make a stiff dough. • Form tablespoons of the dough into 6-inch (15-cm) ropes. • Make each rope into a pretzel shape by twisting the two ends around each other, then bringing both back near to the center of the strip, about 1 inch (2.5-cm) apart. • Transfer to the cookie sheets, spacing 1 inch (2.5 cm) apart. • Bake until just golden, 12–15 minutes. • Transfer to racks to cool.

1 cup (100 g) finely chopped dried apricots

⅓ cup (90 ml) freshly squeezed orange juice

5 tablespoons butter

1⅓ cups (200 g) all-purpose (plain) flour

1 teaspoon baking powder

¼ teaspoon salt

¼ cup (50 g) granulated sugar

2 large egg yolks, lightly beaten

2 oz (60 g) semisweet (dark) chocolate, finely grated

Makes: 20–24 cookies
Preparation: 45 minutes
Cooking: 12–15 minutes
Level: 2

FENNEL COOKIES

354

Preheat the oven to 350°F (180°C/gas 4).
• Butter four cookie sheets. • Mix the flour and salt in a medium bowl. • Melt the chocolate in a double boiler over barely simmering water. • Beat the butter and sugar in a large bowl with an electric mixer at high speed until creamy. • Add the vanilla, milk, and egg, beating until just blended. • Mix in the dry ingredients and chocolate. • Choose a design plate for your cookie press; slide it into the head and lock in place. Press out the cookies, spacing about 1½ inches (4 cm) apart on the prepared cookie sheets. Place a few fennel seeds at the center of each cookie. • Bake until just colored and crisp, 8–10 minutes. • Transfer to racks to cool.

2 cups (300 g) all-purpose (plain) flour
¼ teaspoon salt
2 oz (60 g) semisweet (dark) chocolate, coarsely chopped
½ cup (125 g) butter, softened
1 cup (200 g) granulated sugar
1 teaspoon vanilla extract (essence)
2 tablespoons milk
1 large egg, lightly beaten
2 tablespoons fennel seeds

Makes: 40–48 cookies
Preparation: 50 minutes
Cooking: 8–10 minutes
Level: 1

DIPPED CITRUS TWISTS

Preheat the oven to 350°F (180°C/gas 4).
• Line three cookie sheets with parchment
paper. • Mix the flour, baking powder, and salt
in a medium bowl. • Beat the butter and sugar
in a large bowl with an electric mixer at high
speed until creamy. • Add the egg, beating until
just blended. • Finely grate 2 oz (60 g) of the
chocolate and beat into the mixture. • Beat in
the orange zest. • Mix in the dry ingredients
to form a soft dough. • Turn the dough out onto
a lightly floured surface and knead until
smooth. • Form tablespoons of the dough
into 8-inch (20-cm) ropes. • Fold in half and
twist, pressing the ends of the rope together.
• Transfer to the prepared cookie sheets,
placing them 2 inches (5 cm) apart. • Bake
until just firm, 10–12 minutes. • Transfer to
racks to cool. • Melt the remaining chocolate
in a double boiler over barely simmering water.
• Dip in the tops of cookies and let set
for 30 minutes.

3 cups (450 g) all-purpose (plain) flour

2 teaspoons baking powder

¼ teaspoon salt

¾ cup (180 g) butter, softened

½ cup (100 g) granulated sugar

1 large egg

8 oz (250 g) milk chocolate

1 tablespoon finely shredded orange zest

Makes: about 30 cookies
Preparation: 40 minutes
  + 30 minutes to set
Cooking: 10–12 minutes
Level: 2

COCONUT CRESCENTS

Blanch the pistachios in boiling water for 1 minute. Drain well and use a clean cloth to rub off the skins. • Let cool, then transfer to a food processor and process until very finely chopped. • Place the flour on a work surface and make a well in the center. • Cut in the butter, coconut, confectioners' sugar, and the egg and egg yolk to make a smooth dough. • Wrap in plastic wrap (cling film) and refrigerate for at least 2 hours. • Divide the dough into balls the size of walnuts. Form into crescent shapes, wrap individually in plastic wrap, and refrigerate for 1 hour more.
• Preheat the oven to 350°F (180°C/gas 4).
• Butter and flour a baking sheet. • Sprinkle the cookies with the sugar. Dip in the finely chopped pistachios until well coated.
• Arrange on the prepared baking sheet.
• Bake until firm to the touch, 15–20 minutes.
• Cool the cookies completely on the baking sheet.

1¼ cups (190 g) pistachios, shelled

1⅓ cups (200 g) all-purpose (plain) flour

⅓ cup (90 g) butter, softened

2 tablespoons freshly grated coconut

⅓ cup (50 g) confectioners' (icing) sugar

1 large egg + 1 large egg yolk

½ cup (100 g) granulated sugar

Makes: 15–20 cookies
Preparation: 40 minutes + 3 hours to chill
Cooking: 15–20 minutes
Level: 1

CINNAMON PINE NUT COOKIES

360

Preheat the oven to 350°F (180°C/gas 4).
• Butter two cookie sheets. • Sift the flour,
baking powder, cinnamon, and salt into a
medium bowl. • Stir in the sugar. • Beat the
eggs in a large bowl with an electric mixer
on high speed until pale and thick. • Beat in
the butter and lemon zest until well blended.
• Mix in the dry ingredients and enough milk
to make a stiff dough. • Break off balls of
dough the size of walnuts and form into
4-inch (10-cm) ropes. Shape the ropes into
disks and sprinkle with the pine nuts. • Place
on the prepared cookie sheets, about 1 inch
(2.5 cm) apart. • Bake until just golden,
15–20 minutes. • Transfer to racks to cool.

2²/₃ cups (400 g) all-purpose (plain) flour

2 teaspoons baking powder

½ teaspoon ground cinnamon

⅛ teaspoon salt

¾ cup (150 g) granulated sugar

3 large eggs

⅓ cup (90 g) butter, softened

Finely grated zest of ½ lemon

3 tablespoons milk

2 tablespoons pine nuts

Makes: 25–30 cookies
Preparation: 20 minutes
Cooking: 15–20 minutes
Level: 2

FROSTED BRANDY CRUNCH

Cookies: Preheat the oven to 350°F (180°C/gas 4). • Separate two of the eggs, place the whites in a large bowl, and set aside for the frosting. • Mix the flour in a large bowl. • Break in the remaining egg and add the yolks, butter, salt, and brandy. • Gradually work these ingredients into the flour, first with a fork, then by hand until the dough is smooth and elastic. • Divide the dough into 4 or 5 portions and roll each one into a long cylinder about as thick as a finger. Cut into ½-inch (1-cm) thick slices. • Grease a baking sheet with the remaining butter and bake until they are pale golden brown, about 15 minutes. • Remove from the oven and place on wire racks to cool. • Frosting: Add the confectioners' sugar and lemon juice to the reserved egg whites and mix until smooth. • Set aside 7 tablespoons of this frosting in a small bowl. • Working fast (so that the frosting doesn't have time to set), add the baked dough pieces to the frosting left in the large bowl and stir gently to coat all over. • Place 4–6 little slices on each of the

Cookies
- 3 large eggs
- 1²⁄₃ cups (250 g) all-purpose (plain) flour
- ½ cup (125 g) butter, softened
- ¼ teaspoon salt
- 3 tablespoons brandy

Frosting
- 2²⁄₃ cups (400 g) confectioners' (icing) sugar)
- 1 tablespoon freshly squeezed lemon juice

- 15 confectioners' or ice cream wafers

Makes: about 15 cookies
Preparation: 20 minutes + 4 hours to stand
Cooking: 15 minutes
Level: 2

confectioners' or ice cream wafers. • Spoon
some of the extra frosting over each one.
• Set aside for several hours before serving.

CINNAMON ROSETTES

Preheat the oven to 350°F (180°C/gas 4).
• Set out two cookie sheets. • Mix the flour, cinnamon, and salt in a medium bowl. • Beat the butter, cream cheese, and sugar in a large bowl with an electric mixer at high speed until creamy. • Add the vanilla and egg yolk, beating until just blended. • Mix in the dry ingredients until well blended. • Choose a design plate for your cookie press; slide it into the head and lock in place. • Press out the cookies, spacing 1 inch (2.5 cm) apart on the cookie sheets. • Bake until just golden, 12–15 minutes. • Transfer to racks to cool.

1   cup (150 g) all-purpose (plain) flour

½   teaspoon ground cinnamon

¼   teaspoon salt

½   cup (125 g) butter, softened

¼   cup (60 g) cream cheese, softened

½   cup (100 g) granulated sugar

½   teaspoon vanilla extract (essence)

1   large egg yolk

Makes: about 20 cookies
Preparation: 30 minutes
Cooking: 12–15 minutes
Level: 1

CHERRY PETITS FOURS

Dust two cookie sheets with rice flour.
• Mix the almonds, confectioners' sugar, egg whites, and salt in a large bowl until smooth.
• Fit a pastry bag with a ½-inch (1-cm) star tip. Fill the pastry bag, twist the opening tightly closed, and squeeze out rosettes, spacing 1 inch (2.5 cm) apart on the prepared cookie sheets. • Place a piece of candied cherry on top of each cookie. • Refrigerate for 30 minutes. • Preheat the oven to 475°F (250°C/gas 9). • Bake until lightly browned at the edges, about 5 minutes. • Transfer to racks to cool.

1¼ cups (125 g) finely ground almonds

¾ cup (125 g) confectioners' (icing) sugar

2 large egg whites

⅛ teaspoon salt

12 candied cherries, chopped

Makes: about 25 cookies
Preparation: 25 minutes + 30 minutes to chill
Cooking: 3–5 minutes
Level: 1

HAZELNUT HORSESHOES

Preheat the oven to 375°F (190°C/gas 5).
• Set out three cookie sheets. • Mix the flour
and salt in a medium bowl. • Beat the butter
and sugar in a large bowl with an electric
mixer at high speed until creamy.
• Add the egg, vanilla, and almond extract,
beating until just blended. • Mix in the dry
ingredients and ground hazelnuts. • Fit a
pastry bag with a ½-inch (1-cm) star tip.
Fill the pastry bag, twist the opening tightly
closed, and squeeze out generous 1-inch
(2.5-cm) tall arches (horseshoes), spacing
1 inch (2.5 cm) apart on the cookie sheets.
• Bake until golden and firm at the edges,
8–10 minutes. • Transfer to racks to cool.

2 cups (300 g) all-purpose (plain) flour

⅛ teaspoon salt

1 cup (250 g) butter, softened

¾ cup (150 g) granulated sugar

1 large egg

1 teaspoon vanilla extract (essence)

¼ teaspoon almond extract (essence)

1 cup (150 g) finely ground hazelnuts

Makes: about 50 cookies
Preparation: 30 minutes
Cooking: 8–10 minutes
Level: 1

ALMOND FLOWER COOKIES

Preheat the oven to 375°F (190°C/gas 5).
• Butter four cookie sheets. • Mix the flour and salt in a medium bowl. • Beat the butter, sugar, and vanilla in a large bowl with an electric mixer at high speed until creamy.
• Gradually mix in the dry ingredients and ground almonds to form a smooth dough.
• Insert a flower design plate into your cookie press by sliding it into the head and locking in place. Press out the cookies, spacing about 1 inch (2.5 cm) apart on the prepared cookie sheets. • Bake until golden brown and firm at the edges, 10–15 minutes. • Transfer to racks to cool.

3 cups (450 g) all-purpose (plain) flour

½ teaspoon salt

1½ cups (375 g) butter, softened

1¼ cups (250 g) granulated sugar

1 tablespoon vanilla extract (essence)

1½ cups (200 g) finely ground almonds

Makes: about 60 cookies
Preparation: 30 minutes
Cooking: 10–15 minutes
Level: 1

GINGER ROPES

Mix both flours, the ginger, baking powder, and salt in a large bowl. • Use a pastry blender to cut in the butter until the mixture resembles coarse crumbs. • Stir in the brown sugar and walnuts. • Mix in the egg to form a smooth dough. • Cover with plastic wrap (cling film) and refrigerate for 30 minutes. • Preheat the oven to 350°F (180°C/gas 4). • Butter three cookie sheets. • Form tablespoons of the dough into 6-inch (15-cm) ropes and fold the ropes in half. • Twist the dough and place 1½ inches (4 cm) apart on the prepared cookie sheets. • Bake until lightly browned and firm to the touch, 12–15 minutes. • Place on racks to cool.

1 cup (150 g) all-purpose (plain) flour
½ cup (75 g) whole-wheat (wholemeal) flour
1 tablespoon ground ginger
1 teaspoon baking powder
¼ teaspoon salt
½ cup (125 g) butter, cut up
⅓ cup (70 g) firmly packed light brown sugar
¼ cup (25 g) finely chopped walnuts
1 large egg, lightly beaten

Makes: 36–40 cookies
Preparation: 30 minutes + 30 minutes to chill
Cooking: 12–15 minutes
Level: 1

374

GINGER LEMON CRISPS

376

Preheat the oven to 375°F (190°C/gas 5).
• Butter four cookie sheets. • Mix the flour, ginger, cloves, and salt in a medium bowl.
• Beat the butter, sugar, and vanilla in a large bowl with an electric mixer at high speed until creamy. • Add the egg and lemon zest and juice, beating until just blended. • Mix in the dry ingredients to form a stiff dough.
• Choose a design plate for your cookie press; slide it into the head and lock in place. Press out the cookies, spacing about 1 inch (2.5 cm) apart on the prepared cookie sheets.
• Decorate each cookie with crystallized ginger and sprinkle with sugar crystals.
• Bake until firm to the touch and golden at the edges, 10–12 minutes. • Transfer to racks to cool.

3 cups (450 g) all-purpose (plain) flour
2 teaspoons ground ginger
¼ teaspoon ground cloves
¼ teaspoon salt
1½ cups (375 g) butter, softened
1¼ cups (250 g) granulated sugar
1 teaspoon vanilla extract (essence)
1 large egg
1 tablespoon finely grated lemon zest
1 tablespoon freshly squeezed lemon juice
1 tablespoon chopped candied ginger
1 tablespoon colored sugar crystals

Makes: about 60 cookies
Preparation: 30 minutes
Cooking: 10–12 minutes
Level: 2

FAIRY GLEN COOKIES

Preheat the oven to 350°F (180°C/gas 4).
• Butter three cookie sheets. • Beat the egg
whites and salt in a large bowl with an electric
mixer at medium speed until soft peaks form.
• With mixer at high speed, gradually add the
sugar, beating until stiff glossy peaks form.
• Use a large rubber spatula to fold in the
almonds. • Heat the marmalade in a small
saucepan over low heat until liquid. Let cool
slightly. • Carefully fold the marmalade into
the batter. • Fit a pastry bag with a ½-inch
(1-cm) star tip. Fill the pastry bag and twist
the opening tightly closed. Squeeze out
generous 1½-inch (4-cm) rosettes spacing
2 inches (5 cm) apart on the prepared cookie
sheets. • Decorate with cherry halves.
• Bake until just golden, 10–15 minutes.
• Transfer to racks to cool.

3 large egg whites
⅛ teaspoon salt
1¾ cups (350 g)
    granulated sugar
3⅓ cups (330 g) finely
    ground almonds
¼ cup (60 g) orange
    marmalade
20 candied cherries,
    cut in half

Makes: about 40 cookies
Preparation: 25 minutes
Cooking: 10–15 minutes
Level: 1

CHOCOLATE ALMOND LOGS

Preheat the oven to 350°F (180°C/gas 4).
• Line two cookie sheets with rice paper.
• Beat the egg whites in a large bowl with an electric mixer at high speed until stiff peaks form. • Use a large rubber spatula to fold in the superfine sugar, almonds, and almond extract. • Fit a pastry bag with a ½-inch (1-cm) plain tip. Fill the pastry bag, twist the opening tightly closed, and pipe out 3-inch (8-cm) long lines spaced 1½ inches (4 cm) apart on the prepared cookie sheets.
• Bake until golden brown, 15–20 minutes.
• Cool on the cookie sheets for 1 minute.
• Transfer to racks to cool completely. • Tear away the excess rice paper from around the edges. • Melt the chocolate in a double boiler over barely simmering water. • Drizzle the chocolate in a zigzag pattern over the logs.

2   large egg whites
1   cup (200 g) superfine (caster) sugar
1¾ cups (275 g) finely ground almonds
½ teaspoon almond extract (essence)
4   oz (125 g) semisweet (dark) chocolate, coarsely chopped

Makes: about 20 cookies
Preparation: 30 minutes
Cooking: 15–20 minutes
Level: 1

NUT SPRITZ COOKIES

Preheat the oven to 300°F (150°C/gas 2).
• Line two cookie sheets with parchment
paper. • Mix the flour, hazelnuts, almonds, and
salt in a large bowl. • Stir in the egg, orange
juice, orange zest, and 1 tablespoon of maple
syrup to form a soft, smooth dough. • Fit a
pastry bag with a plain 1-inch (2.5-cm) tip.
Spoon the mixture into the pastry bag and
squeeze out half moons and wreaths spacing
2 inches (5 cm) apart on the prepared cookie
sheets. • Bake until lightly golden, 12–15
minutes. • Transfer to racks to cool. • Warm
the preserves in a small saucepan over low
heat. • Brush over the warm cookies and
sprinkle with the pistachios.

3 tablespoons all-purpose (plain) flour

1⅓ cups (200 g) finely ground hazelnuts

⅔ cup (100 g) finely ground almonds

⅛ teaspoon salt

1 large egg, lightly beaten

½ cup (120 ml) freshly squeezed orange juice

1 tablespoon finely grated orange zest

1½ tablespoons maple or corn (golden) syrup

3 tablespoons apricot preserves

2 tablespoons finely chopped pistachios

Makes: about 30 cookies
Preparation: 30 minutes
Cooking: 12–15 minutes
Level: 2

ANISEED COOKIES

Line two cookie sheets with parchment paper.
• Mix the flour, cornstarch, and aniseed in a
large bowl. • Beat the eggs, sugar, and salt in
a double boiler over barely simmering water
with an electric mixer at high speed until pale
and thick. Remove from the heat and continue
beating until the mixture has cooled. • Use
a large rubber spatula to fold the dry
ingredients into the batter, followed by
enough water to obtain a soft dough. • Fit
a pastry bag with a ¼-inch (5-mm) plain tip.
Fill the pastry bag, twist the opening tightly
closed, and squeeze out ¾-inch (2-cm) round
cookies, spacing 1½ inches (4 cm) apart on
the prepared cookie sheets. • Set aside,
covered, at room temperature until a thin
crust has formed, about 12 hours. • Preheat
the oven to 275°F (140°C/gas 1). • Bake
until lightly browned, 25–30 minutes.
• Transfer to racks to cool.

½ cup (75 g) all-purpose (plain) flour

2 tablespoons cornstarch (cornflour)

1 tablespoon ground aniseeds

2 large eggs

½ cup (100 g) granulated sugar

¼ teaspoon salt

1 tablespoon water + extra, as required

Makes: about 20 cookies
Preparation: 1 hour
+ 12 hours to rest
Cooking: 25–30 minutes
Level: 2

NUTMEG SPRITZ COOKIES

386

Preheat the oven to 350°F (180°C/gas 4).
• Set out two cookie sheets. • Mix the flour, half the nutmeg, and salt in a medium bowl.
• Beat the butter, cream cheese, and sugar in a large bowl with an electric mixer at high speed until creamy. • Add the almond extract and egg yolk, beating until just blended.
• Mix in the dry ingredients until well blended.
• Choose a design plate for your cookie press; slide it into the head and lock in place.
• Press out the cookies, spacing 1 inch (2.5 cm) apart on the cookie sheets. Dust the cookies with the remaining nutmeg. • Bake until just golden, 12–15 minutes. • Transfer to racks to cool.

1   cup (150 g) all-purpose (plain) flour
½ teaspoon freshly grated nutmeg
⅛ teaspoon salt
½ cup (125 g) butter, softened
¼ cup (60 g) cream cheese, softened
½ cup (100 g) granulated sugar
½ teaspoon almond extract (essence)
1   large egg yolk

Makes: about 34 cookies
Preparation: 30 minutes
Cooking: 12–15 minutes
Level: 1

LADYFINGERS

Preheat the oven to 325°F (170°C/gas 3).
• Line two cookie sheets with parchment
paper. • Mix the flour and salt in a medium
bowl. • Beat the eggs, ½ cup (100 g) of sugar,
and vanilla in a double boiler over barely
simmering water. Beat until the batter falls off
the beaters in ribbons. • Use a large rubber
spatula to fold in the dry ingredients. • Fit a
pastry bag with a ½-inch (1-cm) star tip. Fill
the pastry bag, twist the opening tightly
closed, and squeeze out 3 x ¾-inch
(8 x 2-cm) lengths, spacing them 1 inch
(2.5 cm) apart on the prepared cookie sheets.
• Sprinkle with the remaining superfine sugar.
• Bake until crisp and dry to the touch, 10–15
minutes. • Cool on the sheets until the
cookies firm slightly. • Transfer to racks
to finish cooling.

⅔ cup (100 g) all-purpose (plain) flour

⅛ teaspoon salt

3 large eggs

¾ cup (150 g) superfine (caster) sugar

½ teaspoon vanilla extract (essence)

Makes: 30–35 cookies
Preparation: 30 minutes
Cooking: 10–15 minutes
Level: 2

POPPY SEED S-BEND COOKIES

Mix the flour, baking powder, and salt in a medium bowl. • Beat the butter and sugar in a large bowl with an electric mixer at high speed until creamy. • Add the aniseeds and lemon zest. • With mixer at high speed, beat the egg, egg yolk, and 2 tablespoons of milk until frothy in a large bowl. • Beat the egg mixture into the batter. • Mix in the dry ingredients to form a smooth dough. • Divide the dough in half. • Form into 8-inch (20-cm) logs, wrap in plastic wrap (cling film), and refrigerate for 30 minutes. • Preheat the oven to 375°F (190°C/gas 5). • Line two cookie sheets with parchment paper. • Slice the dough ½-inch (1-cm) thick. • Roll each slice into a 6-inch (15-cm) log and form into an S-shape, flattening slightly. • Place on the cookie sheets. • Mix the egg white and remaining milk in a small bowl. • Brush over the cookies and sprinkle with poppy seeds. • Bake until just golden at the edges, 8–10 minutes. • Transfer to racks to cool.

1⅓ cups (200 g) all-purpose (plain) flour

1 teaspoon baking powder

⅛ teaspoon salt

½ cup (125 g) butter, softened

½ cup (100 g) granulated sugar

1 teaspoon ground aniseeds

1 teaspoon finely grated lemon zest

1 large egg + 1 large egg yolk + 1 large egg white

2 tablespoons + 1 teaspoon milk

2 tablespoons poppy seeds

Makes: about 32 cookies
Preparation: 40 minutes + 30 minutes to chill
Cooking: 8–10 minutes
Level: 2

BUTTER WREATHS

Preheat the oven to 375°F (190°C/gas 5).
• Set out three cookie sheets. • Mix the flour, baking powder, and salt in a medium bowl.
• Beat the butter and sugar in a large bowl with an electric mixer at high speed until creamy. • Add the vanilla and egg, beating until just blended. • Mix in the dry ingredients. • Fit a pastry bag with a 3/4-inch (2-cm) plain tip. Fill the pastry bag, twist the opening tightly closed, and squeeze out 1 1/2-inch (4-cm) wreaths, spacing 1 inch (2.5 cm) apart on the cookie sheets. • Press the sugar strands and balls into the tops of the cookies in a decorative manner. • Bake until the edges are just golden, 8–10 minutes. • Transfer to racks to cool.

1 1/4 cups (180 g) all-purpose (plain) flour

1/2 teaspoon baking powder

1/8 teaspoon salt

1/2 cup (125 g) butter, softened

3/4 cup (150 g) granulated sugar

1/2 teaspoon vanilla extract (essence)

1 large egg

Silver and colored balls, to decorate

2 tablespoons sugar strands, to decorate

Makes: 35–40 cookies
Preparation: 25 minutes
Cooking: 8–10 minutes
Level: 1

CHERRY-TOPPED SHORTBREAD

394

Preheat the oven to 325°F (170°C/gas 3).
• Butter a cookie sheet. • Mix the flour and salt in a medium bowl. • Beat the butter, sugar, and vanilla in a large bowl with an electric mixer at high speed until creamy.
• Mix in the dry ingredients and milk.
• Fit a pastry bag with a $\frac{1}{2}$-inch (1-cm) star tip. Fill the pastry bag, twist the opening tightly closed, and squeeze rosettes onto the prepared cookie sheet. Press a piece of cherry into the top of each one. • Bake until golden and firm to the touch, 20–25 minutes.
• Transfer the cookies to racks to cool.

$1\frac{1}{4}$ cups (180 g) all-purpose (plain) flour

$\frac{1}{8}$ teaspoon salt

$\frac{3}{4}$ cup (180 g) butter, softened

$\frac{1}{4}$ cup (50 g) granulated sugar

$\frac{1}{2}$ teaspoon vanilla extract (essence)

2 teaspoons milk

2 tablespoons chopped candied cherries

Makes: about 16 cookies
Preparation: 25 minutes
Cooking: 20–25 minutes
Level: 1

ALMOND BUTTER WHIRLS

Preheat the oven to 325°F (170°C/gas 3).
• Butter a cookie sheet. • Mix the flour, baking powder, and salt in a medium bowl. • Beat the butter, confectioners' sugar, and vanilla in a large bowl with an electric mixer at high speed until creamy. • Mix in the dry ingredients until well blended. • Fit a pastry bag with a ½-inch (1-cm) star tip. Fill the pastry bag, twist the opening tightly closed, and squeeze out flat whirls, spacing 1 inch (2.5 cm) apart on the prepared cookie sheet.
• Place a half cherry on top of each whirl.
• Bake until lightly browned, 15–20 minutes.
• Cool on the sheet until the cookies firm slightly. Transfer to racks and let cool completely.

1⅓ cups (200 g) all-purpose (plain) flour

½ teaspoon baking powder

⅛ teaspoon salt

¾ cup (180 g) butter, softened

⅓ cup (50 g) confectioners' (icing) sugar

⅓ teaspoon almond extract (essence)

8 candied cherries, cut in half

Makes: about 16 cookies
Preparation: 25 minutes
Cooking: 15–20 minutes
Level: 2

PIPED VANILLA COOKIES

Preheat the oven to 375°F (190°C/gas 5).
• Set out three cookie sheets. • Beat the
butter and ½ cup (100 g) of sugar in a large
bowl with an electric mixer at high speed
until creamy. • Add the vanilla and egg,
beating until just blended. • Mix in the flour
and salt to form a soft dough. • Choose a
design plate for your cookie press; slide it into
the head and lock in place. Press out the
cookies, spacing 1 inch (2.5 cm) apart on the
cookie sheets. • Sprinkle with the remaining
sugar. • Bake until just golden at the edges,
about 10 minutes. • Transfer to racks
and let cool completely.

1 cup (250 g) butter,
   softened
½ cup (100 g)
   + 2 tablespoons
   granulated sugar
1½ teaspoons vanilla
   extract (essence)
1 large egg
2 cups (300 g) all-
   purpose (plain) flour
⅛ teaspoon salt

Makes: about 48 cookies
Preparation: 40 minutes
Cooking: 10 minutes
Level: 1

ORANGE BUTTER COOKIES

Beat the butter and sugar in a large bowl with an electric mixer at high speed until creamy.
• Add the egg yolk, beating until just blended.
• Mix in the flour, salt, and orange juice until well blended. • Refrigerate for 1 hour.
• Preheat the oven to 375°F (190°C/gas 5).
• Butter two cookie sheets. • Fit a pastry bag with a 1-inch (2.5-cm) star tip. Fill the pastry bag, twist the opening tightly closed, and squeeze out four long strips on each sheet, spacing well. • Use a sharp knife to score each strip at 2½-inch (6-cm) intervals. • Bake until just golden, 8–10 minutes. • Cut up the cookies along the scored lines. • Cool on the sheet until the cookies firm slightly. Transfer to racks to finish cooling.

⅔ cup (150 g) butter, softened

½ cup (100 g) granulated sugar

1 large egg yolk, lightly beaten

2 cups (300 g) all-purpose (plain) flour

⅛ teaspoon salt

2 tablespoons freshly squeezed orange juice

Makes: about 36 cookies
Preparation: 40 minutes
+ 1 hour to chill
Cooking: 8–10 minutes
Level: 2

GLAZED COOKIE TREES

Butter Cookies: Preheat the oven to 375°F
(190°C/gas 5). • Set out two cookie sheets.
• Mix the flour and salt in a medium bowl.
• Beat the butter and sugar in a large bowl
with an electric mixer at high speed until
creamy. • Add the egg yolk, beating until just
blended. • Beat in the sour cream, almond
extract, and dry ingredients to form a smooth
dough. • Insert a tree design plate into your
cookie press by sliding it into the head and
locking in place. Press out the cookies, spacing
about ½ inch (1 cm) apart on the cookie sheets.
• Bake until lightly browned, 8–10 minutes.
• Orange Glaze: While the cookies are in the
oven, mix the confectioners' sugar and orange
juice in a small bowl. • Warm the apricot
preserves in a small saucepan over low heat.
• Brush the cookies with a little preserves,
followed by the orange glaze. • Bake until the
glaze begins to crystallize, 5 minutes. • Cool
on the sheets until the cookies firm slightly.
Transfer to racks to finish cooling.

Butter Cookies

1 cup (150 g) all-purpose
  (plain) flour
⅛ teaspoon salt
⅓ cup (90 g) butter,
  softened
¼ cup (50 g) granulated
  sugar
1 large egg yolk,
  lightly beaten
2 tablespoons sour cream
¼ teaspoon almond
  extract (essence)

Orange Glaze

6 tablespoons
  confectioners' (icing)
  sugar
2 tablespoons freshly
  squeezed orange juice
¼ cup (60 g) apricot
  preserves

Makes: about 26 cookies
Preparation: 45 minutes
Cooking: 13–15 minutes
Level: 2

GLAZED LEMON
S-BEND COOKIES

Cookies: Use a wooden spoon to mix the flour, egg yolks, butter, lemon juice, sugar, and salt in a large bowl to form a smooth dough. • Press the dough into a disk, wrap in plastic wrap (cling film), and refrigerate for 30 minutes. • Preheat the oven to 350°F (180°C/gas 4). • Butter two cookie sheets. • Form the dough into 1-inch (2.5-cm) long logs and place 1 inch (2.5 cm) apart on the prepared cookie sheets. • Shape the logs into S-shapes. • Bake until just golden, 8–10 minutes. • Lemon Glaze: Place the confectioners' sugar in a medium bowl. Beat in ¼ cup (60 ml) of lemon juice and the zest until smooth, adding extra lemon juice as needed to make a good glazing consistency. • Drizzle the glaze over the cookies.

Cookies

2⅔ cups (400 g) all-purpose (plain) flour

3 large egg yolks

⅔ cup (180 g) butter, softened

2 tablespoons freshly squeezed lemon juice

¾ cup (150 g) granulated sugar

¼ teaspoon salt

Lemon Glaze

1 cup (150 g) confectioners' (icing) sugar

5 tablespoons freshly squeezed lemon juice, + more, as required

2 teaspoons finely grated lemon zest

Makes: about 25 cookies
Preparation: 35 minutes + 30 minutes to chill
Cooking: 8–10 minutes
Level: 1

PARTY COOKIES

406

Cookies: Preheat the oven to 350°F (180°C/gas 4). • Lightly oil two cookie sheets. • Beat the butter and confectioners' sugar in a large bowl with an electric mixer at high speed until creamy. • With mixer at low speed, gradually beat in the flour and salt. • Continue beating for 2–3 minutes until smooth and light. • Fit a pastry bag with a $3/4$-inch (2-cm) star tip. Fill the pastry bag, twist the opening tightly closed, and squeeze 2-inch (5-cm) lines and rosettes spacing them 2 inches (5 cm) apart on the prepared cookie sheets. • Bake until lightly browned, 6–8 minutes. • Cool the cookies on the sheet for 1 minute. Transfer to racks to cool. • Lemon Glaze: Place the confectioners' sugar in a small bowl and mix with the lemon juice until smooth. • Drizzle over the cookies. • Sprinkle with the sugar confetti.

Cookies

1 cup (250 g) butter, softened

½ cup (75 g) confectioners' (icing) sugar

1¼ cups (180 g) all-purpose (plain) flour

⅛ teaspoon salt

Lemon Glaze

⅔ cup (100 g) confectioners' (icing) sugar

1 tablespoon freshly squeezed lemon juice

1 tablespoon sugar confetti

Makes: about 35 cookies
Preparation: 25 minutes
Cooking: 6–8 minutes
Level: 1

ORANGE LADYFINGERS

Preheat the oven to 375°F (190°C/gas 5).
• Line two cookie sheets with parchment
paper. • Mix the flour and salt in a medium
bowl. • Beat the eggs, superfine sugar, and
orange zest in a large bowl with an electric
mixer at high speed until pale and very thick.
• Use a large rubber spatula to fold in the dry
ingredients. • Fit a pastry bag with a ½-inch
(1-cm) star tip. Fill the pastry bag, twist the
opening tightly closed, and squeeze out 2-inch
(5-cm) lines, spacing them 3 inches (8 cm)
apart on the prepared cookie sheets.
• Bake until just golden, 5–10 minutes.
• Transfer to racks to cool.

⅓ cup (50 g) all-purpose
(plain) flour

⅛ teaspoon salt

2 large eggs

⅓ cup (70 g) superfine
(caster) sugar

Finely grated zest
of 1 orange

Makes: about 20 cookies
Preparation: 15 minutes
Cooking: 5–10 minutes
Level: 1

LEMON ROSETTES

Preheat the oven to 350°F (180°C/gas 4).
• Butter two cookie sheets. • Mix the flour, baking powder, and salt in a large bowl.
• Stir in the sugar. • Add the egg, beating until just blended. • Stir in the oil, cream, honey, and lemon zest. • Fit a pastry bag with a ½-inch (1-cm) star tip. Fill the pastry bag, twist the opening tightly closed, and squeeze out generous 1½-inch (4-cm) rosettes, spacing 1 inch (2.5 cm) apart onto the prepared cookie sheets. • Bake until just golden at the edges, 10–15 minutes. • Transfer to racks to cool. • Dot the tops of the cookies with lemon curd and decorate with the candied lemon zest.

1⅔ cups (250 g) all-purpose (plain) flour

½ teaspoon baking powder

⅛ teaspoon salt

½ cup (100 g) granulated sugar

1 large egg

⅓ cup (90 ml) sunflower oil

¼ cup (60 ml) light (single cream

1 teaspoon honey

Finely grated zest of 1 lemon

¼ cup (60 g) lemon curd

3 tablespoons candied lemon zest

Makes: about 25 cookies
Preparation: 25 minutes
Cooking: 10–15 minutes
Level: 1

PINEAPPLE COOKIES

412

Preheat the oven to 400°F (200°C/gas 6).
• Set out two cookie sheets. • Mix the flour, baking powder, and salt in a medium bowl.
• Beat the butter and sugar in a large bowl with an electric mixer at high speed until creamy. • Add the egg, beating until just blended. • Mix in the dry ingredients, followed by the pineapple juice. • Insert a star-shaped design plate into a cookie press by sliding it into the head and locking it in place. Press out the cookies, spacing about 1 inch (2.5 cm) apart on the prepared cookie sheets. • Bake until just golden at the edges, 8–10 minutes.
• Cool on the sheets until the cookies firm slightly. Transfer to racks and let cool completely.

2¼ cups (330 g) all-purpose (plain) flour

½ teaspoon baking powder

¼ teaspoon salt

1 cup (250 g) butter, softened

¾ cup (150 g) granulated sugar

1 large egg

1 tablespoon fresh or canned pineapple juice

Makes: 32–36 cookies
Preparation: 25 minutes
Cooking: 8–10 minutes
Level: 1

ORANGE ESSES

Mix the flour and salt in a large bowl. • Stir in the ground hazelnuts, sugar, and orange zest. • Use a pastry blender to cut in the butter until the mixture resembles fine crumbs. • Mix in the egg whites to form a stiff dough. • Divide the dough in half. Form the dough into two disks, wrap in plastic wrap (cling film), and refrigerate for 30 minutes. • Preheat the oven to 350°F (180°C/gas 4). • Butter three cookie sheets. • Pinch off balls of dough the size of walnuts and shape into rounded S-shape cookies. Place on the prepared cookie sheets, spacing 1 inch (2.5 cm) apart. • Bake until golden brown, 12–15 minutes. • Transfer to racks to cool.

¾ cup (125 g) all-purpose (plain) flour

⅛ teaspoon salt

1⅓ cups (200 g) finely ground hazelnuts

1 cup (200 g) granulated sugar

1 tablespoon finely grated orange zest

½ cup (125 g) butter, cut up

2 large egg whites, lightly beaten

Makes: about 40 cookies
Preparation: 25 minutes
  + 30 minutes to chill
Cooking: 12–15 minutes
Level: 1

LIME ESSES

Mix the flour and salt in a large bowl.
• Stir in the ground almonds, sugar, and lime zest. • Use a pastry blender to cut in the butter until the mixture resembles fine crumbs. • Mix in the egg whites to form a stiff dough. • Divide the dough in half. Form the dough into two disks, wrap in plastic wrap (cling film), and refrigerate for 30 minutes.
• Preheat the oven to 350°F (180°C/gas 4).
• Butter three cookie sheets. • Pinch off balls of dough the size of walnuts and shape into rounded S-shape cookies. Place the cookies on the prepared cookie sheets, spacing 1 inch (2.5 cm) apart. • Bake until golden brown, 12–15 minutes. • Transfer to racks to cool.

¾ cup (125 g) all-purpose (plain) flour

⅛ teaspoon salt

1⅓ cups (200 g) finely ground almonds

1 cup (200 g) granulated sugar

1 tablespoon finely grated lime zest

½ cup (125 g) butter, cut up

2 large egg whites, lightly beaten

Makes: about 40 cookies
Preparation: 25 minutes
  + 30 minutes to chill
Cooking: 12–15 minutes
Level: 1

LEMON RINGS

Preheat the oven to 350°F (180°C/gas 4).
• Line three cookie sheets with parchment
paper. • Use a wooden spoon to mix the flour,
sugar, eggs, milk, vanilla, butter, lemon zest,
and salt in a large bowl to make a smooth
dough. • Break off balls of dough the size of
walnuts and form into 4-inch (10-cm) ropes.
Form the ropes into 1½-inch (4-cm) rings and
place 1 inch (2.5 cm) apart on the prepared
cookie sheets. • Bake until just golden,
15–20 minutes. • Cool the cookies
completely on the cookie sheets.

3⅓ cups (500 g) all-
purpose (plain) flour

¾ cup (150 g) granulated
sugar

2 large eggs

½ cup (125 ml) milk

1 teaspoon vanilla extract
(essence)

⅓ cup (90 g) butter,
softened

Finely grated zest
of 1 lemon

⅛ teaspoon salt

Makes: about 45 cookies
Preparation: 25 minutes
Cooking: 15–20 minutes
Level: 1

ITALIAN WHOLE-WHEAT COOKIES

Preheat the oven to 350°F (180°C/gas 4).
• Butter two cookie sheets. • Mix the flour, baking powder, and salt in a medium bowl.
• Mix the honey and olive oil in a large bowl until well blended. • Add the vanilla and egg, beating until just blended. • Mix in the dry ingredients to form a soft dough. • If the dough is stiff, add the milk. • Fit a pastry bag with ½-inch (1-cm) star tip. Fill the pastry bag, twist the opening tightly closed, and squeeze out small rosettes, spacing 2 inches (5 cm) apart on the prepared cookie sheets.
• Bake until lightly browned, 15–20 minutes.
• Transfer to racks to cool. • Dust with the confectioners' sugar.

1¼ cups (180 g) whole-wheat (wholemeal) flour

½ teaspoon baking powder

⅛ teaspoon salt

2 tablespoons honey

⅓ cup (90 ml) extra-virgin olive oil

½ teaspoon vanilla extract (essence)

1 large egg

2 tablespoons milk

⅓ cup (50 g) confectioners' (icing) sugar, to dust

Makes: about 28 cookies
Preparation: 25 minutes
Cooking: 15–20 minutes
Level: 1

PINWHEEL COOKIES

Mix the flour, baking soda, cinnamon, and salt
in a large bowl. • Cut in the butter until the
mixture resembles fine crumbs. • Stir in the
½ cup (100 g) of sugar, the almonds, dried
currants, caraway seeds, if using. • Add the
egg and mix until firm. • Refrigerate for
30 minutes. • Preheat the oven to 400°F
(200°C/gas 6). • Butter two cookie sheets.
• Roll out the dough to a 6 x 8-inch
(15 x 20-cm) rectangle. • Brush lightly
with water. Sprinkle with the remaining sugar.
• Cut the dough into ½ x 6-inch (1 x 15-cm)
long strips and shape into ropes. Form each
rope into a tight circular coil and place on the
cookie sheets, flattening slightly. • Bake until
golden brown, 10–12 minutes. • Transfer
to racks to cool.

2½ cups (375 g) all-
purpose (plain) flour

½ teaspoon baking soda
(bicarbonate of soda)

1 teaspoon ground
cinnamon

⅛ teaspoon salt

1 cup (250 g) butter,
softened

6 tablespoons granulated
sugar

⅔ cup (100 g) finely
ground almonds

½ cup (90 g) dried
currants

2 teaspoons caraway
seeds (optional)

1 large egg,
lightly beaten

2 teaspoons water

Makes: about 30 cookies
Preparation: 40 minutes
+ 30 minutes to chill
Cooking: 10–12 minutes
Level: 2

ALMOND GARLANDS

424

Preheat the oven to 350°F (180°C/gas 4).
• Set out two cookie sheets. • Mix the flour,
baking powder, and salt in a medium bowl.
• Beat the butter and sugar in a large bowl
with an electric mixer at high speed until
creamy. • Add the egg yolk and almond
extract, beating until just blended. • Mix
in the dry ingredients and almonds until well
blended. • Fit a pastry bag with a ½-inch
(1-cm) star tip. Fill the pastry bag, twist the
opening tightly closed, and squeeze out
2-inch rings onto the cookie sheets, spacing
1 inch (2.5 cm) apart. • Bake until golden
brown, 8–10 minutes. • Cool on the sheets
until the cookies firm slightly. Transfer to
racks and let cool completely.

1½ cups (225 g) all-
    purpose (plain) flour
½ teaspoon baking
    powder
⅛ teaspoon salt
1 cup (250 g) butter,
    softened
½ cup (100 g) granulated
    sugar
1 large egg yolk
½ teaspoon almond
    extract (essence)
⅓ cup (50 g) finely
    ground almonds

Makes: about 35 cookies
Preparation: 25 minutes
Cooking: 8–10 minutes
Level: 1

MINT SPRITZERS

Preheat the oven to 400°F (200°C/gas 6).
• Butter two cookie sheets. • Mix the flour
and salt in a medium bowl. • Beat the butter,
sugar, egg, and vanilla and mint extracts
in a large bowl with an electric mixer at high
speed. • Mix in the dry ingredients, followed
by the food coloring. • Refrigerate for
30 minutes. • Insert a clover-shaped design
plate into your cookie press by sliding it into
the head and locking in place. Press out the
cookies, spacing about 1 inch (2.5 cm) apart
on the prepared cookie sheet. • Bake until just
golden at the edges, 8–10 minutes. • Working
quickly, press a chocolate into the center of
each cookie. • Cool on the sheets until the
cookies firm slightly. Transfer to racks
and let cool.

1 cup (150 g) all-purpose
   (plain) flour
⅛ teaspoon salt
½ cup (125 g) butter,
   softened
⅓ cup (70 g) granulated
   sugar
½ large egg,
   lightly beaten
½ teaspoon vanilla extract
   (essence)
½ teaspoon mint extract
   (essence)
   Few drops green food
   coloring
30 Hershey kisses

Makes: about 30 cookies
Preparation: 25 minutes
   + 30 minutes to chill
Cooking: 8–10 minutes
Level: 2

FILLED
COOKIES

CHOCOLATE SANDWICHES

430

Mix the flour, custard powder, cocoa, and salt in a medium bowl. • Beat the butter and granulated sugar in a large bowl with an electric mixer at high speed until creamy. • Add the egg, beating until just blended. • Mix in the dry ingredients. • Press the dough into a disk, wrap in plastic wrap (cling film), and refrigerate for 30 minutes. • Preheat the oven to 350°F (180°C/gas 4). • Butter two cookie sheets. • Roll the dough out ¼-inch (5-mm) thick. Cut into rectangles. • Arrange the cookies 1 inch (2.5 cm) apart on the prepared sheets. Prick all over with a fork and sprinkle with the superfine sugar. • Bake until lightly browned, 10–12 minutes. • Cool completely on the sheets. • Stick the cookies together in pairs with the buttercream.

1 cup (150 g) all-purpose (plain) flour

⅓ cup (50 g) custard powder

2 tablespoons unsweetened cocoa powder

⅛ teaspoon salt

½ cup (125 g) butter, softened

1 cup (200 g) granulated sugar

1 large egg

Superfine (caster) sugar, to sprinkle

½ recipe Italian buttercream flavored with 2 tablespoons cocoa (see page 698)

Makes: about 12 cookies
Preparation: 15 minutes
  + 30 minutes to chill
Cooking: 10–12 minutes
Level: 1

FILLED CHOCOLATE COOKIES

Preheat the oven to 375°F (190°C/gas 5).
• Butter two cookie sheets. • Mix the flour and cocoa in a medium bowl. • Beat the butter and sugar in a large bowl with an electric mixer at medium speed until creamy. • Add the egg yolk, beating until just blended. • Mix in the dry ingredients. • Form the dough into two equal-size disks, wrap in plastic wrap (cling film), and refrigerate for 30 minutes. • Roll out the dough on a lightly floured surface to 1/4-inch (5-mm) thick. • Use a 2-inch (5-cm) cutter to cut out 20 disks and a 1 1/2-inch (4-cm) cutter to cut out another 20 disks. • Place the larger disks on the cookie sheets with a piece of chocolate in the center of each. Cover with the smaller circles, molding them over the chocolate. Press around the edges with a fork to seal. • Bake until firm and spread, 10–12 minutes. • Cool on the sheet for 5 minutes. • Transfer to racks to cool completely.

1 2/3 cups (250 g) self-rising flour

2 tablespoons unsweetened cocoa powder

2/3 cup (150 g) butter, softened

3/4 cup (150 g) granulated sugar

1 large egg yolk

20 chocolate drops (buttons) or small squares of semisweet (dark) chocolate

Makes: about 20 cookies
Preparation: 20 minutes
+ 30 minutes to chill
Cooking: 10–12 minutes
Level: 2

MARZIPAN COOKIES

Mix the flour, ginger, baking soda, and salt in a medium bowl. • Heat the honey and sugar over low heat until the sugar has dissolved. • Let cool for 5 minutes. • Stir in the dry ingredients, almonds, and candied peel. • Cover with a clean cloth and let rest for 12 hours. • Preheat the oven to 375°F (190°C/gas 3). • Line two cookie sheets with parchment paper. • Filling: Knead the marzipan and preserves until smooth. Work in the almonds and lemon peel. • Divide the cookie dough in two equal portions. Roll out into two 12 x 6-inch (30 x 15-cm) rectangles. • Cover with the marzipan and sprinkle with currants. • Roll the dough up tightly to form logs about 2 inches (5 cm) in diameter. Cut into slices ½-inch (1-cm) thick. Transfer to the cookie sheets, cut-side up. • Bake until just golden, 15–20 minutes. • Let cool completely. • Top with the frosting, pistachios, and candied fruit.

2⅓ cups (350 g) all-purpose (plain) flour
1 tablespoon ginger
2 teaspoons baking soda
½ teaspoon salt
1 cup (250 g) honey
¾ cup (150 g) sugar
1⅓ cups (200 g) finely ground almonds
¾ cup (75 g) chopped candied peel

Filling
8 oz (250 g) marzipan
1 cup (250 g) white currant preserves
1 cup (100 g) chopped almonds
½ cup (50 g) chopped lemon peel
½ cup (90 g) dried currants
1 recipe chocolate frosting (see 697)
4 tablespoons chopped pistachios
2 tablespoons chopped candied fruit

Makes: 30–35 cookies
Preparation: 1 hour
  + 12 hours to rest
Cooking: 15–20 minutes
Level: 2

CHOCOLATE LOGS

Logs: Mix the flour, cocoa, and salt in a large bowl. • Use a pastry blender to cut in the butter until the mixture resembles fine crumbs. • Stir in the sugar and vanilla. • Add the milk to form a stiff dough. • Form the dough into a log 1 inch (2.5 cm) in diameter, wrap in plastic wrap (cling film), and refrigerate for 30 minutes. • Preheat the oven to 400°F (200°C/gas 6). • Butter a cookie sheet. • Slice the dough into 2-inch (5-cm) lengths and place 1 inch (2.5 cm) apart on the prepared cookie sheet. • Bake until lightly browned and firm to the touch, 20–25 minutes. • Transfer to racks to cool. • Frosting: Mix the cocoa with the water until smooth. • Beat the butter in a medium bowl until creamy. • Beat the confectioners' sugar and the cocoa mixture until smooth. • Spread the cookies with the frosting. • Draw the tines of a fork across the frosting to resemble the bark of a log.

Logs
- 3/4 cup (125 g) all-purpose (plain) flour
- 1/3 cup (50 g) unsweetened cocoa powder
- 1/8 teaspoon salt
- 1/3 cup (90 g) butter
- 1/4 cup (50 g) granulated sugar
- 1/2 teaspoon vanilla extract (essence)
- 2 tablespoons milk

Frosting
- 2 tablespoons unsweetened cocoa powder
- 1 tablespoon boiling water
- 1/2 cup (125 g) butter, softened
- 2 cups (300 g) confectioners' (icing) sugar

Makes: 14–16 cookies
Preparation: 30 minutes + 30 minutes to chill
Cooking: 20–25 minutes
Level: 1

COFFEE NUTS

438

Preheat oven to 350°F (180°C/gas 4). • Line two baking sheets with parchment paper. • Mix the flour and baking powder in a medium bowl. Rub in the margarine finely and then add the sugar. • Beat the egg yolk and add gradually with the coffee essence to make a stiff paste—you may not need all the egg. • Bind the mixture together with lightly floured hands, then roll into small balls about the size of a walnut. • Place on the prepared baking sheets, spacing well. • Bake until pale golden brown, about 10 minutes. • Transfer to wire racks and let cool completely. • When cold, sandwich together with the coffee buttercream.

1   cup (150 g) all-purpose (plain) flour
1   teaspoon baking powder
⅓   cup (90 g) margarine
¼   cup + 1 tablespoon (60 g) granulated sugar
1   large egg yolk
1   teaspoon coffee extract (essence)
1   recipe coffee buttercream (see page 699)

Makes: about 12 cookies
Preparation: 15 minutes
Cooking: 10 minutes
Level: 1

COCONUT COOKIES

Preheat the oven to 350°F (180°C/gas 4).
• Set out two cookie sheets. • Mix the flour,
baking soda, and salt in a medium bowl. Stir
in the coconut. • Beat the butter, brown sugar,
and vanilla in a large bowl with an electric
mixer at high speed until creamy. • Add the
egg, beating until just blended. • With mixer
at low speed, gradually add the dry
ingredients. • Form the dough into balls
the size of walnuts and place 1 inch (2.5 cm)
apart on the sheets. • Use your thumb to
make a slight hollow in each center and fill
with a small amount of preserves. • Bake
until golden brown, 12–15 minutes.
• Transfer to racks to cool.

1¼ cups (180 g) all-purpose (plain) flour

2 teaspoons baking soda (bicarbonate of soda)

¼ teaspoon salt

⅓ cup (40 g) shredded (desiccated) coconut

½ cup (125 g) butter, softened

½ cup (100 g) firmly packed light brown sugar

1 teaspoon vanilla extract (essence)

1 large egg

½ cup (125 g) raspberry or strawberry preserves (jam)

Makes: 25–30 cookies
Preparation: 20 minutes
Cooking: 12–15 minutes
Level: 1

HAZELNUT SPIRALS

Refrigerate four cookie sheets. • Mix the flour, baking powder, and salt in a medium bowl. • Beat the butter and sugar in a large bowl with an electric mixer at high speed until creamy. Add the brandy and vanilla. • Add the eggs one at a time beating until just blended after each addition. • Mix in the dry ingredients to form a soft dough. • Mix the chocolate hazelnut spread and coffee liqueur in a small bowl. • Roll the dough out into a large rectangle about ½-inch (1-cm) thick. • Spread evenly with the chocolate mixture and roll the dough up tightly from the long side. • Wrap in plastic wrap (cling film) and refrigerate for 30 minutes. • Preheat the oven to 375°F (190°C/gas 5). • Cut the dough into ½-inch (1-cm) thick slices. • Place 1 inch (2.5 cm) apart on the cookie sheets. • Bake until lightly browned and firm to the touch, 8–10 minutes. • Cool on the cookie sheets for 5 minutes. Transfer to racks to cool.

3⅓ cups (500 g) all-purpose (plain) flour
½ teaspoon baking powder
¼ teaspoon salt
1 cup (250 g) butter, softened
¾ cup (150 g) granulated sugar
1 tablespoon brandy
1 teaspoon vanilla extract (essence)
2 large eggs
¼ cup (60 g) chocolate hazelnut spread (Nutella)
1 tablespoon coffee liqueur

Makes: 60–65 cookies
Preparation: 60 minutes + 30 minutes to chill
Cooking: 8–10 minutes
Level: 2

MOCHA PINWHEELS

Mix the flour, baking powder, and salt in a medium bowl. • Beat $1/4$ cup (60 g) of butter and 2 tablespoons of sugar in a medium bowl with an electric mixer at high speed until creamy. • Mix in $3/4$ cup (125 g) of the dry ingredients. • Stir the coffee granules into the remaining flour. • Beat the remaining butter and sugar until creamy. • Mix in the coffee mixture. • Roll out both doughs on a lightly floured work surface into rectangles $1/4$-inch (5-mm) thick. • Brush the plain dough with the milk. • Top with the coffee dough and roll up tightly from the long side. Wrap in plastic wrap (cling film) and refrigerate for at least 30 minutes. • Preheat the oven to 350°F (180°C/gas 4). • Butter two cookie sheets. • Slice the dough $1/4$ inch (5 mm) thick and place 1 inch (2.5 cm) apart on the prepared cookie sheets. • Bake until just golden, 12–15 minutes. • Transfer to racks to cool.

$1^2/_3$ cups (250 g) all-purpose (plain) flour

1 teaspoon baking powder

$1/8$ teaspoon salt

$1/2$ cup (125 g) butter, softened

$1/3$ cup (70 g) granulated sugar

2 teaspoons instant coffee granules

2 teaspoons milk

Makes: about 25 cookies
Preparation: 1 hour
 + 30 minutes to chill
Cooking: 12–15 minutes
Level: 1

MELTING MOMENTS

Mix the flour, custard powder, sugar, rice flour, baking powder, and salt in a large bowl. • Use a pastry blender to cut in the butter until the mixture resembles coarse crumbs. Stir in the milk to form a firm dough. • Press the dough into a disk, wrap in plastic wrap (cling film), and refrigerate for 30 minutes. • Preheat the oven to 350°F (180°C/gas 4). • Set out two cookie sheets. • Transfer the dough to a lightly floured surface and roll out to a ¼-inch (5-mm) thick. • Use a 1½-inch (4-cm) cookie cutter to cut out the cookies. • Gather the dough scraps, re-roll, and continue cutting out the cookies until all the dough is used. • Transfer the cookies to the cookie sheets, spacing 1 inch (2.5 cm) apart. • Bake until lightly browned, 12–15 minutes. • Transfer to racks to cool. • Stick pairs of cookies together with the buttercream.

1²/₃ cups (250 g) all-purpose (plain) flour

1¼ cups (180 g) custard powder

1 cup (200 g) granulated sugar

½ cup (75 g) rice flour

1 teaspoon baking powder

⅛ teaspoon salt

¾ cup (180 g) butter, cut up

¼ cup (60 ml) milk

1 recipe Italian buttercream (see page 698)

Makes: about 15 cookies
Preparation: 15 minutes + 30 minutes to chill
Cooking: 12–15 minutes
Level: 1

COFFEE SANDWICHES

Preheat the oven to 375°F (190°C/gas 5).
• Butter two cookie sheets. • Mix the flour, cocoa, baking powder, and salt in a medium bowl. • Beat the butter, sugar, and vanilla in a large bowl with an electric mixer at high speed until creamy. • Mix in the dry ingredients to form a stiff dough. • Form the dough into balls the size of walnuts and place 1 inch (2.5 cm) apart on the prepared cookie sheets. Use a fork to flatten them slightly.
• Bake until firm to the touch, 10–15 minutes.
• Cool on the sheets until the cookies firm slightly. Transfer to racks to finish cooling.
• Stick the cookies together in pairs with the buttercream.

3/4 cup (125 g) all-purpose (plain) flour
1 tablespoon unsweetened cocoa powder
1/2 teaspoon baking powder
1/8 teaspoon salt
1/2 cup (125 g) butter, softened
1/2 cup (50 g) granulated sugar
1/2 teaspoon vanilla extract (essence)
1 recipe coffee buttercream (see page 699)

Makes: 12–15 cookies
Preparation: 20 minutes
Cooking: 10–15 minutes
Level: 1

DATE CRUNCHIES

Preheat oven to 350°F (180°C/gas 4).
• Line two cookie sheets with parchment paper. • Beat the margarine and sugar in an electric mixer on high speed until pale and creamy. • Work in the oats, baking powder, salt, and 1 tablespoon of water. Squeeze the dough together with your hands and roll out thinly on a floured surface, taking care that the mixture does not stick to the board. • Cut into rounds with a 2-inch (5-cm) plain cookie cutter. • Transfer to the prepared cookie sheets. Bake until pale golden brown, 15–20 minutes. • Place the dates and remaining water in a saucepan and simmer until of a spreading consistency. • Sandwich the cookies together with the date filling.

¼ **cup (60 g) margarine**
4 **tablespoons granulated sugar**
4 **oz (125 g) rolled oats**
½ **teaspoon baking powder**
Pinch of salt
¼ **cup (60 ml) water**
½ **cup (100 g) dates, pitted and chopped**

Makes: about 12 cookies
Preparation: 30 minutes
Cooking: 8–10 minutes
Level: 1

FILLED
COOKIES

FILLED HAZELNUT CRUNCHIES

452

Refrigerate three cookie sheets. • Mix the flour and salt in a large bowl. Stir in the superfine sugar and hazelnuts. • Dot the butter evenly over the mixture. • Use a pastry blender to cut in the butter until the mixture resembles coarse crumbs. • Add the eggs, beating until just blended. • Turn out onto a lightly floured surface and work into a smooth dough. Knead gently once or twice (too much kneading causes cracks when cutting out shapes). • Shape into a ball, wrap in plastic wrap (cling film), and refrigerate for 1 hour. • Roll out small portions of dough to ¼-inch (5-mm) thick. • Use a cutter to stamp into 1-inch (2.5-cm) disks. Gather the dough scraps, re-roll, and continue cutting out cookies until all the dough is used. • Use a metal spatula to transfer the cookies onto the chilled baking sheets, placing them 1½ inches (4 cm) apart. • Preheat the oven to 375°F (190°C/gas 5). • Bake until just golden, 12–15 minutes. • Cool the cookies on the cookie sheets for 2 minutes. Transfer to rack and let cool completely. • Spread half the cookies with a little of the preserves and sandwich together.

3 cups (450 g) all-purpose (plain) flour

⅛ teaspoon salt

1 cup (200 g) superfine (caster) sugar

1⅓ cups (130 g) finely ground hazelnuts

1 cup (250 g) cold butter, cut up

2 large eggs, lightly beaten

¾ cup (180 g) strawberry or raspberry preserves

Makes: about 30 cookies
Preparation: 40 minutes + 1 hour to chill
Cooking: 12–15 minutes
Level: 2

APRICOT BRANDY MACAROONS

Cookies: Preheat the oven to 275°F (140°C/gas 1). • Butter two cookie sheets. • Place the flour in a medium bowl. Stir in the walnuts. • Beat the egg whites and salt in a large bowl until frothy. • Add the sugar, beating until stiff peaks form. • Fold in the dry ingredients. • Fit a pastry bag with a ¾-inch (2-cm) plain tip. Fill the pastry bag, twist the opening tightly closed, and squeeze out mounds the size of walnuts, spacing them 1 inch (2.5 cm) apart on the sheets. • Bake until the cookies are set and lightly browned, 20–25 minutes. • Transfer to racks and let cool completely. • Filling: Melt the chocolate with the cream in a double boiler over barely simmering water. • Stir in the brandy. • Plunge the pan into a bowl of ice water and stir until the mixture has cooled. • With mixer at high speed, beat until creamy. • Stick the cookies together in pairs with the filling. Roll in the pistachios.

Cookies

⅓ cup (50 g) all-purpose (plain) flour

2 cups (300 g) finely ground walnuts

3 large egg whites

¼ teaspoon salt

¾ cup (150 g) granulated sugar

Filling

8 oz (250 g) white chocolate, coarsely chopped

¼ cup (60 ml) heavy (double) cream

2 tablespoons apricot brandy

2 tablespoons finely chopped pistachios

Makes: about 20 cookies
Preparation: 30 minutes
Cooking: 20–25 minutes
Level: 2

HONEY FILLED COOKIES

Cookies: Mix the flour, confectioners' sugar, and salt in a large bowl. Cut in the butter until the mixture resembles coarse crumbs. Add the water to form a stiff dough. • Press the dough into a disk, wrap in plastic wrap (cling film), and refrigerate for 30 minutes. • Preheat the oven to 375°F (190°C/gas 5). • Line two cookie sheets with parchment paper. • Roll out the dough on a lightly floured surface to 1/8-inch (3-mm) thick. • Use a 2 1/2-inch (6-cm) cookie cutter to cut out cookies. • Transfer to the cookie sheets. • Bake until just golden, 10–12 minutes. • Transfer to racks and let cool completely. • Spice Filling: Place the sugar, cinnamon, cloves, orange zest, and water in a medium saucepan. • Cook, without stirring, until the mixture reaches 238°F (114°C), or the soft-ball stage. • Stir in the vinegar, discard the cloves, cinnamon stick, and orange zest, and remove from the heat. • Let cool completely. • Stick the cookies together in pairs with the spice filling.

Cookies

2 1/4 cups (330 g) all-purpose (plain) flour

2/3 cup (100 g) confectioners' (icing) sugar

1/8 teaspoon salt

1 cup (250 g) butter, softened

1 tablespoon warm water + more as needed

Spice Filling

2 cups (400 g) firmly packed dark brown sugar

1 stick cinnamon

2 cloves

Zest of 1 orange, in one piece

1 cup (250 ml) water

1/4 teaspoon white vinegar

Makes: about 30 cookies
Preparation: 55 minutes + 30 minutes to chill
Cooking: 10–12 minutes
Level: 2

MARZIPAN HONEY DROPS

Cookies: Mix the all-purpose and rye flours, baking soda, cinnamon, nutmeg, ginger, and salt in a large bowl. • Heat the honey and sugar in a small saucepan over low heat until the sugar has dissolved completely. Cool for 15 minutes. • Use a wooden spoon to work the honey mixture into the dry ingredients to form a smooth dough. • Cover with a clean cloth and let rest at room temperature for 12 hours. • Preheat the oven to 350°F (180°C/gas 4). • Line two cookie sheets with parchment paper. • Filling: Knead the marzipan, confectioners' sugar, and lemon juice and zest until smooth. • Roll the dough out on a lightly floured surface into three 12 x 4-inch (30 x 10-cm) strips. • Shape the marzipan filling into logs of the same length. Place on the dough strips and fold over to seal. • Slice 1 inch (2.5 cm) thick and place cut-side up on the cookie sheets. • Bake until just golden at the edges, 12–15 minutes. • Transfer to racks. • Toast the cornstarch in a frying pan until lightly golden, 3–4 minutes. Add the confectioners' sugar and water and bring to a boil, stirring constantly. • Drizzle over the cookies while warm.

Cookies

1 cup (150 g) all-purpose (plain) flour

2/3 cup (100 g) rye flour

1 teaspoon baking soda

1 teaspoon cinnamon

1/2 teaspoon finely grated nutmeg

1/4 teaspoon ground ginger

1/4 teaspoon salt

1 cup (250 ml) honey

1/4 cup (50 g) granulated sugar

Filling

14 oz (400 g) marzipan, softened

2/3 cup (100 g) confectioners' (icing) sugar

1/2 teaspoon lemon juice

1 teaspoon finely grated lemon zest

1 tablespoon cornstarch (cornflour)

1 tablespoon confectioners' (icing) sugar

3/4 cup (180 ml) hot water

Makes: 35–40 cookies
Preparation: 1 hour
  + 12 hours to rest
Cooking: 12–15 minutes
Level: 3

BLACK SUGAR COOKIES

Mix the flour, cocoa, and salt in a large bowl.
• Use a pastry blender to cut in the butter
until the mixture resembles coarse crumbs.
• Mix in the cream. • Press the dough into
a disk, wrap in plastic wrap (cling film), and
refrigerate for 30 minutes. • Preheat the oven
to 375°F (190°C/gas 5). • Line two cookie
sheets with parchment paper. • Roll out the
dough on a lightly floured surface to ⅛-inch
(3 mm) thick. • Use a 1½-inch (4-cm) cookie
cutter to cut out the cookies. Gather the
dough scraps, reroll, and continue cutting out
cookies until all the dough is used. • Use a
spatula to transfer the cookies to the cookie
sheet, spacing them 1½ inches (4-cm) apart.
• Sprinkle with the sugar. • Bake until just
firm to the touch, 8–10 minutes. • Transfer
to racks to cool. • Filling: Melt the chocolate
in a double boiler over barely simmering
water. Remove from the heat and mix in the
confectioners' sugar and cream. • Stick the
cookies together in pairs with the filling.
• Let the cookies stand for 30 minutes to set.

1 cup (150 g) all-purpose (plain) flour
4 tablespoons unsweetened cocoa powder
⅛ teaspoon salt
⅓ cup (90 g) butter, cut up
5 tablespoons light (single) cream
⅓ cup (70 g) granulated sugar, to sprinkle

Filling
2 oz (60 g) semisweet (dark) chocolate, coarsely chopped
1 cup (150 g) confectioners' (icing) sugar
1 tablespoon light (single) cream

Makes: 12–14 cookies
Preparation: 40 minutes + 1 hour to chill and set
Cooking: 8–10 minutes
Level: 2

SUGAR COOKIES WITH PINK FILLING

462

Cookies: Place the flour and salt in a large bowl. • Use a pastry blender to cut in the butter until the mixture resembles coarse crumbs. • Mix in the cream. • Press the dough into a disk, wrap in plastic wrap (cling film), and refrigerate for 30 minutes. • Preheat the oven to 375°F (190°C/gas 3). • Line two cookie sheets with parchment paper. • Roll out the dough on a lightly floured surface to 1/8-inch (3-mm) thick. • Use a 1 1/2-inch (4-cm) cookie cutter to cut out the cookies. Gather the dough scraps, reroll, and continue cutting out cookies until all the dough is used. • Use a spatula to transfer the cookies to the cookie sheet, spacing them 1 1/2 inches (4 cm) apart. • Bake until just golden at the edges, 8–10 minutes. • Transfer to racks to cool. • Pink Filling: Mix the confectioners' sugar, butter, cream, vanilla, and red food coloring in a small bowl. • Stick the cookies together in pairs with the filling.• Dust with the confectioners' sugar.

1 cup (150 g) all-purpose (plain) flour
1/8 teaspoon salt
1/3 cup (90 g) butter, cut up
1/3 cup (60 ml) light (single) cream
1/3 cup (50 g) confectioners' (icing) sugar, to dust

Pink Filling

1 cup (150 g) confectioners' (icing) sugar
1 tablespoon butter, softened
1 tablespoon light (single) cream
1/2 teaspoon vanilla extract (essence)
   Few drops red food coloring

Makes: about 12 cookies
Preparation: 40 minutes + 30 minutes to chill
Cooking: 8–10 minutes
Level: 2

RASPBERRY COOKIES

Cookies: Place the flour in a medium bowl.
• Beat the butter and sugar in a large bowl until creamy. • Mix in the flour, almonds, and lemon zest and juice. • Divide the dough in half. Wrap in plastic wrap (cling film) and refrigerate for 30 minutes. • Roll out half the dough to ⅛-inch (3-mm) thick. • Use a 1½ inch (4 cm) cookie cutter to cut out the cookies. • Place 1 inch (2.5 cm) apart on the sheets. • Use a ¾-inch (2-cm) fluted cutter to cut the centers out of half the cookies. • Refrigerate for 30 minutes. • Preheat the oven to 375°F (190°C/gas 5). • Bake until just golden and the edges are firm, 8–10 minutes. • Let cool on racks. • Glaze: Mix the confectioners' sugar with enough lemon juice to make a smooth glaze. • Spread the cookies with cut-out centers with the glaze. • Set aside until the glaze has dried. • Stick the cookies together in pairs with the preserves.

Cookies

1 cup (150 g) all-purpose (plain) flour

⅔ cup (150 g) butter, softened

½ cup (100 g) granulated sugar

1 cup (150 g) finely ground almonds

1 teaspoon finely grated lemon zest

1 teaspoon freshly squeezed lemon juice

Glaze

⅔ cup (100 g) confectioners' (icing) sugar

1 teaspoon lemon juice, + more, as needed

½ cup (120 g) raspberry or red currant preserves (jam)

Makes: about 16 cookies
Preparation: 45 minutes
**   + 1 hour to chill**
Cooking: 8–10 minutes
Level: 2

STRAWBERRY CINNAMON COOKIES

Preheat the oven to 400°F (200°C/gas 6).
• Butter three cookie sheets. • Mix the flour,
baking powder, cinnamon, and salt in a
medium bowl. • Beat the butter and sugar
in a large bowl with an electric mixer at high
speed until creamy. • Add the eggs and
vanilla, beating until just blended. • Mix in
the dry ingredients. • Fit the pastry bag with
a ½-inch (1-cm) plain tip. Fill the pastry bag,
twist the opening tightly closed, and squeeze
out 2-inch (5-cm) rounds, spacing 1 inch
(2.5 cm) apart on the prepared cookie sheets.
• Press your thumb into each cookie to make
a small hollow. • Bake until just golden,
8–10 minutes. • Transfer to racks to cool.
• Heat the preserves in a small saucepan
over low heat until liquid. • Fill each hollow
with a little of the preserves.

2⅔ cups (350 g) all-purpose (plain) flour
1 teaspoon baking powder
1 teaspoon ground cinnamon
⅛ teaspoon salt
⅓ cup (90 g) butter, softened
½ cup (100 g) granulated sugar
2 large eggs
½ teaspoon vanilla extract (essence)
⅔ cup (180 g) strawberry preserves (jam)

Makes: about 45 cookies
Preparation: 25 minutes
  + 30 minutes to set
Cooking: 8–10 minutes
Level: 2

FROSTED BUTTER COOKIES

Mix the flour, baking powder, and salt in a large bowl. • Beat the butter and sugar in a large bowl with an electric mixer at high speed until creamy. • Add the egg and vanilla, beating until just blended. • Turn the dough out onto a lightly floured surface and knead until smooth. • Press the dough into a disk, wrap in plastic wrap (cling film), and refrigerate for 30 minutes. • Preheat the oven to 350°F (180°C/gas 4). • Butter two cookie sheets. • Roll out the dough to ¼-inch (5-mm) thick. • Use a 1½-inch (4-cm) cookie cutter to cut out the cookies. • Gather the dough scraps, re-roll, and continue cutting out cookies until all the dough is used. • Transfer the cookies to a cookie sheet, placing them 1 inch (2.5 cm) apart. • Bake until lightly browned, 8–10 minutes. • Cool on the sheets until the cookies firm slightly. Transfer to racks to finish cooling. • Warm the raspberry preserves in a small saucepan over low heat until liquid. • Stick the cookies together in pairs with the preserves. • Mix the confectioners' sugar with enough water to make a spreadable frosting. • Spread the tops of the cookies with the frosting and top with a half cherry.

2 cups (300 g) all-purpose (plain) flour

1½ teaspoons baking powder

⅛ teaspoon salt

1 cup (250 g) butter, softened

1½ cups (300 g) granulated sugar

1 large egg

½ teaspoon vanilla extract (essence)

¾ cup (180 ml) raspberry preserves

1 cup (150 g) confectioners' (icing) sugar

1 tablespoon boiling water + more, as needed

10 candied cherries, cut in half

Makes: about 20 cookies
Preparation: 40 minutes
Cooking: 8–10 minutes
Level: 1

LEMON DROPS

Mix the flour, cornstarch, and salt in a medium bowl. • Beat the butter and sugar in a large bowl with an electric mixer at high speed until creamy. • Add the lemon juice and egg yolk, beating until just blended. • Mix in the dry ingredients to make a soft, sticky dough. • Cover with plastic wrap (cling film) and refrigerate for 30 minutes. • Preheat the oven to 350°F (180°C/gas 4). • Line two cookie sheets with parchment paper. • Form the dough into balls the size of walnuts and place 1 inch (2.5 cm) apart on the prepared cookie sheets. Make a slight hollow in each center and fill with a small amount of lemon curd • Bake until just golden, 20–25 minutes. • Transfer to racks to cool.

1³⁄₄ cups (275 g) all-purpose (plain) flour

¹⁄₃ cup (50 g) cornstarch (cornflour)

¹⁄₈ teaspoon salt

1 cup (250 g) butter, softened

¹⁄₄ cup (50 g) granulated sugar

1 tablespoon freshly squeezed lemon juice

1 large egg yolk

¹⁄₂ cup (120 g) lemon curd

Makes: about 30 cookies

Preparation: 20 minutes + 30 minutes to chill

Cooking: 20–25 minutes

Level: 1

SWEET SUMMER KISSES

472

Preheat the oven to 350°F (180°C/gas 4).
• Butter two cookie sheets. • Beat the butter, confectioners' sugar, and vanilla in a large bowl with an electric mixer at high speed until creamy. • Mix in the flour and salt. • Drop tablespoons of the dough 2 inches (5 cm) apart onto the prepared cookie sheets, flattening them slightly with a fork. • Bake until just golden at the edges, 15–20 minutes. • Transfer to racks to cool. • Warm the preserves in a small saucepan over low heat until liquid. • Stick the cookies together in pairs with the preserves.

3/4 cup (180 g) butter, softened

1/2 cup (75 g) confectioners' (icing) sugar

1 teaspoon vanilla extract (essence)

2 cups (300 g) all-purpose (plain) flour

1/8 teaspoon salt

2/3 cup (180 g) apricot preserves (jam)

Makes: about 12 cookies
Preparation: 20 minutes
Cooking: 15–20 minutes
Level: 1

RASPBERRY PINWHEELS

474

Mix the flour and salt in a large bowl. Stir in the almonds and sugar. • Use a pastry blender to cut in the butter until the mixture resembles fine crumbs. • Mix in the egg mixture to form a firm dough. • Turn the dough out onto a lightly floured surface and knead until smooth. • Transfer to a large sheet of parchment paper and roll into a 10 x 14-inch (25 x 35-cm) rectangle. Spread evenly with the preserves and roll up the dough tightly from the long side. • Wrap in plastic wrap (cling film) and refrigerate for at least 30 minutes. • Preheat the oven to 350°F (180°C/gas 4). • Line two cookie sheets with parchment paper. • Slice the dough ½-inch (1-cm) thick and place ½ inch (1 cm) apart on the prepared cookie sheets. • Bake until just golden at the edges, 12–15 minutes.
• Transfer to racks to cool.

2 cups (300 g) all-purpose (plain) flour

⅛ teaspoon salt

½ cup (75 g) finely ground almonds

½ cup (100 g) granulated sugar

⅓ cup (90 g) butter, cut up

1 large egg, lightly beaten with 2 tablespoons cold water

½ cup (120 g) raspberry preserves (jam)

Makes: about 25 cookies
Preparation: 1 hour
 + 30 minutes to chill
Cooking: 12–15 minutes
Level: 2

LEMON CURD COOKIES

Mix the flour and salt in a large bowl. • Cut in the butter until the mixture resembles fine crumbs. • Stir in the granulated sugar, lemon zest and juice, and egg yolks to form a stiff dough. • Press the dough into a disk, wrap in plastic wrap (cling film), and refrigerate for 30 minutes. • Preheat the oven to 350°F (180°C/gas 4). • Butter two cookie sheets. • Roll out the dough to ⅛-inch (3-mm) thick. • Use a 3-inch (8-cm) fluted cookie cutter to cut out the cookies. • Use a 1-inch (2.5-cm) crescent-shaped cookie cutter to cut out the centers from half the cookies. Gather the dough scraps, re-roll, and continue cutting out cookies until all the dough is used. • Transfer the cookies to the sheets. • Bake until golden brown, 8–10 minutes. • Transfer to racks to cool. • Spread the whole cookies with the lemon curd and place the cookies with holes on top.

1½ cups (225 g) all-purpose (plain) flour

⅛ teaspoon salt

⅔ cup (150 g) butter, cut up

⅓ cup (70 g) granulated sugar

1 tablespoon finely grated lemon zest

2 tablespoons freshly squeezed lemon juice

2 large egg yolks

1 cup (250 ml) lemon curd

Makes: 12–15 cookies
Preparation: 45 minutes + 30 minutes to chill
Cooking: 8–10 minutes
Level: 1

APPLE SMILES

Dough: Mix all the ingredients in a large bowl to form a stiff dough. • Filling: Plump the raisins in hot water for 10 minutes. Drain well and pat dry with paper towels. • Preheat the oven to 350°F (180°C/gas 4). • Set out a cookie sheet. • Mix the apples, butter, sugar, and lemon zest and juice in a large saucepan over low heat and stew until the apples begin to soften, about 5 minutes. • Stir in the raisins and let cool completely. • Discard the lemon zest. • Roll the cookie out to ¼-inch (5-mm) thick. • Use a round cookie cutter to stamp out 3-inch (8-cm) circles. • Spread with a heaped teaspoonful of the apple filling, leaving a ½-inch (1-cm) border around the edge. • Brush the border with the beaten egg and fold over, pressing down firmly. • Brush the tops with the remaining egg. • Arrange on the cookie sheet about 1 inch (2.5 cm) apart. • Bake until golden brown, 20–30 minutes. • Cool on the sheet for 2 minutes. Transfer to racks to cool.

Dough

- 1 cup (250 g) quark or ricotta
- 2 cups (300 g) all-purpose (plain) flour
- 1 teaspoon baking powder
- ⅛ teaspoon salt
- ⅓ cup (90 ml) vegetable oil
- 2 tablespoons milk
- ⅓ cup (70 g) sugar
- 1 large egg
- 1 teaspoon finely grated lemon zest
- ½ teaspoon vanilla extract (essence)
- ⅓ cup (90 g) butter

Filling

- 3 tablespoons golden raisins (sultanas)
- 3 medium apples, peeled, cored, and cubed
- 1 tablespoon butter
- ⅓ cup (70 g) sugar
- Grated zest 1 lemon
- 1 teaspoon freshly squeezed lemon juice
- 1 large egg

Makes: 12–15 cookies
Preparation: 1 hour
Cooking: 20–30 minutes
Level: 2

SPICY ALMOND SANDWICHES

Mix the flour, cocoa, allspice, cinnamon, ginger, and salt in a medium bowl. • Beat the butter and sugar in a large bowl with an electric mixer at high speed until creamy. • Add the egg yolk and lemon zest and juice, beating until just blended. • Mix in the dry ingredients and almonds to form a stiff dough. • Press the dough into a disk, wrap in plastic wrap (plastic wrap), and refrigerate for 30 minutes. • Preheat the oven to 350°F (180°C/gas 4). • Set out two cookie sheets. • Roll out the dough on a lightly floured surface to ¼-inch (5-mm) thick. • Use a 2-inch (5-cm) cookie cutter to cut out the cookies. Gather the dough scraps, re-roll, and continue cutting out cookies until all the dough is used. • Transfer the cookies to the cookie sheets, placing them 1 inch (2.5 cm) apart. • Bake until lightly browned and firm to the touch, 15–20 minutes. • Transfer to racks to cool. • Stick the cookies together in pairs with the preserves.

⅔ cup (100 g) all-purpose (plain) flour

2 teaspoons unsweetened cocoa powder

½ teaspoon ground allspice

½ teaspoon ground cinnamon

½ teaspoon ground ginger

⅛ teaspoon salt

¾ cup (180 g) butter, softened

½ cup (100 g) granulated sugar

1 large egg yolk

1 tablespoon finely grated lemon zest

2 tablespoons freshly squeezed lemon juice

2 cups (300 g) finely ground almonds

½ cup (125 g) raspberry preserves (jam)

Makes: 14–16 cookies
Preparation: 25 minutes + 30 minutes to chill
Cooking: 15–20 minutes
Level: 1

PINK DRIZZLERS

Mix the flour, cornstarch, cocoa, cinnamon, allspice, baking soda, ginger, nutmeg, and salt in a medium bowl. • Beat the butter, sugar, and corn syrup in a large bowl with an electric mixer at high speed until creamy. • Add the eggs one at a time beating until just blended after each addition. • Mix in the dry ingredients to form a smooth dough. Press the dough into a disk, wrap in plastic wrap, and refrigerate for 30 minutes. • Preheat the oven to 350°F (180°C/gas 4). • Butter two cookie sheets. • Roll out the dough on a lightly floured surface to 1/2-inch (1-cm) thick. • Use a 2-inch (5-cm) cutter to cut into rounds. • Transfer the cookies to the prepared cookie sheets, placing them 1 inch (2.5 cm) apart. • Bake until firm, 8–10 minutes. • Cool completely on the cookie sheets. • Stick the cookies together in pairs with the preserves. • Mix the confectioners' sugar, water, and food coloring to make a soft frosting. Spread the cookies with the frosting.

1   cup (150 g) all-purpose (plain) flour

3/4   cup (125 g) cornstarch (cornflour)

2   teaspoons unsweetened cocoa powder

1   teaspoon ground cinnamon

1/2   teaspoon allspice

1/2   teaspoon baking soda (bicarbonate of soda)

1/4   teaspoon ground ginger

1/4   teaspoon freshly grated nutmeg

1/4   teaspoon salt

1/2   cup (125 g) butter

3/4   cup (150 g) granulated sugar

1   tablespoon light corn (golden) syrup

2   large eggs

1/2   cup (125 g) raspberry preserves (jam)

2/3   (100 g) confectioners' (icing) sugar

3   teaspoons warm water

Few drops red food coloring

Makes: about 10 cookies
Preparation: 40 minutes
    + 30 minutes to chill
Cooking: 8–10 minutes
Level: 1

FRUITFUL STARS

Mix the flour and salt in a large bowl. • Stir in the granulated and vanilla sugars. • Cut in the butter until the mixture resembles coarse crumbs. • Mix in the egg and egg yolks and vanilla. • Divide the dough in half. • Wrap in plastic wrap (cling film) and refrigerate for 30 minutes. • Preheat the oven to 350°F (180°C/gas 4). • Roll out the dough to ⅛-inch (3-mm) thick. • Use two different sized (1-inch and 2-inch/2.5 and 5-cm) star-shaped cookie cutters to cut out the cookies. Cut out the same number of cookies in each size. • Transfer the cookies to cookie sheets, placing them 1 inch (2.5 cm) apart. • Refrigerate for 10 minutes. • Bake until just golden, 8–12 minutes. • Transfer to racks and let cool completely. • Stick the differently sized cookies together with the preserves—the largest at the bottom, the smallest on top. • Dust with the confectioners' sugar.

3 cups (450 g) all-purpose (plain) flour
⅛ teaspoon salt
1 cup (200 g) granulated sugar
¼ cup (50 g) vanilla sugar (see page 696)
½ cup (125 g) butter, cut up
1 large egg + 3 large egg yolks
1 teaspoon vanilla extract (essence)
3 tablespoons plum or raspberry preserves (jam)
½ cup (75 g) confectioners' (icing) sugar

Makes: about 35 cookies
Preparation: 50 minutes + 30 minutes to chill
Cooking: 8–10 minutes
Level: 2

GYPSY CREAMS

Preheat the oven to 375°F (190°C/gas 5).
• Line two baking sheets with parchment paper. • Beat the margarine, butter, and sugar in an electric mixer at medium speed until pale and creamy. • Melt the syrup in the water and stir into the butter mixture. • With mixer on low speed, gradually beat in the the flour, baking soda, rolled oats, and vanilla. • With lightly-floured hands, roll into small balls about the size of marbles. Place on the prepared baking sheets, spacing well. Press down slightly in the centers to flatten slightly.
• Bake until pale golden brown, 15–20 minutes. • Cool completely on wire racks.
• Sandwich together with the buttercream.

¼ **cup (60 g) margarine**
¼ **cup (60 g) butter**
½ **cup (100 g) granulated sugar**
1 **teaspoon corn (golden) syrup**
3 **teaspoons boiling water**
¼ **teaspoon baking soda (bicarbonate of soda)**
1 **cup (150 g) self-raising flour**
1 **cup (100 g) rolled oats**
½ **teaspoon vanilla extract (essence)**
1 **recipe Italian buttercream (see page 698), made with a few drops of red food coloring**

Makes: about 24 cookies
Preparation: 15 minutes
Cooking: 15–20 minutes
Level: 1

CHOCOLATE CHIP WEDGES

Preheat the oven to 375°F (190°C/gas 5).
• Set out a 14-inch (35-cm) pizza pan. • Sift the flour, baking soda, and salt into a medium bowl. • Beat the butter and both sugars in a large bowl with an electric mixer at high speed until creamy. • Add the vanilla and eggs, beating until just blended. • Mix in the dry ingredients. • Roll the dough out on a floured surface to about twice the diameter of the pan. Place in the prepared pan and sprinkle with the chocolate chips. Fold the overhanging dough over the top. • Bake until lightly browned, 20–25 minutes. • Cool completely in the pan. • Cut into wedges.

2¼ cups (330 g) all-purpose (plain) flour

1 teaspoon baking soda (bicarbonate of soda)

½ teaspoon salt

1 cup (250 g) butter, softened

¾ cup (150 g) granulated sugar

¾ cup (150 g) firmly packed light brown sugar

½ extract (essence)

2 large eggs

1 cup (180 g) semisweet (dark) chocolate chips

Makes: 16–20 wedges
Preparation: 20 minutes
Cooking: 20–25 minutes
Level: 1

COCONUT KISSES WITH CHOCOLATE CREAM

Cookies: Preheat the oven to 300°F (150°C/gas 2). • Set out two cookie sheets. • Sift the flour, baking powder, and salt into a medium bowl. • Beat the butter, sugar, and vanilla in a large bowl with an electric mixer at medium speed until creamy. • Add the egg, beating until just blended. • Mix in the dry ingredients. • Place the coconut in a small bowl. • Roll teaspoons of the dough in the coconut and place 1 inch (2.5 cm) apart on the cookie sheets. • Bake until golden, 18–20 minutes. • Transfer to racks to cool. • Chocolate Filling: Beat the confectioners' sugar and melted butter in a small bowl. • Mix in the cocoa powder. • Stick the cookies together in pairs with the chocolate filling.

Cookies

1⅓ cups (200 g) all-purpose (plain) flour

1 teaspoon baking powder

⅛ teaspoon salt

¾ cup (180 g) butter, softened

⅓ cup (70 g) granulated sugar

½ teaspoon vanilla extract (essence)

1 large egg

3 tablespoons shredded (desiccated) coconut

Chocolate Filling

1 cup (150 g) confectioners' (icing) sugar

½ cup (60 g) butter, melted

1 tablespoon unsweetened cocoa powder

Makes: 15–20 cookies
Preparation: 25 minutes
Cooking: 18–20 minutes
Level: 1

HAZELNUT KISSES

Preheat the oven to 375°F (190°C/gas 5).
• Line two cookie sheets with parchment paper. • Beat the egg whites and salt in a large bowl with an electric mixer at medium speed until frothy. • Gradually add the superfine sugar, beating until stiff glossy peaks form. • Use a large rubber spatula to fold in the confectioners' sugar and hazelnuts. • Fit a pastry bag with a 1-inch (2.5-cm) star tip. Fill the pastry bag, twist the opening tightly closed, and squeeze out 1-inch (2.5-cm) stars spacing 1 inch (2.5 cm) apart on the prepared cookie sheets.
• Bake until pale gold, 8–10 minutes.
• Transfer to racks to cool. • Stick the cookies together in pairs with the chocolate hazelnut cream.

2 large egg whites
⅛ teaspoon salt
2 tablespoons superfine (caster) sugar
⅓ cup (50 g) confectioners' (icing) sugar
1¼ cups (125 g) finely chopped hazelnuts
⅓ cup (90 g) chocolate hazelnut cream (Nutella)

Makes: about 20 cookies
Preparation: 30 minutes
Cooking: 8–10 minutes
Level: 2

BARS AND BROWNIES

CHOCOLATE RASPBERRY BARS

Preheat the oven to 325°F (170°C/gas 3).
• Line a 13 x 9-inch (33 x 23-cm) baking pan with aluminum foil, letting the edges overhang. • Base: Mix the flour, cocoa, and salt in a medium bowl. • Beat the butter, sugar, and vanilla in a large bowl with an electric mixer at high speed until creamy.
• Mix in the dry ingredients. • Press the mixture into the prepared pan to form a smooth, even layer. Prick all over with a fork.
• Bake until firm to the touch, 15–20 minutes.
• Increase the oven temperature to 375°F (190°C/gas 5). • Filling: Mix the preserves and liqueur in a small bowl and spread it evenly over the base. Sprinkle with the chocolate chips. • Process the finely ground almonds, egg whites, sugar, and almond extract in a food processor or blender until well blended.
• Pour the mixture over the preserves and sprinkle with the flaked almonds. • Bake until lightly browned, 20–25 minutes. • Using the foil as handles, lift onto a rack and let cool completely. • Remove the foil and cut into bars.

Base

1   cup (150 g) all-purpose (plain) flour

2 tablespoons unsweetened cocoa powder

¼   teaspoon salt

½   cup (125 g) butter, softened

½   cup (100 g) granulated sugar

½   teaspoon vanilla extract (essence)

Filling

½   cup (120 g) raspberry preserves (jam)

1   tablespoon raspberry liqueur

1   cup (180 g) semisweet (dark) chocolate chips

1   cups (150 g) finely ground almonds

4   large egg whites

1   cup (200 g) granulated sugar

½   teaspoon almond extract (essence)

2   tablespoons flaked almonds

Makes: about 30 bars
Preparation: 25 minutes
Cooking: 35–45 minutes
Level: 1

CHOCOLATE ALMOND SQUARES

Preheat the oven to 350°F (180°C/gas 4).
• Butter a 13 x 9-inch (33 x 23-cm) baking pan. • Beat 3 of the egg whites in a large bowl with an electric mixer at high speed until soft peaks form. • Gradually add 1 cup (200 g) of the sugar, beating until stiff glossy peaks form. • Use a large rubber spatula to fold in the almonds, chocolate, and vanilla. • Spread the mixture evenly in the prepared pan. • Beat the remaining egg white and remaining sugar until frothy. Brush over the top. • Bake until lightly browned, 20–25 minutes. • Cool completely in the pan. If liked, spread with the frosting. • Cut into squares.

4 large egg whites

1¼ cups (250 g) granulated sugar

2 cups (300 g) finely ground almonds

2 oz (60 g) milk chocolate, finely grated

1 teaspoon vanilla extract (essence)

1 recipe chocolate frosting (see page 697), made with milk chocolate (optional)

Makes: about 30 squares
Preparation: 30 minutes
Cooking: 20–25 minutes
Level: 1

PECAN BROWNIES

500

Preheat the oven to 350°F (180°C/gas 4).
• Line a deep 13 x 9-inch (33 x 23-cm) baking pan with aluminum foil, letting the edges overhang. • Mix the flour, baking powder, and salt in a medium bowl. • Melt the butter and chocolate in a double boiler over barely simmering water. • Remove from the heat and stir in the sugar. • Add the eggs one at a time, beating until just blended after each addition. • Mix in the dry ingredients, vanilla, and pecans. • Spoon the batter into the prepared pan. • Bake until dry on top and almost firm to the touch, 25–30 minutes. Do not overbake. • Cool completely in the pan. • Using the foil as handles, lift onto a cutting board. Peel off the foil. Cut into squares.

3 cups (450 g) all-purpose (plain) flour

2 teaspoons baking powder

¼ teaspoon salt

½ cup (125 g) butter, cut up

4 oz (125 g) semisweet (dark) chocolate, coarsely chopped

2 cups (400 g) granulated sugar

4 large eggs

1 teaspoon vanilla extract (essence)

¾ cup (125 g) coarsely chopped pecans

Makes: about 30 brownies
Preparation: 20 minutes
Cooking: 25–30 minutes
Level: 1

CHOCOLATE ORANGE BARS

Preheat the oven to 350°F (180°C/gas 4).
• Butter an 11 x 7-inch (28 x 18-cm) baking pan. • Mix the flour, cocoa, baking powder, and salt in a medium bowl. • Beat the butter and brown sugar in a large bowl with an electric mixer at high speed until creamy.
• Add the eggs and orange zest, beating until just blended. • Mix in the dry ingredients, orange juice, and dates. • Spoon the mixture into the prepared pan. • Bake until a toothpick inserted into the center comes out clean, 30–35 minutes. • Cool completely in the pan. • Cut into bars.

1½ cups (225 g) all-purpose (plain) flour
3 tablespoons unsweetened cocoa powder
2 teaspoons baking powder
¼ teaspoon salt
½ cup (125 g) butter, softened
¾ cup (150 g) firmly packed light brown sugar
3 large eggs
1 tablespoon finely grated orange zest
¾ cup (180 ml) freshly squeezed orange juice
1 cup (100 g) finely chopped pitted dates

Makes: about 30 bars
Preparation: 20 minutes
Cooking: 30–35 minutes
Level: 1

CRUNCHY COCONUT SQUARES

Base: Preheat the oven to 325°F (170°C/gas 3). • Line two cookie sheets with parchment paper. • Mix the flour, baking powder, and salt in a large bowl. • Stir in the sugar. • Use a pastry blender to cut in the butter until the mixture resembles fine crumbs. • Stir in the egg yolk mixture and knead into a stiff dough, adding more water if needed. • Wrap in plastic wrap (cling film) and refrigerate for 30 minutes. • Topping: Beat the egg white with an electric mixer at medium speed until frothy. With mixer at high speed, gradually add the confectioners' sugar, beating until stiff. • Roll out the dough on a lightly floured surface to ¼-inch (5-mm) thick. Cut into 3 x 8-inch (8 x 20-cm) strips. • Spread with the topping and sprinkle with coconut. Sprinkle with sprinkles or nuts, if using. • Cut the strips in half lengthwise and into 1½-inch (4-cm) squares. • Use a spatula to transfer the cookies to the prepared cookie sheets, placing them 1 inch (2.5 cm) apart. • Bake until lightly golden, 15–20 minutes. • Transfer to racks to cool.

Base

1⅓ cups (200 g) all-purpose (plain) flour

1 teaspoon baking powder

¼ teaspoon salt

5 tablespoons granulated sugar

½ cup (125 g) butter, cut up

1 large egg yolk, lightly beaten with 2 tablespoons cold water

Topping

1 large egg white

½ cup (75 g) confectioners' (icing) sugar, sifted

3 tablespoons shredded (desiccated) coconut

Colored sprinkles, chopped Brazil nuts, or hazelnuts (optional)

Makes: about squares
Preparation: 40 minutes + 30 minutes to chill
Cooking 15–20 minutes
Level: 1

BUTTER CURRANT SQUARES

Mix the flour, confectioners' sugar, and salt in a large bowl. • Use a pastry blender to cut in the butter until the mixture resembles fine crumbs. • Add the whole egg to form a stiff dough. • Divide the dough in half. Press each half into a disk, wrap in plastic wrap (cling film), and refrigerate for 30 minutes. • Preheat the oven to 400°F (200°C/gas 6). • Butter two cookie sheets. • Roll out one disk on a lightly floured surface into a 14 x 12-inch (35 x 30-cm) rectangle. Sprinkle with the currants. • Roll out the remaining dough to the same dimensions and place on top of the currants, pressing down lightly. • Cut into squares. • Use a spatula to transfer the cookies to the prepared cookie sheets, placing them 1 inch (2.5 cm) apart. Brush with the remaining beaten egg yolk. • Bake until golden brown 10–12 minutes. • Transfer to racks to cool.

2⅓ cups (350 g) all-purpose (plain) flour

⅔ cup (100 g) confectioners' (icing) sugar

⅛ teaspoon salt

¾ cup (180 g) butter, cut up

1 large egg + 1 large egg yolk, lightly beaten

⅓ cup (45 g) dried currants

Makes: about 30 squares
Preparation: 15 minutes + 30 minutes to chill
Cooking: 10–12 minutes
Level: 1

PRUNE SQUARES

Preheat the oven to 350°F (180°C/gas 4).
• Butter a 9-inch (23-cm) square baking pan.
• <u>Base</u>: Mix the flour, baking powder, and salt in a large bowl. • Beat the butter and brown sugar in a large bowl with an electric mixer at high speed until creamy. • Add the vanilla and egg, beating until just blended. • Mix in the dry ingredients. • <u>Filling</u>: Bring the prunes and water to a boil in a large saucepan. • Reduce the heat and simmer for 3 minutes. • Drain well and transfer the prunes to a food processor or blender. Add the honey and lemon zest and juice and process until smooth. • Firmly press half of the cookie base into the prepared pan to form a smooth, even layer. Spread with the prune filling. Sprinkle with the remaining cookie base. • Bake until lightly browned, about 50 minutes. • Cool completely before cutting into squares.

Base

1²/₃ cups (250 g) all-purpose (plain) flour

1 teaspoon baking powder

½ teaspoon salt

³/₄ cup (180 g) butter, softened

1½ cups (300 g) firmly packed light brown sugar

1 teaspoon vanilla extract (essence)

1 large egg, lightly beaten

Filling

1¼ cups (310 g) pitted prunes

2 cups (500 ml) water

¼ cup (60 g) honey

Finely grated zest and juice of ¼ lemon

Makes: about 20 squares
Preparation: 30 minutes
Cooking: 50 minutes
Level: 1

CURRANT SQUARES

Mix the flour, baking powder, and salt in a medium bowl. Stir in the sugar. • Use a pastry blender to cut in the shortening until the mixture resembles fine crumbs. • Stir in the currants. • Mix in enough water to form a stiff dough. • Press the dough into a disk, wrap in plastic wrap (cling film), and refrigerate for 30 minutes. • Preheat the oven to 400°F (200°C/gas 6). • Butter a cookie sheet. • Roll out the dough on a lightly floured surface to 1/4-inch (5-mm) thick. • Use a sharp knife to cut the dough into 2-inch (5-cm) squares. • Use a spatula to transfer the cookies to the prepared cookie sheet, placing them 1 inch (2.5 cm) apart. • Bake until golden, about 10 minutes. • Transfer to racks to cool.

3/4 cup (125 g) all-purpose (plain) flour

1/2 teaspoon baking powder

1/8 teaspoon salt

4 tablespoons granulated sugar

1/3 cup (90 g) vegetable shortening or lard

1/2 cup (90 g) dried currants

2 tablespoons ice water + more, as needed

Makes: about 12 squares
Preparation: 40 minutes + 30 minutes to chill
Cooking: 8–10 minutes
Level: 1

GOLDEN WALNUT SQUARES

Preheat the oven to 350°F (180°C/gas 4).
• Butter an 8-inch (20-cm) baking pan.
Base: Mix the flour and brown sugar in a large bowl. • Use a pastry blender to cut in the butter until the mixture resembles coarse crumbs. • Firmly press the mixture into the prepared pan to form a smooth, even layer.
• Bake until lightly browned, 10–15 minutes.
• Cool the base completely in the pan.
Topping: Mix the orange and lemon juices with enough water to make $2/3$ cup (150 ml) of liquid. • Simmer the apricots in this liquid in a medium saucepan until softened, about 15 minutes. • Drain the apricots, reserving the liquid in a small bowl. • Finely chop the apricots and return to the saucepan. Add both zests, the brown sugar, cornstarch, and $1/4$ cup (60 ml) of the apricot liquid. • Bring to a boil and simmer for 1 minute, stirring constantly. Let cool, then spread over the base. Sprinkle with walnuts. • Bake until golden brown, 15–20 minutes. • Cool completely before cutting into bars.

Base

1 cup (150 g) all-purpose (plain) flour

$3/4$ cup (150 g) firmly packed light brown sugar

5 tablespoons cold butter, cut up

Topping

Zest and juice of 1 orange

Zest and juice of $1/2$ lemon

Water

$3/4$ cup (75 g) dried apricots

$1/3$ cup (70 g) firmly packed light brown sugar

2 teaspoons cornstarch (cornflour)

$1/2$ cup (75 g) finely chopped walnuts

Makes: about 20 bars
Preparation: 30 minutes
Cooking: 25–35 minutes
Level: 2

GINGER CHERRY SQUARES

514

Preheat the oven to 300°F (150°C/gas 2).
• Butter an 11 x 7-inch (28 x 18-cm) baking
pan. • Mix the flour, baking powder, and salt
in a medium bowl. • Stir in the dried fruit and
ginger. • Beat the butter and sugar in a large
bowl with an electric mixer at high speed until
creamy. • Add the egg. • Mix in the dry
ingredients. • Spoon the mixture into
the prepared pan. • Bake until golden brown,
40–45 minutes. • Cool completely before
cutting into bars.

1 cup (150 g) all-purpose
   (plain) flour
1 teaspoon baking
   powder
1/8 teaspoon salt
1 cup (100 g) finely
   chopped mixed dried
   fruit
1/2 cup (50 g) finely
   chopped crystallized
   ginger
1/2 cup (125 g) butter,
   softened
3/4 cup (150 g) granulated
   sugar
1 large egg

Makes: about 20 bars
Preparation: 10 minutes
Cooking: 40–45 minutes
Level: 1

GLAZED DIAMONDS

Preheat the oven to 350°F (180°C/gas 4).
• Butter a 13 x 9-inch (33 x 23-cm) baking pan. • Mix the flour, cinnamon, baking powder, baking soda, and salt in a large bowl. • Stir in the brown sugar. • Add the eggs, beating until just blended. • Beat in the butter and sour cream. • Stir in the dates and walnuts.
• Spoon the mixture into the prepared pan.
• Bake until golden brown and a toothpick inserted into the center comes out clean, 20–25 minutes. • Cool completely in the pan.
Lemon Glaze: Mix the confectioners' sugar, butter, and lemon juice in a small bowl.
• Add enough water to create a smooth glaze.
• Spread the glaze over the cooled cake.
• Cut lengthwise into long strips. Cut the strips into diamonds by running the knife diagonally from one side of the pan to the other.

$1^2/_3$ cups (250 g) all-purpose (plain) flour

1 teaspoon ground cinnamon

1 teaspoon baking powder

$^1/_2$ teaspoon baking soda (bicarbonate of soda)

$^1/_2$ teaspoon salt

1 cup (200 g) firmly packed brown sugar

2 large eggs

1 cup (250 g) butter, melted

$^1/_2$ cup (125 ml) sour cream

$1^1/_3$ cups (140 g) finely chopped dates

$^3/_4$ cup (75 g) finely chopped walnuts

Lemon Glaze

$1^1/_2$ cups (225 g) confectioners' (icing) sugar

3 tablespoons butter, melted

1 tablespoon freshly squeezed lemon juice

1 tablespoon water

Makes: about 30 bars
Preparation: 25 minutes
Cooking: 20–25 minutes
Level: 1

DRIED FRUIT SQUARES

Preheat the oven to 375°F (190°C/gas 5).
• Line an 8-inch (20-cm) baking pan with
aluminum foil, letting the edges overhang.
• Mix the flour, baking powder, and salt in
a medium bowl. • Mix the pears, apricots,
honey, and applesauce in a large bowl.
• Beat in the oil and eggs until well blended.
• Mix in the dry ingredients. • Spoon the
mixture into the prepared pan. • Sprinkle with
the almonds. • Bake until just golden and a
toothpick inserted into the center comes
out clean, 25–30 minutes. • Using the foil
as handles, lift onto a rack to cool.
• Cut into squares.

1½ cups (225 g) whole-wheat (wholemeal) flour

1½ teaspoons baking powder

¼ teaspoon salt

3 large firm-ripe pears, peeled, cored, and finely chopped

1½ cups (150 g) finely chopped dried apricots

2 tablespoons honey

1 tablespoon applesauce

2 tablespoons vegetable oil

2 large eggs, lightly beaten

½ cup (50 g) flaked almonds, to decorate

Makes: about 16 squares
Preparation: 20 minutes
Cooking: 25–30 minutes
Level: 1

MIDDLE EASTERN SQUARES

Preheat the oven to 350°F (180°C/gas 4).
• Line a 13 x 9-inch (33 x 23-cm) baking pan with aluminum foil, letting the edges overhang. • Date Filling: Cook the dates with the brown sugar and water in a saucepan over medium heat until the sugar has dissolved completely. • Remove from the heat and add the vanilla and cinnamon. • Transfer to a food processor or blender and chop until smooth.
• Let cool completely. Oat Crust: Mix the flour, brown sugar, cinnamon, baking soda, and salt in a large bowl. • Use a pastry blender to cut in the butter until the mixture resembles coarse crumbs. Stir in the oats and walnuts.
• Firmly press half the mixture into the prepared pan to form a smooth, even layer.
• Pour the filling over the oat crust and sprinkle with the remaining oat crust mixture.
• Bake until lightly browned, 30–35 minutes.
• Using the foil as handles, lift onto a rack and let cool completely. • Cut into squares.

Date Filling

1 lb (500 g) pitted dates
1 cup (200 g) firmly packed dark brown sugar
1 cup (250 ml) water
½ teaspoon vanilla extract (essence)
½ teaspoon ground cinnamon

Oat Crust

1½ cups (225 g) all-purpose (plain) flour
1 cup (200 g) firmly packed dark brown sugar
1 teaspoon ground cinnamon
½ teaspoon baking soda (bicarbonate of soda)
⅛ teaspoon salt
1 cup (250 g) butter, cut up
⅔ cup (150 g) old-fashioned rolled oats
½ cup (50 g) finely chopped walnuts

Makes: about 30 squares
Preparation: 30 minutes
Cooking: 30–35 minutes
Level: 1

CHOCOLATE RICE SQUARES

Set out a 10½ x 15½-inch (26 x 36-cm) jelly-roll pan. • Melt the butter and sugar in a large saucepan over medium heat. • Remove from the heat and stir in the dates, cherries, raisins, and rice krispies until well mixed. • Spoon the mixture evenly into the pan, pressing down firmly. • Refrigerate until set, about 2 hours. • Melt the chocolate in a double boiler over barely simmering water. Pour the chocolate over the and let stand until set, about 30 minutes. • Use a sharp knife to cut into squares.

½ cup (125 g) butter, cut up

½ cup (100 g) granulated sugar

1¾ cups (175 g) finely chopped pitted dates

⅔ cup (70 g) finely chopped candied cherries

⅓ cup (60 g) golden raisins (sultanas)

2 cups (200 g) rice krispies

8 oz (250 g) semisweet (dark) chocolate, coarsely chopped

Makes: about 20 squares
Preparation: 15 minutes
+ 2 hours 30 minutes to chill and set
Level: 1

COCONUT SQUARES

Preheat the oven to 350°F (180°C/gas 4).
• Butter an 11 x 7-inch (28 x 18-cm) baking pan. • Mix the flour, baking powder, and salt in a large bowl. • Stir in the coconut, walnuts, almonds, oats, and sugar. • Use a pastry blender to cut in the butter until the mixture resembles fine crumbs. • Dissolve the corn syrup in the milk in a small saucepan over low heat. Add the egg, beating until just blended. • Pour the egg mixture into the dry ingredients and mix well. • Spread the mixture evenly in the baking pan. • Bake until golden brown, 40–45 minutes. • Cool completely before cutting into bars.

$^3/_4$ cup (125 g) all-purpose (plain) flour

$^1/_2$ teaspoon baking powder

$^1/_2$ teaspoon salt

$^1/_2$ cup (60 g) shredded (desiccated) coconut

$^1/_2$ cup (50 g) finely chopped walnuts

2 tablespoons finely ground almonds

$^1/_3$ cup (50 g) old-fashioned rolled oats

$^3/_4$ cup (150 g) granulated sugar

$^1/_2$ cup (125 g) butter, cut up

1 tablespoon light corn syrup (golden) syrup

1 tablespoon milk

1 large egg

Makes: about 20 squares
Preparation: 15 minutes
Cooking: 40–45 minutes
Level: 1

WHOLE-WHEAT ORANGE BARS

Preheat the oven to 350°F (180°C/gas 4).
• Butter an 8-inch (20-cm) square baking pan.
• Heat the milk in a small saucepan over low heat. • Pour the milk into a large bowl, add the dates, and let soak for 15 minutes. • Mix the flour, baking powder, cinnamon, and salt in a medium bowl. • Beat the egg, butter, sugar, and orange zest into the date mixture.
• Mix in the dry ingredients, followed by the orange flesh until well blended. • Spoon the batter into the prepared pan. • Bake until a toothpick inserted into the center comes out clean, 35–40 minutes. • Cool completely before cutting into bars.

$2/3$ **cup (150 ml) milk**

$1/2$ **cup (100 g) finely chopped dates**

$3/4$ **cup (125 g) whole-wheat (wholemeal) flour**

$1/2$ **teaspoon baking powder**

$1/2$ **teaspoon ground cinnamon**

$1/8$ **teaspoon salt**

1 **large egg, lightly beaten**

$1/4$ **cup (60 g) butter, melted**

5 **tablespoons raw sugar**

Finely grated zest and chopped flesh of 1 orange

Makes: 16–20 bars
Preparation: 20 minutes + 15 minutes to soak the dates
Cooking: 35–40 minutes
Level: 1

HAZELNUT BARS
WITH COFFEE GLAZE

Base: Mix the flour, hazelnuts, and salt in a large bowl. • Beat the butter and confectioners' sugar in a large bowl with an electric mixer at high speed until creamy. • Mix in the dry ingredients, followed by the hazelnuts.
• Press the dough into a disk, wrap in plastic wrap (cling film), and refrigerate for 30 minutes. • Preheat the oven to 375°F (190°C/gas 5). • Butter two cookie sheets.
• Roll out the dough on a lightly floured surface to ¼-inch (5-mm) thick. • Coffee Glaze: Beat the egg white and coffee in a small bowl. Brush all over the dough. • Cut into 3 x 1½-inch (8 x 4-cm) bars and use a spatula to transfer to the prepared cookie sheets, placing them 1 inch (2.5 cm) apart.
• Bake until firm to the touch, 12–15 minutes.
• Transfer to racks and let cool completely.

Base

1²/₃ cups (250 g) all-purpose (plain) flour

1¼ cups (125 g) finely chopped hazelnuts

⅛ teaspoon salt

¾ cup (200 g) butter, softened

1 cup (150 g) confectioners' (icing) sugar

Coffee Glaze

1 large egg white, lightly beaten

1 tablespoon instant coffee granules dissolved in 2 teaspoons hot water

Makes: about 30 bars
Preparation: 40 minutes + 30 minutes to chill
Cooking: 12–15 minutes
Level: 1

MOCHA BROWNIES

Preheat the oven to 350°F (180°C/gas 4).
• Butter a 9-inch (23-cm) square baking pan.
• Mix the flour, baking powder, and salt in a
large bowl. • Melt the butter with the brown
sugar in a medium saucepan over low heat,
stirring constantly. • Stir in the coffee mixture.
• Remove from the heat and let cool for 5
minutes. • Add the vanilla and eggs, beating
until just blended. • Stir in the dry
ingredients, chocolate, and walnuts. • Spoon
the mixture into the prepared pan. • Bake
until dry on the top and almost firm to the
touch, 20–25 minutes. Do not overbake.
• Cool completely before cutting into bars.

1 cup (150 g) all-purpose (plain) flour

1 teaspoon baking powder

1/8 teaspoon salt

1/2 cup (125 g) butter, cut up

1 1/3 cups (270 g) firmly packed light or dark brown sugar

1 tablespoon instant coffee granules dissolved in 1 tablespoon hot water

1 teaspoon vanilla extract (essence)

2 large eggs, lightly beaten

5 oz (150 g) semisweet (dark) chocolate, coarsely chopped

2 tablespoons coarsely chopped walnuts

Makes: about 20 brownies
Preparation: 15 minutes
Cooking: 20–25 minutes
Level: 1

NUTTY COFFEE SQUARES

Preheat the oven to 350°F (180°C/gas 4).
• Butter an 8-inch (20-cm) square baking pan.
• Place the almonds in a large bowl and pour in enough hot water to cover them completely. Let stand for 5 minutes. • Use a slotted spoon to scoop the nuts out of the water and place on a clean cloth. • Gently rub the nuts to remove the skins. Pick out the skins and discard them. • Finely chop the almonds.
• Bring 2 tablespoons of water, the granulated sugar, and the coffee granules to a boil in a small saucepan until the sugar and coffee have dissolved completely. • Stir in the almonds. • Remove from the heat and set aside. • Beat the egg whites and salt in a large bowl with an electric mixer at high speed until stiff peaks form. • Use a large rubber spatula to fold into the almond mixture. • Spoon the batter into the prepared pan. • Bake until a toothpick inserted into the center comes out clean, 35–40 minutes.
• Cool completely before cutting into squares.
• Dust with the confectioners' sugar.

1⅓ cups (200 g) whole almonds
Boiling water
¾ cup (150 g) granulated sugar
2 teaspoons instant coffee granules
2 large egg whites
⅛ teaspoon salt
Confectioners' (icing) sugar, to dust

Makes: about 16 squares
Preparation: 40 minutes
Cooking: 35–40 minutes
Level: 2

GINGER BARS

Preheat the oven to 325°F (170°C/gas 3).
• Butter a 13 x 9-inch (33 x 23-cm) baking
pan. • Mix the flour, ginger, cream of tartar,
baking soda, and salt in a large bowl. • Use
a pastry blender to cut in the butter until the
mixture resembles coarse crumbs. • Stir in
the oats and brown sugar. • Firmly press the
mixture into the prepared pan to form a
smooth, even layer. • Bake until lightly
browned, 20–30 minutes. • Cool completely
before cutting into bars.

2 cups (300 g) whole-wheat (wholemeal) flour

1 tablespoon ground ginger

1½ teaspoon cream of tartar

¾ teaspoon baking soda (bicarbonate of soda)

⅛ teaspoon salt

1¼ cups (310 g) butter, cut up

⅓ cup (50 g) old-fashioned rolled oats

1½ cups (300 g) firmly packed light brown sugar

Makes: about 30 bars
Preparation: 20 minutes
Cooking: 20–30 minutes
Level: 1

CINNAMON HEARTIES

Base: Preheat the oven to 375°F (190°C/gas 5). • Butter three cookie sheets. • Mix the flour and salt in a medium bowl. • Beat the butter and sugar in a large bowl with an electric mixer at high speed until creamy. • Mix in the dry ingredients and almond extract. The mixture should be slightly crumbly. • Press into a disk, wrap in plastic wrap (cling film), and refrigerate for 1 hour, or until the mixture can be formed into a firm, smooth dough. • Roll out the dough on a lightly floured surface to a 12 x 8-inch (30 x 20-cm) rectangle. • Topping: Mix the superfine sugar, cinnamon, and almonds in a small bowl. • Brush the cookies with the beaten egg white and sprinkle with the topping. • Cut into 3 x 1-inch (8 x 2.5-cm) bars. • Use a spatula to transfer the bars to the prepared cookie sheets, placing them ½ inch (1 cm) apart. Bake until just golden, 12–15 minutes. • Cool on the sheet until slightly firmed. Transfer to racks to cool.

Base
- 1²/₃ cups (250 g) all-purpose (plain) flour
- ⅛ teaspoon salt
- ¾ cup (180 g) butter, softened
- ⅓ cup (70 g) granulated sugar
- 1 teaspoon almond extract (essence)

Topping
- ⅓ cup (70 g) superfine (caster) sugar
- ½ teaspoon ground cinnamon
- ⅔ cup (100 g) coarsely chopped blanched almonds, toasted
- 1 large egg white, lightly beaten

Makes: about 30 bars
Preparation: 15 minutes + 1 hour to chill
Cooking: 12–15 minutes
Level: 1

GLAZED ALMOND BARS

Base: Preheat the oven to 350°F (180°C/gas 4). • Butter and flour two cookie sheets. • Mix the flour, baking soda, and salt in a large bowl. • Heat the honey in a medium saucepan over low heat until liquid. Stir in the sugar, cinnamon, cloves, both almonds, and the candied lemon and orange peel. • Remove from the heat. • Mix in the dry ingredients and kirsch. • Shape the warm mixture into a ball and knead on a lightly floured surface until smooth. If it is sticky, add more flour. • Roll out the dough to ¼-inch (5-mm) thick. Use a sharp knife to cut into bars. • Place the bars on the prepared baking sheets. • Bake until lightly browned, 15–20 minutes. • Transfer the cookies to racks and let cool to warm. Glaze: Mix the confectioners' sugar with the water in a small bowl. Add lemon juice and rum to make a pouring consistency. Add more water if needed. • Brush the glaze on the hot cookies and let cool completely.

Base

4 cups (600 g) all-purpose (plain) flour
1 teaspoon baking soda
¼ teaspoon salt
1 cup (250 ml) honey
1½ cups (300 g) granulated sugar
1 tablespoon cinnamon
1 teaspoon ground cloves
1½ cups (150 g) finely chopped blanched almonds
1½ cups (150 g) finely chopped unblanched almonds
⅔ cup (70 g) chopped candied lemon peel
⅔ cup (70 g) chopped candied orange peel
⅓ cup (90 ml) kirsch

Glaze

1⅓ cups (200 g) confectioners' (icing) sugar
1 tablespoon hot water + more, as needed
1 tablespoon freshly squeezed lemon juice
1 tablespoon dark rum

Makes: about 50 bars
Preparation: 30 minutes
Cooking: 15–20 minutes
Level: 2

MERINGUE SQUARES

Preheat the oven to 350°F (190°C/gas 5).
• Butter a 10-inch (25-cm) square baking pan.
• Mix the flour, confectioners' sugar, and salt
in a large bowl. • With an electric mixer at
medium speed, beat in the butter and whole
egg until well blended. • Firmly press the
mixture into the prepared pan to form a
smooth, even layer. • Bake for 10 minutes.
• Reduce the oven temperature to 300°F
(150°C/gas 2). • Warm the preserves in a
small saucepan over low heat until liquid.
• Spread the preserves over the base. • With
mixer at medium speed, beat the egg whites
in a large bowl until soft peaks form. • With
mixer at high speed, gradually add the
superfine sugar and cinnamon, beating until
stiff glossy peaks form. • Spread the meringue
on top of preserves. • Bake until the meringue
is lightly browned, 20–25 minutes. • Cool
in the pan for 15 minutes. • Cut into squares
and let cool.

^{2}/$_{3}$ cup (100 g) all-purpose (plain) flour
^{1}/$_{2}$ cup (75 g) confectioners' (icing) sugar
^{1}/$_{8}$ teaspoon salt
^{1}/$_{3}$ cup (90 g) butter, softened
1 large egg + 2 large egg whites
^{3}/$_{4}$ cup (200 g) raspberry preserves (jam)
^{1}/$_{2}$ cup (100 g) superfine (caster) sugar
1 teaspoon ground cinnamon

Makes: about 25 squares
Preparation: 30 minutes
Cooking: 30–35 minutes
Level: 1

APRICOT BARS

Preheat the oven to 350°F (180°C/gas 4).
• Butter a 10½ x 15½-inch (26 x 36-cm) jelly-roll pan. • <u>Topping</u>: Melt the butter in a small saucepan over medium heat. Stir in the brown sugar and oats until well blended. <u>Base</u>: Mix the flour, baking powder, and salt in a large bowl and stir in the sugar. Use a pastry blender to cut in the butter until the mixture resembles fine crumbs. • Firmly press the mixture into the prepared pan. • Heat the preserves in a small saucepan over medium heat until liquid. Spread over the cookie base. • Sprinkle with the topping. • Bake until lightly browned, 25–30 minutes. • Cool completely before cutting into bars.

Topping

½ cup (125 g) butter, cut up

1 cup (200 g) firmly packed dark brown sugar

½ cup (75 g) old-fashioned rolled oats

Base

3²⁄₃ cups (550 g) all-purpose (plain) flour

2 teaspoons baking powder

¼ teaspoon salt

¾ cup (150 g) granulated sugar

1 cup (250 g) butter, cut up

½ cup (125 g) apricot preserves (jam)

Makes: about 25 bars
Preparation: 20 minutes
Cooking: 25–30 minutes
Level: 1

SEED AND NUT BARS

Preheat the oven to 375°F (190°C/gas 5).
• Butter an 11 x 7-inch (28 x 18-cm) baking
pan. • Melt the butter with the honey and raw
sugar in a large saucepan over low heat,
stirring constantly. • Bring to a boil and
simmer until the sugar has dissolved
completely. • Stir in the oats, walnuts, raisins,
pumpkin seeds, sunflower seeds, sesame
seeds, coconut, cinnamon, and salt. • Spoon
the mixture evenly into the prepared pan.
• Bake until just golden, 30–35 minutes.
• Cool completely before cutting into bars.

⅓ cup (90 g) butter, softened
⅓ cup (90 g) honey
½ cup (100 g) raw sugar (Demerara or Barbados)
1½ cups (225 g) old-fashioned rolled oats
½ cup (50 g) coarsely chopped walnuts
½ cup (90 g) raisins
2 tablespoons pumpkin seeds
2 tablespoons sunflower seeds
2 tablespoons sesame seeds
2 tablespoons shredded (desiccated) coconut
¾ teaspoon ground cinnamon
⅛ teaspoon salt

Makes: about 20 bars
Preparation: 20 minutes
Cooking: 30–35 minutes
Level: 1

CORN FLAKE SQUARES

Preheat the oven to 350°F (180°C/gas 4).
• Butter an 8-inch (20-cm) square baking pan.
• Mix the corn flakes, butter, sugar, cherries, ginger, and salt in a medium bowl . • Firmly press the mixture into the pan. • Bake until golden brown, 25–30 minutes. • Let cool before cutting into squares.

³/₄ cup (90 g) corn flakes

¹/₂ cup (125 g) butter, melted

¹/₂ cup (100 g) firmly packed dark brown sugar

¹/₂ cup (50 g) candied green cherries

¹/₂ teaspoon ground ginger

¹/₈ teaspoon salt

Makes: about 16 squares
Preparation: 10 minutes
Cooking: 25–30 minutes
Level: 1

CANDIED PINEAPPLE BARS

548

Preheat the oven to 350°F (180°C/gas 4).
• Butter a 13 x 9-inch (33 x 23-cm) baking pan. • Mix the flour, ground ginger, and salt in a medium bowl. • Beat the butter and brown sugar in a large bowl with an electric mixer at high speed until creamy. • Use a wooden spoon to mix in the dry ingredients until the mixture resembles coarse crumbs. Transfer half the mixture to a small bowl and set aside. • Add the egg to the remaining mixture and mix to form a smooth dough. • Firmly press the dough into the prepared pan to form a smooth, even layer. • Sprinkle with the crystallized pineapple and ginger. Top with the reserved crumb mixture. • Bake until golden, 45–50 minutes. • Cool in the pan for 15 minutes then cut into bars. • Serve warm.

2 cups (300 g) all-purpose (plain) flour
1 teaspoon ground ginger
1/8 teaspoon salt
1 cup (250 g) butter, softened
3/4 cup (150 g) firmly packed soft brown sugar
1 large egg, lightly beaten
1 cup (150 g) chopped candied pineapple
1/2 cup (50 g) finely chopped candied ginger

Makes: about 30 bars
Preparation: 30 minutes
Cooking: 45–50 minutes
Level: 1

CRANBERRY AND PECAN SQUARES

Preheat the oven to 350°F (180°C/gas 4).
• Butter a 9-inch (23-cm) square baking pan.
• Mix the flour, cinnamon, and salt in a
medium bowl. • Mix the butter and sugar in
a medium bowl. • Add the egg, beating until
just blended. • Mix in the dry ingredients,
pecans, and cranberries until well blended.
• Spread the mixture in the prepared pan.
• Bake until just golden and a toothpick
inserted into the center comes out clean,
30–35 minutes. • Cool completely in the
pan. • Dust with the confectioners' sugar
and cut into squares.

1 cup (150 g) all-purpose (plain) flour
½ teaspoon ground cinnamon
⅛ teaspoon salt
¼ cup (60 g) butter, melted
¾ cup (150 g) granulated sugar
1 large egg, lightly beaten
⅔ cup (70 g) finely chopped pecans
½ cup (125 g) fresh or frozen cranberries
2 tablespoons confectioners' (icing) sugar, to dust

Makes: about 20 squares
Preparation: 20 minutes
Cooking: 30–35 minutes
Level: 1

GLAZED CRANBERRY SQUARES

<u>Base</u>: Preheat the oven to 350°F (180°C/gas 4). • Butter a 9-inch (23-cm) square baking pan. • Sift the flour and salt into a medium bowl. • Mix the butter and sugar in a medium bowl. • Add the egg, beating until just blended. • Mix in the dry ingredients, walnuts, and cranberries. • Spread the mixture in the prepared pan. • Bake for 30–35 minutes, or until golden and a toothpick inserted into the center comes out clean. • Cool completely in the pan. • Cut into squares. • <u>Glaze</u>: Mix the confectioners' sugar and water in a small bowl. Add the food coloring until well blended. Drizzle the glaze over the cookies.

Base

1¼ cups (180 g) all-purpose (plain) flour

⅛ teaspoon salt

½ cup (125 g) butter, melted

¾ cup (150 g) granulated sugar

1 large egg, lightly beaten

⅔ cup (70 g) finely chopped walnuts

½ cup (125 g) fresh or frozen cranberries

Glaze

1 cup (150 g) confectioners' (icing) sugar

2 tablespoons hot water + more, as needed

3 drops red food coloring

Makes: about 20 squares
Preparation: 20 minutes
Cooking: 30–35 minutes
Level: 1

DIAMOND COOKIES

554

Mix the flour, granulated sugar, vanilla sugar, lemon zest, and salt in a medium bowl. • Use a pastry blender to cut in the butter until the mixture resembles coarse crumbs. • Make a well in the center and add the egg, mixing until a dough is formed. • Turn out onto a lightly floured surface and knead in the candied cherries, candied peel, and nuts. Knead until smooth. • Return to the bowl, cover with plastic wrap, and refrigerate for 30 minutes. • Preheat the oven to 350°F (180°C/gas 4). • Line two cookie sheets with parchment paper. • Roll out the dough ½-inch (1-cm) thick. Cut into diamond shapes. • Use a metal spatula to transfer to the prepared cookie sheets, spacing 1 inch (2.5 cm) apart. • Mix the egg yolk and water in a small bowl. • Brush the cookies with the egg yolk mixture. • Bake until lightly browned, 12–15 minutes. • Cool on the sheets for 10 minutes. Transfer to racks and let cool completely.

2 cups (300 g) all-purpose (plain) flour
½ cup (100 g) granulated sugar
1 tablespoon vanilla sugar (see page 696)
Grated zest of ½ lemon
¼ teaspoon salt
¾ cup (180 g) cold butter, cut up
1 large egg, lightly beaten
1 tablespoon candied cherries, chopped
2 tablespoons mixed candied peel, chopped
2 tablespoons sugared nuts, crushed
1 large egg yolk, to brush
½ cup (125 ml) water

Makes: 40 cookies
Preparation: 45 minutes + 30 minutes to chill
Cooking: 12–15 minutes
Level: 2

GLAZED ALMOND BARS

Base: Beat the whole egg and yolk, sugar, and salt in a large bowl with an electric mixer at high speed until creamy. • Mix in the chocolate, coffee, almonds, and baking powder to form a stiff dough. • Press the dough into a disk, wrap in plastic wrap (cling film) , and refrigerate for 30 minutes. • Preheat the oven to 350°F (180°C/gas 4). • Butter a 10-inch (25-cm) square baking pan. • Press the dough into the baking pan in an even layer. • Glaze: With mixer at medium speed, beat the egg white and salt in a small bowl until frothy. • With mixer at high speed, gradually beat in the confectioners sugar until stiff glossy peaks form. • Spread the glaze evenly over the dough. • Bake until firm, 15–20 minutes. • Cut into bars while still hot.

Base

1 large egg + 1 large egg yolk

¾ cup (150 g) granulated sugar

2 oz (60 g) semisweet (dark) chocolate, grated

1 teaspoon instant coffee granules dissolved in 1 teaspoon warm water

⅛ teaspoon salt

2 cups (300 g) finely ground almonds

¼ teaspoon baking powder

Glaze

1 large egg white

⅛ teaspoon salt

⅓ cup (50 g) confectioners' (icing) sugar

Makes: about 18 bars
Preparation: 30 minutes
 + 30 minutes to chill
Cooking: 15–20 minutes
Level: 1

NUTTY OAT FINGERS

Preheat the oven to 400°F (200°C/gas 6).
• Butter an 8-inch (20-cm) square baking pan.
• Melt the chocolate and margarine in
a heavy-based saucepan over low heat.
• Remove from the heat and stir in the rolled
oats, corn syrup, sugar, salt, and vanilla. Mix
thoroughly. • Pack firmly into the prepared
pan. Sprinkle with the nuts. • Bake until pale
golden brown, 12–15 minutes. • Remove from
oven and mark into fingers, but leave to cool
in the pan. • Turn out and cut into fingers.

2 oz (60 g) semisweet (dark) chocolate

3 tablespoons (45 g) margarine

2 cups (250 g) rolled oats

2 tablespoons corn (golden) syrup

3 tablespoons granulated sugar

¼ teaspoon salt

1 teaspoon vanilla extract (essence)

3 tablespoons chopped toasted nuts

Makes: about 20 fingers
Preparation: 10 minutes
Cooking: 12–15 minutes
Level: 1

■■■ *Use the nuts of your choice to top these fingers; walnuts, hazelnuts, almonds, pecans, or macademias are all good choices.*

MOCHA NUT BROWNIES

Preheat oven to 350°F (180°C/gas 4).
• Line a deep 10-inch (25-cm) square baking pan with parchment paper. • Melt the chocolate in a double boiler over barely simmering heat. • Mix the flour, cocoa, coffee, and baking powder in a medium bowl. • Beat the butter, sugar, and vanilla in a large bowl with an electric mixer on high speed until pale and creamy. • Add the eggs one at a time, beating until just combined after each addition. • With mixer on low speed, gradually beat in chocolate and mixed dry ingredients. Stir in two-thirds of the pecans. • Spoon the batter into the prepared baking pan and sprinkle with the remaining nuts. • Bake until the brownies begin to pull away from the sides of the pan, 25–30 minutes. Test with a skewer, they should still be still quite soft but not raw. • Cool in the baking tray on a wire rack and then refrigerate before cutting into squares.

4 oz (125 g) semisweet (dark) chocolate, chopped

1 cup (150 g) all-purpose (plain) flour

1 tablespoon unsweetened cocoa powder

2 teaspoons instant coffee granules

½ teaspoon baking powder

4 large eggs

1 tablespoon vanilla extract (essence)

2 cups (400 g) granulated sugar

¾ cup (200 g) butter

1½ cups (225 g) pecans coarsely chopped

Makes: about 24 brownies
Preparation: 15 minutes
Cooking: 25–30 minutes
Level: 1

CHERRY SHORTBREAD

Preheat the oven to 325°F (170°C/gas 3).
• Butter an 11 x 7-inch (28 x 18-cm) baking
pan. • Mix the flour, baking powder, and salt
in a medium bowl. • Beat the butter and
2/3 cup (130 g) sugar in a large bowl with
an electric mixer at high speed until creamy.
• Add the egg yolks, beating until just
blended. • Beat in the corn syrup and rum.
• Mix in the dry ingredients to form a stiff
dough. • Divide the dough in half. Firmly
press one half into the prepared pan to form a
smooth, even layer. Sprinkle with the cherries.
• Roll out the remaining dough on a lightly
floured surface into an 11 x 7-inch (28 x 18-
cm) rectangle. Place the dough on top of the
cherries. • Sprinkle with the remaining sugar.
• Bake until pale gold, 35–40 minutes. • Cool
completely before cutting into squares.

2½ cups (375 g) all-purpose (plain) flour

½ teaspoon baking powder

⅛ teaspoon salt

1 cup (250 g) butter, softened

3/4 cup (150 g) granulated sugar

2 large egg yolks

1 tablespoon light corn syrup (golden) syrup

1 tablespoon dark rum

½ cup (50 g) finely chopped candied cherries

Makes: about 25 squares
Preparation: 30 minutes
Cooking: 35–40 minutes
Level of difficulty: 1

CHOCOLATE CHIP SHORTBREAD

Preheat the oven to 325°F (170°C/gas 3).
• Butter two 9-inch (23-cm) springform pans.
• Mix the flour, confectioners' sugar, cornstarch, and salt in a large bowl. • Use a pastry blender to cut in the butter until the mixture resembles coarse crumbs. • Stir in the chocolate chips. • Firmly press the mixture into the prepared pans to form smooth, even layers. • Bake until just golden, 15–20 minutes. • Cool for 5 minutes in the pan. • Loosen and remove the springform sides. Let cool completely. • Cut each round into sixteen wedges.

1¾ cups (275 g) all-purpose (plain) flour

½ cup (75 g) confectioners' (icing) sugar

2 tablespoons cornstarch (cornflour)

¼ teaspoon salt

1 cup (250 g) butter, cut up

2 cups (360 g) semisweet (dark) chocolate chips

Makes: about 32 wedges
Preparation: 20 minutes
Cooking: 15–20 minutes
Level of difficulty: 1

GINGER SHORTBREAD

Preheat the oven to 325°F (170°C/gas 3).
• Butter an 11 x 7-inch (28 x 18-cm) baking pan. • Mix the flour, baking powder, and salt in a medium bowl. • Beat the butter and $2/3$ cup (130 g) sugar in a large bowl with an electric mixer at high speed until creamy.
• Add the egg yolks, beating until just blended. • Beat in the corn syrup and brandy.
• Mix in the dry ingredients to form a stiff dough. • Divide the dough in half. Firmly press one half into the prepared pan to form a smooth, even layer. Sprinkle with the ginger.
• Roll out the remaining dough on a lightly floured surface into an 11 x 7-inch (28 x 18-cm) rectangle. Place the dough on top of the ginger. • Sprinkle with the remaining sugar.
• Bake until pale gold, 35–40 minutes.
• Cool completely before cutting into squares.

2½ cups (375 g) all-purpose (plain) flour

½ teaspoon baking powder

⅛ teaspoon salt

1 cup (250 g) butter, softened

¾ cup (150 g) granulated sugar

2 large egg yolks

1 tablespoon light corn syrup (golden) syrup

1 tablespoon brandy

½ cup (50 g) finely chopped crystallized ginger

Makes: about 25 squares
Preparation: 30 minutes
Cooking: 35–40 minutes
Level: 1

POLENTA LEMON WEDGES

Preheat the oven to 350°F (180°C/gas 4).

• Butter a 9-inch (23-cm) springform pan.

• Mix the flour, polenta, and salt in a medium bowl. • Use a pastry blender to cut in the butter until the mixture resembles coarse crumbs. • Stir in the ground almonds and granulated sugar. • Mix in the egg yolks, lemon zest and juice, and almond extract to form a stiff dough. • Firmly press the dough into the prepared pan to form a smooth even layer. Sprinkle with the chopped almonds and raw sugar. • Use a sharp knife to score the cookie into 16 wedges. • Bake for 20 minutes. • Reduce the oven temperature to 300°F (150°C/gas 2). • Bake until pale gold and firm to the touch, 20–25 minutes more. • Use a sharp knife to cut into 16 wedges along the scored lines. • Loosen and remove the pan sides and bottom. Transfer to racks and let cool completely.

$2/3$ cup (100 g) all-purpose (plain) flour

$2/3$ cup (100 g) polenta (finely ground yellow cornmeal)

$1/8$ teaspoon salt

$1/2$ cup (125 g) butter, cut up

1 cup (150 g) finely ground almonds

$1/2$ cup (100 g) granulated sugar

2 large egg yolks, lightly beaten

Finely grated zest and juice of 1 lemon

$1/2$ teaspoon almond extract (essence)

2 tablespoons finely chopped almonds

2 tablespoons raw sugar (Barbados or Demerara)

Makes: about 16 wedges
Preparation: 35 minutes
Cooking: 40–45 minutes
Level: 1

SHORTBREAD WALNUT DIAMONDS

Preheat the oven to 350°F (180°C/gas 4).
• Butter a 10 x 15-inch (25 x 36-cm) jelly-roll pan. • Mix the flour, cinnamon, ginger, and salt in a medium bowl. • Beat the butter and sugar in a large bowl with an electric mixer at high speed until creamy. • Add the almond extract and egg yolk, beating until just blended. • Mix in the dry ingredients to form a smooth dough. • Firmly press the dough into the prepared pan to form a smooth even layer. • Beat the egg white and water in a small bowl and brush it over the dough. Sprinkle with walnuts. • Score the dough into 1-inch (2.5-cm) diamonds. • Bake until lightly browned, 15–20 minutes. • Cool completely in the pan. • Cut along the lines and divide into diamonds.

2 cups (300 g) all-purpose (plain) flour
1 teaspoon ground cinnamon
1 teaspoon ground ginger
⅛ teaspoon salt
1 cup (250 g) butter, softened
1 cup (200 g) granulated sugar
1 teaspoon almond extract (essence)
1 large egg, separated
1 tablespoon cold water
1 cup (100 g) finely chopped walnuts

Makes: about 18 cookies
Preparation: 20 minutes
Cooking: 15–20 minutes
Level: 1

WAFERS AND MACAROONS

ORANGE WAFERS

Toast the sesame seeds in a frying pan over medium heat, until lightly browned, 5–7 minutes. • Mix the flour and salt in a medium bowl. • Beat the butter, confectioners' sugar, and orange zest in a large bowl with an electric mixer at high speed until creamy. • Gradually beat in the egg whites. • Mix in the dry ingredients and sesame seeds. Refrigerate for 1 hour. • Preheat the oven to 350°F (180°C/gas 4). • Butter two cookie sheets. • Butter two rolling pins. • Drop teaspoons of the dough 2 inches (5 cm) apart on the prepared cookie sheets. Use a thin spatula to spread the batter to about 3 inches (8 cm) in diameter. • Do not place more than five cookies on each sheet. • Bake until the edges are lightly golden, 5–6 minutes. • Working quickly, use a spatula to place the cookies over a rolling pin. • Slide each cookie off the pin onto a rack to finish cooling. • Butter the cookie sheets again and continue to bake in batches until all the batter has been used.

1 cup (100 g) sesame seeds

$2/3$ cup (100 g) all-purpose (plain) flour

$1/8$ teaspoon salt

$1/3$ cup (90 g) butter, softened

$2/3$ cup (100 g) confectioners' (icing) sugar

2 tablespoons vanilla sugar (see page 696)

Finely grated zest of 1 orange

3 large egg whites, lightly beaten

Makes: about 26 cookies
Preparation: 50 minutes + 1 hour to chill
Cooking: 5–6 minutes
Level: 3

FRUIT WAFERS
WITH CHOCOLATE

Preheat the oven to 350°F (180°C/gas 4).
• Line four cookie sheets with parchment
paper. • Mix the flour and salt in a medium
bowl. • Melt the butter with the sugar and
honey in a medium saucepan over low heat,
stirring often, until the sugar has dissolved
completely. • Increase the heat and bring the
mixture almost to a boil. • Remove from the
heat and mix in the almonds and dried fruit.
• Add the dry ingredients all at once and stir
until well blended. • Drop teaspoons of the
dough 3 inches (8 cm) apart onto the
prepared cookie sheets, flattening them
slightly. • Bake until golden brown on top
and slightly darker brown at the edges,
8–10 minutes. • Cool on the sheets until
the cookies firm slightly. Transfer to racks
to finish cooling. • Melt the chocolate in
a double boiler over barely simmering water.
• Brush one side of the cookies with the
melted chocolate and let stand until set,
about 30 minutes.

¾ cup (125 g) all-purpose (plain) flour

⅛ teaspoon salt

½ cup (125 g) butter, cut up

¾ cup (150 g) granulated sugar

2 teaspoons honey

½ cup (50 g) flaked almonds, toasted

⅔ cup (70 g) finely chopped dried cranberries

⅔ cup (70 g) finely chopped dried pineapple

⅔ cup (70 g) finely chopped dried apricots

4 oz (125 g) semisweet (dark) chocolate, coarsely chopped

Makes: about 45 cookies
Preparation: 25 minutes +
 30 minutes to stand
Cooking: 8–10 minutes
Level: 2

HAZELNUT WAFERS WITH WHITE CHOCOLATE

Preheat the oven to 325°F (170°C/gas 3).
• Spread the hazelnuts on a baking sheet.
Toast until lightly golden, about 7 minutes.
• Transfer to a food processor with ¼ cup
(50 g) of sugar and process until very finely
chopped. • Increase the oven temperature to
375°F (170°C/gas 3). • Set out three cookie
sheets. • Melt the butter with the honey,
cream, and remaining sugar in a small
saucepan over low heat until the sugar has
dissolved. • Bring to a boil and simmer for
2 minutes. • Remove from the heat and stir in
the nut mixture and salt. • Drop teaspoons of
the mixture 3 inches (8 cm) apart onto the
cookie sheets. • Bake until golden brown,
8–10 minutes. • Cool on the sheets until the
cookies firm slightly. Transfer to racks and let
cool completely. • Melt the chocolate in a
double boiler over barely simmering water.
• Brush one side of the cookies with the
melted chocolate and let stand until set,
about 30 minutes.

1   lb (500 g) hazelnuts
1   cup (200 g) granulated
    sugar
1   cup (250 g) butter,
    softened
½ cup (125 g) honey
½ cup (125 ml) heavy
    (double) cream
⅛ teaspoon salt
6   oz (180 g) white
    chocolate, coarsely
    chopped

Makes: 30–40 cookies
Preparation: 20 minutes +
   30 minutes to set
Cooking: 8–10 minutes
Level: 3

ORANGE THINS

Preheat the oven to 375°F (190°C/gas 5).
• Line two cookie sheets with parchment
paper. • Mix the flour, cornstarch, and salt
in a medium bowl. • Use a whisk to beat the
eggs, superfine sugar, and orange zest in a
double boiler over barely simmering water
until pale and very thick. • Transfer to a
medium bowl. • Use a large rubber spatula to
fold in the dry ingredients. • Fit a pastry bag
with a ½-inch (1-cm) plain tip. Fill the pastry
bag, twist the opening tightly closed, and
squeeze out 3-inch (8-cm) lines, spacing
2 inches (5 cm) apart on the prepared cookie
sheets. • Sprinkle with the sugar crystals.
• Bake until just golden, 8–10 minutes.
• Cool the cookies on the cookie sheets
for 5 minutes. Transfer to racks and
let cool completely.

1½ cups (180 g) all-
   purpose (plain) flour

½ cup (75 g) cornstarch
   (cornflour)

⅛ teaspoon salt

3 large eggs,
   lightly beaten

1 cup (200 g) superfine
   (caster) sugar

2 teaspoons finely grated
   orange zest

2 tablespoons sugar
   crystals

Makes: 30–35 cookies
Preparation: 40 minutes
Cooking: 8–10 minutes
Level of difficulty: 1

CHOCOLATE-GLAZED MACAROONS

582

Mix the flour, baking powder, and salt in a large bowl. • Beat the egg whites in a large bowl with an electric mixer at medium speed until frothy. • With mixer at high speed, gradually add the superfine sugar, beating until stiff, glossy peaks form. • Use a large rubber spatula to fold in the almonds, grated chocolate, and candied peel, followed by the dry ingredients. Mix until well blended. • Drop spoonfuls of the mixture on a sheet of rice paper placed on a baking sheet. Use a thin metal spatula to spread the mixture to $1/2$-inch (1-cm) thick. • Refrigerate for 2 hours. • Preheat the oven to 300°F (150°C/gas 2). • Bake until firm to the touch, 20–25 minutes. • Transfer to racks to cool. • Tear off the extra rice paper from around the cookies. • Melt both types of chocolate separately in a double boiler over barely simmering water. • Drizzle the over the macaroons, swirling with a knife to create a marbled effect.

2 tablespoons all-purpose (plain) flour

1 teaspoon baking powder

$1/8$ teaspoon salt

4 large egg whites

$1 1/2$ cups (300 g) superfine (caster) sugar

$2 1/2$ cups (250 g) finely ground almonds

3 oz (90 g) semisweet (dark) chocolate, coarsely grated

1 cup (100 g) mixed candied peel, finely chopped

Rice paper, cut into 2-inch (5-cm) rounds

3 oz (90 g) semisweet (dark) chocolate, coarsely chopped

3 oz (90 g) white chocolate, coarsely chopped

Makes: about 15 cookies
Preparation: 30 minutes + 2 hours to chill
Cooking: 20–25 minutes
Level of difficulty: 2

SICILIAN MACAROONS

Preheat the oven to 375°F (190°C/gas 5).
• Line a cookie sheet with parchment paper.
• Mix the almonds with the egg white in a food processor to form a smooth paste.
• Mix the vanilla sugar, granulated sugar, and the orange and almond extracts in a small bowl. Gradually work the mixture into the almond paste until soft. • Form the mixture into balls the size of walnuts. • Place 2 inches (5 cm) apart on the prepared cookie sheet, flattening slightly. • Lightly press an almond into the top of each cookie. Brush with the water and dust with confectioners' sugar.
• Bake until golden and slightly firm to the touch, 15–20 minutes. • Transfer the cookies on the parchment paper to racks and cool until slightly firm. • Peel off the paper and let cool completely.

1 cup (150 g) blanched almonds, toasted and finely ground

½ cup (100 g) vanilla sugar (see page 696)

¼ cup (60 g) granulated sugar

½ teaspoon orange extract (essence)

2 large egg whites

½ teaspoon almond extract (essence)

15 blanched almonds or almond halves

1 teaspoon water

Confectioners' (icing) sugar, to dust

Makes: 12–15 cookies
Preparation: 40 minutes
Cooking: 15–20 minutes
Level of difficulty: 2

HAZELNUT MOMENTS

Preheat the oven to 300°F (150°C/gas 2).
• Line two cookie sheets with parchment
paper. • Beat the egg whites in a medium
bowl with an electric mixer at medium speed
in a bowl over barely simmering water. With
mixer at high speed, gradually beat in the
granulated and vanilla sugars. • Mix in the
ground hazelnuts, nutmeg, and lemon juice
and beat until frothy. The mixture should
remain just warm to the touch. • Remove
from the water and beat with an electric mixer
until stiff and glossy. • Mix in the ground
hazelnuts. • Fill a pastry bag fitted with a
1/2-inch (1-cm) plain tip and squeeze out 1-inch
(2.5-cm) rounds onto the prepared cookie
sheets. Press a hazelnut into the center of
each cookie. • Brush lightly with water and
dust with the confectioners' sugar. • Bake
until lightly golden around the edges and just
firm to the touch, 15–20 minutes. • Transfer
on the parchment paper to racks and cool
until the cookies firm slightly. • Peel off the
paper and let cool completely.

2   large egg whites
1/2   cup (100 g) granulated
      sugar
2   tablespoons vanilla
      sugar (see page 696)
1   cup (150 g) finely
      ground shelled
      hazelnuts, toasted
      + 25–30 hazelnuts
1/4   teaspoon freshly grated
      nutmeg
1   teaspoon freshly
      squeezed lemon juice
1   teaspoon water
4   tablespoons
      confectioners' (icing)
      sugar, to dust

Makes: 25–30 cookies
Preparation: 50 minutes
Cooking: 18–20 minutes
Level of difficulty: 2

LEMON AND ALMOND MERINGUES

Preheat the oven to 250°F (130°C/gas ½).
• Line two cookie sheets with parchment paper. • Beat the egg whites and salt in a large bowl with an electric mixer at medium speed until soft peaks form. With mixer at high speed, gradually add the superfine sugar and lemon juice, beating until stiff glossy peaks form. • Stir together the finely ground nuts and cornstarch and fold into the mixture. • Fit a pastry bag with a ½-inch (1-cm) star tip. Fill the pastry bag, twist the opening tightly closed, and squeeze out small mounds, spacing 1 inch (2.5 cm) apart on the prepared cookie sheets. • Sprinkle with the flaked almonds and dust with the confectioners' sugar. • Bake until the meringues are dry to the touch, 50–60 minutes. • Turn off the oven. Leave in the oven for 30 minutes more. • Using the parchment paper as handles, lift the meringues onto a rack. Carefully peel off the paper and let cool completely.

2 large egg whites
⅛ teaspoon salt
½ cup (100 g) superfine (caster) sugar
1 teaspoon freshly squeezed lemon juice
3 tablespoons finely ground almonds, toasted
1 teaspoon cornstarch (cornflour)
2 tablespoons flaked almonds, to sprinkle
2 tablespoons confectioners' (icing) sugar, to dust

Makes: 20–25 meringues
Preparation: 30 minutes
Cooking: 50–60 minutes
  + 30 minutes to rest
Level: 2

MOCHA MERINGUES

Preheat the oven to 300°F (150°C/gas 2).
• Line a cookie sheet with parchment paper.
• Beat the egg whites and salt in a large bowl with an electric mixer at medium speed until frothy. • With mixer at high speed, gradually add the superfine sugar, beating until stiff glossy peaks form. • Use a large rubber spatula to fold in the coffee extract, pecans, and cornstarch. • Fit a pastry bag with a 1/2-inch (1-cm) star tip. Fill the pastry bag, twist the opening tightly closed, and squeeze out 2-inch (5-cm) stars, spacing 2 inches (5-cm) apart on the prepared cookie sheet.
• Bake until the meringues are crisp and lightly browned, about 20 minutes. • Cool the meringues completely in the oven with the door ajar.

2   **large egg whites**
1/8   **teaspoon salt**
1   **cup (200 g) superfine (caster) sugar**
1   **teaspoon coffee extract (essence)**
1/2   **cup (50 g) coarsely chopped pecans**
1   **tablespoon cornstarch (cornflour)**

Makes: about 15 cookies
Preparation: 30 minutes
Cooking: 20 minutes
Level of difficulty: 2

PISTACHIO ORANGE MACAROONS

Preheat the oven to 350°F (180°C/gas 4).
• Line two cookie sheets with parchment
paper and grease them with almond oil.
• Sift the flour and salt into a medium bowl.
• Process $2/3$ cup (100 g) of pistachios in a
food processor until finely chopped. • Transfer
to a large bowl and mix in the granulated
sugar, candied peel, and orange zest. • Mix in
the dry ingredients. • Beat the egg whites in a
large bowl with an electric mixer at medium
speed until frothy. • With mixer at high speed,
gradually beat in the superfine sugar, beating
until stiff, glossy peaks form. • Mix in the
pistachios. • Drop teaspoons of the mixture
$1^1/2$ inches (4 cm) apart onto the prepared
cookie sheets. • Sprinkle with the 2
tablespoons of chopped pistachios. • Bake
until the macaroons are lightly golden and
the bottoms are firm and just browned, 10–12
minutes. • Dust with the confectioners' sugar
and let cool on the parchment. • Transfer to
racks to cool completely.

$1/3$ cup (50 g) all-purpose (plain) flour

$1/8$ teaspoon salt

$2/3$ cup (100 g) pistachios + 2 tablespoons chopped pistachios

$3/4$ cup (150 g) granulated sugar

3 tablespoons finely chopped candied orange peel

1 tablespoon finely grated orange zest

3 large egg whites

$1/4$ cup (50 g) superfine (caster) sugar

2 tablespoons confectioners' (icing) sugar, to dust

Makes: 25–30 cookies
Preparation: 20 minutes
Cooking: 10–12 minutes
Level of difficulty: 1

LIGHT LEMON MACAROONS

Preheat the oven to 350°F (150°C/gas 2).
• Butter two cookie sheets. • Beat the egg whites in a large bowl with an electric mixer at high speed until stiff peaks form. • Use a large rubber spatula to fold the almonds, sugar, flour, lemon zest, vanilla, and salt into the beaten whites. • Fit a pastry bag with a 1/2-inch (1-cm) plain tip. Fill the pastry bag, twist the opening tightly closed, and squeeze out small mounds, spacing 1 inch (2.5 cm) apart on the prepared cookie sheets. • Bake until lightly golden, 20–25 minutes. • Cool on the sheets for 5 minutes. Transfer to racks and let cool completely.

4   large egg whites

2½ cups (250 g) finely chopped almonds

1¼ cups (250 g) granulated sugar

1   tablespoon whole-wheat (wholemeal) flour

Finely grated zest of 1 lemon

½   teaspoon vanilla extract (essence)

⅛   teaspoon salt

Makes: about 25 cookies
Preparation: 25 minutes
Cooking: 20–25 minutes
Level of difficulty: 2

CHOCOLATE ALMOND MACAROONS

Preheat the oven to 325°F (170°C/gas 3).
• Line three cookie sheets with rice paper.
• Sprinkle the almonds onto a large baking
sheet. Toast until lightly golden, about
7 minutes. • Set aside to cool completely.
Lower the oven to 275°F (140°C/gas 1).
• Beat the egg whites in a large bowl with
an electric mixer at medium speed until
frothy. • With mixer at high speed, gradually
add the sugar, cream of tartar, vanilla, and salt
and beat until stiff glossy peaks form. • Use
a large rubber spatula to fold in the chocolate
and almonds. • Drop teaspoons of the batter
1½ inches (4 cm) apart onto the prepared
cookie sheets. • Bake until lightly browned,
20–25 minutes. • Cool the cookies completely
on the cookie sheets. Tear away the excess
paper from around the macaroons.

2 cups (200 g) slivered almonds

3 large egg whites

1 cup (200 g) superfine (caster) sugar

⅛ teaspoon cream of tartar

¼ teaspoon vanilla extract (essence)

⅛ teaspoon salt

4 oz (125 g) semisweet (dark) chocolate, finely grated

Makes: about 40 cookies
Preparation: 40 minutes
Cooking: 20–25 minutes
Level of difficulty: 1

NUTTY RAW SUGAR MACAROONS

Preheat the oven to 325°F (170°C/gas 3).

• Line a cookie sheet with parchment paper.

• Spread the almonds on a large baking sheet. Toast until lightly browned, about 7 minutes.

• Transfer the nuts to a food processor, add the raw sugar, and process until finely ground.

• Transfer to a large bowl and stir in the aniseed. • Beat the egg white and almond extract in a medium bowl until stiff peaks form. • Use a large spatula to fold in the nut mixture. • Form the dough into balls the size of walnuts and place 1 inch (2.5 cm) apart on the prepared cookie sheet, flattening slightly.

• Sprinkle the tops of the cookies with the pine nuts, pressing them into the dough.

• Bake until golden and dry to the touch, 20–25 minutes. • Transfer to racks to cool.

$^2/_3$ cup (100 g) blanched almonds

½ cup (100 g) raw sugar (Barbados or Demerara)

½ teaspoon ground aniseed

¼ teaspoon almond extract (essence)

1 large egg white

1 tablespoon pine nuts

Makes: 15–18 cookies
Preparation: 35 minutes
Cooking 20–25 minutes
Level of difficulty: 1

WALNUT CRISPS

600

Preheat the oven to 325°F (170°C/gas 3).
• Line three cookie sheets first with
parchment paper and then with rice paper.
• Spread the walnuts on a large baking sheet.
Toast for 7 minutes, or until lightly golden.
• Process in a food processor with $1/3$ cup
(50 g) of sugar until finely ground. • Beat the
eggs and the remaining sugar in a large bowl
with an electric mixer at high speed until pale
and thick. • Mix in the lemon zest and juice
and ground walnuts. • Drop rounded
teaspoons of the mixture onto the prepared
cookie sheets, spacing them $1^1/2$ inches
(4 cm) apart. • Bake until lightly browned,
12–15 minutes. • Transfer the cookies still
on the parchment paper to racks to cool.
• Tear away the excess rice paper from
around the cookies.

$2^1/3$ cups (350 g) walnut
halves

$1^1/3$ cups (270 g)
granulated sugar

3 large eggs

Finely grated zest and
juice of $1/2$ lemon

Makes: 35–40 cookies
Preparation: 20 minutes
Cooking: 12–15 minutes
Level of difficulty: 2

ORANGE MACAROON DRIZZLERS

Macaroons: Preheat the oven to 325°F (170°C/gas 3). • Line three cookie sheets with parchment paper. • Sprinkle the almonds on a large baking sheet. Toast until lightly golden, 7 minutes. • Lower the oven temperature to 275°F (140°C/gas 1). • Process the almonds in a food processor until very finely chopped. • Beat the egg whites, superfine sugar, and vanilla sugar in a double boiler over barely simmering water with an electric mixer at high speed until stiff peaks form. • Add the orange zest and juice. • Remove from the heat. • Use a rubber spatula to fold the almonds and bread crumbs into the batter. • Drop teaspoons of the batter 1 inch (2.5 cm) apart onto the prepared cookie sheets. • Bake until pale golden, 20–25 minutes. The macaroons should still be soft; they will harden while cooling. • Transfer to racks to cool. • Glaze: Heat the marmalade in a small saucepan and drizzle over the cooled macaroons. Set aside. • Melt the chocolate in a double boiler over barely simmering water. • Drizzle the chocolate over the macaroons.

Macaroons

1¼ cups (180 g) blanched almonds

3 large egg whites

¾ cup (150 g) superfine (caster) sugar

1 tablespoon vanilla sugar (see page 696)

Finely grated zest of 1 orange

1 tablespoon freshly squeezed orange juice

½ cup (60 g) fine dry bread crumbs

Glaze

2 tablespoons orange marmalade

2 oz (60 g) semisweet (dark) chocolate, coarsely chopped

Makes: about 50 cookies
Preparation: 30 minutes
Cooking: 20–25 minutes
Level of difficulty: 2

HAZELNUT MERINGUES

604

Preheat the oven to 325°F (170°C/gas 3).
• Line two cookie sheets with parchment
paper. • Spread the hazelnuts on a large
baking sheet. Toast until lightly golden, about
7 minutes. • Reduce the oven temperature to
250°F (130°C/gas $\frac{1}{2}$). • Place the nuts
in a food processor with $\frac{1}{2}$ cup (100 g) of
superfine sugar and process until finely
ground. • Beat the egg whites and salt in a
large bowl with an electric mixer at medium
speed until soft peaks form. • With mixer at
high speed, gradually add the remaining
superfine sugar, beating until stiff glossy
peaks form. • Use a large rubber spatula to
fold in the hazelnuts. • Drop teaspoons of the
mixture 2 inches (5 cm) apart on the
prepared cookie sheets. • Bake until the
meringues are dry and crisp, 25–35 minutes.
• Transfer while still on the parchment paper
to wire racks to cool.

2 cups (300 g) hazelnuts
1 cup (200 g) superfine
   (caster) sugar
4 large egg whites
¼ teaspoon salt

Makes: 30–35 cookies
Preparation: 20 minutes
Cooking: 25–35 minutes
Level of difficulty: 1

CHOCOLATE CINNAMON MACAROONS

606

Preheat the oven to 325°F (170°C/gas 3).
• Spread the almonds on a large baking sheet.
Toast until lightly golden, about 7 minutes.
Leave the oven on. • Let the almonds cool
completely. • Transfer the nuts to a food
processor and process until finely ground.
• Melt half the chocolate in a double boiler
over barely simmering water. • Mix the ground
almonds, sugar, cocoa, and cinnamon in
a large bowl and make a well in the center.
• Mix in the melted chocolate and enough
egg white to form a soft, but not sticky paste.
• Refrigerate for 30 minutes. • Line two cookie
sheets with parchment paper. • Spoon scant
tablespoons of the mixture 1 inch (2.5 cm)
apart onto the prepared cookie sheets,
flattening them slightly. • Brush the tops with
a little water and dust with the confectioners'
sugar. • Bake until just firm to the touch,
10–12 minutes. • Transfer to racks to cool.
• Melt the remaining chocolate in a double
boiler over barely simmering water. • Dip the
macaroons halfway into the melted chocolate.
• Let dry on parchment paper for 30 minutes.

1 cup (150 g) blanched almonds

6 oz (180 g) milk chocolate, coarsely chopped

½ cup (100 g) granulated sugar

1 tablespoon unsweetened cocoa powder

¼ teaspoon ground cinnamon

2 large egg whites, lightly beaten

1 teaspoon water

2 tablespoons confectioners' (icing) sugar

Makes: 20–24 cookies
Preparation: 40 minutes +
 1 hour to chill and set
Cooking: 10–12 minutes
Level of difficulty: 2

WHITE FOAM MERINGUES

Preheat the oven to 300°F (150°C/gas 2).
• Line two cookie sheets with parchment
paper. • Mix the egg whites and brown sugar
in a large bowl over barely simmering water,
stirring until the sugar has dissolved and the
mixture is warm to the touch. • Remove the
bowl from the heat and whisk with an electric
mixer until thick and cool, about 15–20
minutes. • Fold in 1 tablespoon of nuts.
• Drop tablespoons of the mixture 2 inches
(5 cm) apart onto the prepared cookie sheets.
• Sprinkle with the remaining nuts. • Bake
until crisp and dry to the touch, 12–15
minutes. • Cool completely in the oven
with the door ajar.

4 large egg whites
1 cup (200 g) firmly
   packed light brown
   sugar
2 tablespoons coarsely
   chopped hazelnuts

Makes: about 12 meringues
Preparation: 30 minutes
Cooking: 15 minutes
Level of difficulty: 2

CANDIED PEEL MACAROONS

Soak the candied peel in the orange liqueur for 1 hour. • Drain, reserving the liqueur. • Preheat the oven to 375°F (190°C/gas 5). • Line two cookie sheets with parchment paper. • Mix the flour, baking powder, and salt in a medium bowl. • Beat the butter and sugar in a large bowl with an electric mixer at high speed until creamy. • Add the lemon extract. • With mixer at high speed, beat in the egg whites and the reserved orange liqueur. • Mix in the dry ingredients. • Fit a pastry bag with a 1/2-inch (1-cm) plain tip. Fill the pastry bag, twist the opening tightly closed, and squeeze out 1 1/2-inch (4-cm) mounds, spacing 2 inches (5 cm) apart on the prepared cookie sheets. • Lightly press a piece of candied peel into the top of each cookie. • Bake until golden brown, 8–10 minutes. • Cool on the sheets until the cookies firm slightly. Transfer to racks and let cool completely.

2 tablespoons finely chopped mixed candied peel

2 tablespoons orange liqueur

1 cup (150 g) all-purpose (plain) flour

1/4 teaspoon baking powder

1/8 teaspoon salt

1/2 cup (125 g) butter, softened

3/4 cup (150 g) granulated sugar

1/2 teaspoon lemon extract (essence)

2 egg whites, lightly beaten

Makes: about 30 cookies
Preparation: 30 minutes
+ 1 hour to soak
Cooking: 8–10 minutes
Level of difficulty: 2

MACADAMIA MACAROONS

Preheat the oven to 350°F (180°C/gas 4).
• Butter a cookie sheet. • Beat the egg whites
and salt in a large bowl with an electric mixer
at medium speed until frothy. • With mixer at
high speed, gradually add the sugar, beating
until stiff glossy peaks form. • Use a large
rubber spatula to fold in the coconut and
macadamia nuts. • Drop teaspoons of the
mixture 1 inch (2.5 cm) apart onto the
prepared cookie sheet. • Bake until lightly
golden, 10–15 minutes. • Transfer to
racks to cool.

2   large egg whites
1/8 teaspoon salt
3/4 cup (150 g) granulated
     sugar
1½ cups (185 g) shredded
     (desiccated) coconut
1   cup (100 g) coarsely
     chopped macadamia
     nuts

Makes: about 15 cookies
Preparation: 20 minutes
Cooking: 10–15 minutes
Level of difficulty: 1

PINE NUT MACAROONS

614

Line a cookie sheet with parchment paper.
• Place small heaps of pine nuts (about 10 pine nuts per heap) on the prepared cookie sheet. • Mix the almonds, sugar, and vanilla in a large bowl. • Beat the egg whites in a large bowl with an electric mixer at high speed until stiff peaks form. • Use a large rubber spatula to fold the beaten whites into the almond mixture. • Drop teaspoons of the mixture on top of the pine nuts to cover them completely. • Refrigerate for 30 minutes. • Preheat the oven to 300°F (150°C/gas 2). • Bake until set, 18–20 minutes. • Turn off the oven. Cool the meringues completely in the oven with the door ajar.

¾ cup (150 g) pine nuts

1½ cups (150 g) finely chopped almonds

1¼ cups (250 g) granulated sugar

½ teaspoon vanilla extract (essence)

2 large egg whites

Makes: about 16 cookies
Preparation: 20 minutes + 30 minutes to chill
Cooking: 18–20 minutes
Level of difficulty: 1

POPPY SEED MACAROONS

Preheat the oven to 325°F (170°C/gas 3).
• Line a cookie sheet with rice paper. • Spread the nuts on a large baking sheet. • Toast until lightly golden, about 7 minutes. • Increase the oven temperature to 375°F (190°C/gas 5).
• Transfer the almonds to a food processor, add the sugar, and process until finely ground.
• Stir together the almond mixture and flour in a medium bowl. • Beat the egg whites and salt in a large bowl with an electric mixer at high speed until stiff peaks form. • Use a large rubber spatula to fold in the dry ingredients and vanilla. • Fit a pastry bag with a 1-inch (2.5-cm) star tip. Fill the pastry bag, twist the opening tightly closed, and squeeze out 1-inch (2.5-cm) stars 1 inch (2.5-cm) apart on the prepared cookie sheet. Sprinkle with the poppy seeds. • Bake until pale gold, 12–15 minutes. • Cool on the sheets until the cookies firm slightly. • Transfer to racks on the rice paper, tearing away the excess paper, and let cool completely.

3/4 cup (120 g) blanched almonds

1 cup (200 g) granulated sugar

2 tablespoons all-purpose (plain) flour

2 large egg whites

1/8 teaspoon salt

1/2 teaspoon vanilla extract (essence)

1 tablespoon poppy seeds

Makes: 14–16 cookies
Preparation: 30 minutes
Cooking: 12–15 minutes
Level of difficulty: 2

MINI MERINGUES

Preheat the oven to 300°F (150°C/gas 4).
• Line two cookie sheets with aluminum foil.
• Process the almonds in a food processor
until finely chopped. • Beat the egg whites,
confectioners' sugar, and salt in a large bowl
placed over barely simmering water with an
electric mixer at high speed until stiff peaks
form. • Remove the bowl from the water. Stir
in the almond extract and chopped almonds.
• Drop teaspoons of the mixture 1 inch (2.5
cm) apart onto the prepared cookie sheets.
• Bake until crisp, 10–15 minutes.
• Transfer the meringues on the
foil to racks and let cool.

1¼ cups (175 g) blanched almonds

4 large egg whites

⅛ teaspoon salt

2 cups (300 g) confectioners' (icing) sugar

½ teaspoon almond extract (essence)

Makes: about 50 cookies
Preparation: 20 minutes
Cooking: 10–15 minutes
Level of difficulty: 1

LEMON MACAROONS

620

Line a cookie sheet with parchment paper.
• Mix the flour, sugar, egg whites, almonds, candied lemon peel, lemon zest, baking soda, and salt in a large bowl to form a stiff dough. Press the dough into a disk, wrap in plastic wrap (cling film), and refrigerate for 30 minutes. • Roll out the dough on a lightly floured surface to a 12 x 3-inch (30 x 8-cm) rectangle. • Transfer to the prepared cookie sheet and refrigerate for 30 minutes. • Preheat the oven to 300°F (150°C/gas 2). • Cut the dough in half lengthwise and slice into $\frac{1}{2}$-inch (1-cm) strips. • Bake until just golden, 10–15 minutes. • Transfer to racks to cool.

$2\frac{1}{4}$ cups (330 g) all-purpose (plain) flour

$1\frac{3}{4}$ cups (350 g) granulated sugar

4 large egg whites, lightly beaten

$1\frac{1}{3}$ cups (200 g) finely ground almonds

$\frac{2}{3}$ cup (60 g) finely chopped candied lemon peel

Finely grated zest of 1 lemon

1 teaspoon baking soda (bicarbonate of soda)

$\frac{1}{8}$ teaspoon salt

Makes: about 48 cookies
Preparation: 25 minutes
+ 30 minutes to chill
Cooking: 10–15 minutes
Level of difficulty: 1

MUESLI MACAROONS

Preheat the oven to 275°F (140°C/gas 1).
• Line two cookie sheets with parchment or rice paper. • Beat the egg whites and salt in a large bowl with an electric mixer at medium speed until frothy. • With mixer at high speed, gradually beat in the sugar and vanilla, beating until stiff, glossy peaks form. • Fold in the flour, cornstarch, and oat flakes. • Fit a pastry bag with an 1-inch (2.5-cm) tip. Fill the pastry bag, twist the opening tightly closed, and squeeze out small rounds spacing them 1 inch (2.5 cm) apart on the prepared cookie sheets. • Sprinkle with the muesli. • Bake until set and lightly golden, 20–25 minutes.
• Transfer on the parchment paper to racks and let cool completely.

2   large egg whites
⅛   teaspoon salt
¾   cup (150 g) granulated sugar
1   teaspoon vanilla extract (essence)
1   tablespoon all-purpose (plain) flour
2   teaspoons cornstarch (cornflour)
½   cup (75 g) fine oat flakes or wheat flakes
½   cup (75 g) muesli or granola, to sprinkle

Makes: 20–25 cookies
Preparation: 15 minutes
Cooking: 20–25 minutes
Level of difficulty: 1

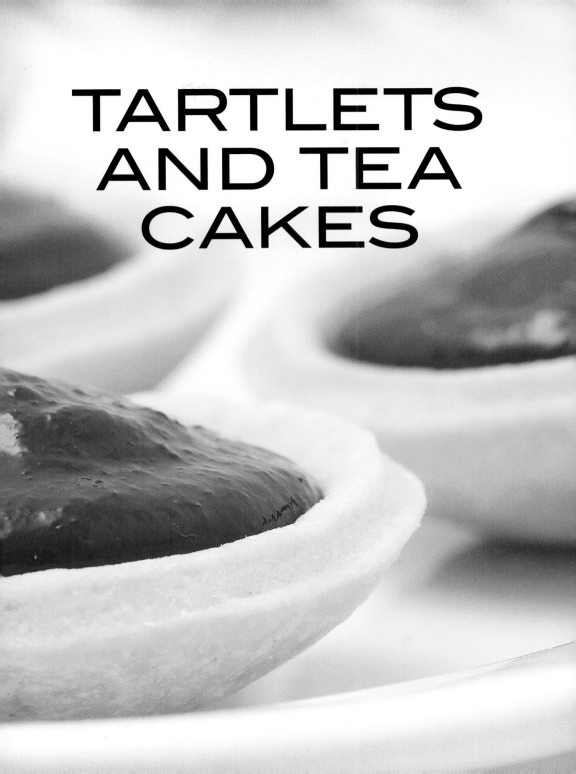

TARTLETS AND TEA CAKES

EGG CUSTARD TARTS

Preheat the oven to 300°F (150°C/gas 2).
• Lightly oil about 20 small tartlet pans (or muffin pans). • Mix the egg yolks and whole eggs in a bowl. Beat slowly with a whisk. Add the sugar and beat until dissolved. • Pour in the milk and cream, and beat until foamy.
• Roll out the pastry and cut it into circles large enough to line the tartlet pans. Press the pastry pieces into the pans. • Fill each tart case with the egg mixture. • Place the tarts on a baking sheet and bake until golden brown, 25–30 minutes. • Let the tarts cool for 10 minutes. • Remove from the pans and place on a rack to cool completely.
• Serve the tarts at room temperature.

2 large eggs + 3 large egg yolks

⅓ cup (90 g) granulated sugar

1 cup (250 ml) milk

2 tablespoons single (light) cream

12 oz (350 g) frozen pastry (flaky or shortcrust), thawed

Makes: about 20 tarts
Preparation: 30 minutes
Cooking: 25–30 minutes
Level: 2

RUM CAKES

628

Cakes: Place the yeast in a small bowl with the water. Stir until dissolved then set aside until frothy, about 10 minutes. • Set out 12 small cake pans or two 12-cup muffin pans. • Preheat the oven to 350°F (180°C/gas 4). • Beat the eggs and sugar with an electric mixer on high speed until pale and creamy. • With mixer on low, gradually beat in the oil, butter, and yeast mixture. • Lastly, beat in the flour and salt. • Knead the dough by hand on a lightly floured surface until soft and elastic. • Fill the pan just under half full, cover, and leave in a warm place to rise. • When the dough has risen to just below the rim of each mold (about 30 minutes), bake in the oven until risen and golden brown, about 15 minutes. • Cool the cakes in the pans for 5 minutes. Transfer to racks and let cool completely. • Rum Syrup: Boil the sugar and water until syrupy, about 10 minutes. • Remove from the heat. Add the lemon and rum and let cool. • Drizzle the rum syrup over the cooled rum cakes.

Cakes

1 oz fresh yeast or 2 (¼-oz/7-g) packages active dry yeast

½ cup (60 ml) warm water

5 large eggs

4 tablespoons sugar

½ cup (125 ml) extra-virgin olive oil

2 tablespoons butter, melted and cooled,

3 cups (450 g) all-purpose (plain flour

⅛ teaspoon salt

Rum Syrup

1½ cups (250 g) granulated sugar

2 cups (500 ml) water

1 lemon, sliced

½ cup (125 ml) rum

Makes: about 12 rum cakes
Preparation: 30 minutes + 30 minutes to rise
Cooking: 15 minutes
Level: 2

CITRUS MADELEINES

Madeleines: Preheat the oven to 350°F (180°C/gas 4). • Butter two 12-cup madeleine pans. • Mix the flour, baking powder, and salt in a medium bowl. • Beat the butter and sugar in a large bowl with an electric mixer at high speed until creamy. • Add the vanilla, egg yolk, and lemon zest and juice, beating until just blended. • Gradually beat in the dry ingredients. • With mixer at high speed, beat the egg white in a medium bowl until stiff peaks form. • Use a large rubber spatula to fold in the beaten white. • Spoon the batter into the prepared pans, filling each cup three-quarters full. • Bake until springy to the touch, 10–12 minutes. • Cool the madeleines in the pan for 15 minutes. • Transfer to racks and let cool completely. • Lemon Drizzle: Melt the butter with the lemon juice in a small saucepan over low heat. • Remove from the heat and beat in the confectioners' sugar. • Drizzle the frosting over the madeleines and let stand for 30 minutes until set.

Madeleines

1 cup (150 g) all-purpose (plain) flour

1 teaspoon baking powder

⅛ teaspoon salt

½ cup (125 g) butter, softened

½ cup (100 g) granulated sugar

½ teaspoon vanilla extract (essence)

1 large egg, separated

Finely grated zest and juice of 1 lemon

Lemon Drizzle

1 tablespoon melted butter

About 4 tablespoons freshly squeezed lemon juice

1 cup (150 g) confectioners' (icing) sugar

Makes: about 20 madeleines
Preparation: 20 minutes + 30 minutes to set
Cooking: 10–12 minutes
Level: 1

COCONUT AND ALMOND TARTLETS

Pastry: Mix the flour and salt in a large bowl.
• Use a pastry blender to cut in the butter and lard until the mixture resembles fine crumbs.
• Mix in enough ice water to form a smooth dough. • Shape into a ball, wrap in plastic wrap (cling film), and refrigerate for at least 30 minutes. • Preheat the oven to 350°F (180°C/gas 4). • Butter twelve small tartlet pans. • Roll out the pastry on a lightly floured surface to ¼-inch (5-mm) thick. Use a pastry cutter to stamp out twelve rounds slightly larger than the tartlet pans. Press the pastry into the prepared pans. • Filling: Heat the raspberry jelly in a small saucepan until liquid. Brush a little jelly over each pastry base. • Beat the egg white in a medium bowl with an electric mixer at high speed until stiff peaks form. Use a rubber spatula to fold in the superfine sugar, coconut, and almonds.
• Spoon the coconut mixture into the pastry bases. • Bake until golden brown, 20–25 minutes. • Cool the tarts completely in the pans.

Pastry

1¼ cups (180 g) all-purpose (plain) flour

⅛ teaspoon salt

¼ cup (60 g) butter, cut up

¼ cup (60 g) lard, cut up, or vegetable shortening

1 tablespoon ice water + more, as needed

Filling

5 tablespoons raspberry jelly

1 large egg white

⅓ cup (70 g) superfine (caster) sugar

2 tablespoons shredded (desiccated) coconut

2 tablespoons finely ground almonds

Makes: 12 tartlets
Preparation: 40 minutes + 30 minutes to chill
Cooking: 20–25 minutes
Level: 2

PLUM CAKELETS

Preheat the oven to 350°F (180°C/gas 4).
• Butter two 12-cup muffin pans. • Cut each
half-plum into three. • Mix the flour, nutmeg,
cinnamon, and salt in a medium bowl. Stir
in the almonds. • Beat the butter and
confectioners' sugar in a large bowl with
an electric mixer at high speed until creamy.
• Mix in the dry ingredients and egg whites.
• Spoon the batter into the prepared pan and
place slices of plum on each one. • Bake until
a toothpick inserted into the centers comes
out clean, 25–30 minutes. • Transfer to
racks to cool.

3 firm-ripe plums, pitted and sliced

½ cup (75 g) all-purpose (plain) flour

1½ teaspoons freshly grated nutmeg

½ teaspoon ground cinnamon

⅛ teaspoon salt

1¼ cups (180 g) finely ground almonds

¾ cup (180 g) butter, softened

1⅔ cups (250 g) confectioners' (icing) sugar

6 large egg whites

Makes: about 24 cakelets
Preparation: 25 minutes
Cooking: 25–30 minutes
Level: 1

BLUEBERRY ALMOND CAKELETS

Preheat the oven to 350°F (180°C/gas 4). • Butter two 12-cup muffin pans. • Mix the flour and salt in a medium bowl. Stir in the almonds. • Beat the butter and confectioners' sugar in a large bowl with an electric mixer at high speed until creamy. • Mix in the dry ingredients and egg whites. • Spoon the batter into the prepared pans and place some blueberries on top of each. • Bake until a toothpick inserted into one comes out clean, 25–30 minutes. • Transfer to racks to cool.

½ cup (75 g) all-purpose (plain) flour

⅛ teaspoon salt

1¼ cups (180 g) finely ground almonds

¾ cup (180 g) butter, softened

1⅔ cups (250 g) confectioners' (icing) sugar

6 large egg whites

½ cup (125 g) blueberries

Makes: about 24 cakelets
Preparation: 25 minutes
Cooking: 25–30 minutes
Level: 1

NUTTY TARTLETS

Pastry: Mix the flour and salt in a medium bowl. Stir in the sugar and orange zest. • Use a pastry blender to cut in the butter until the mixture resembles coarse crumbs. • Mix in the egg yolk to form a smooth dough. • Press the dough into a disk, wrap in plastic wrap (cling film), and refrigerate for 30 minutes. • Preheat the oven to 350°F (180°C/gas 4). • Butter two 12-cup muffin pans. • Roll out the dough on a lightly floured surface to ⅛-inch (3-mm) thick. • Use a fluted cookie cutter to cut out 24 dough rounds. • Press the dough rounds into the prepared pans and prick all over with a fork. • Bake until the pastry is just golden, 10–15 minutes. • Transfer to racks to cool. • Nutty Filling: Mix the sugar with the water in a small saucepan. Wash down the sides of the pan with a pastry brush dipped in cold water to prevent sugar crystals from forming. Simmer over low heat until the syrup is golden, about 10 minutes. • Mix in the pecans, pine nuts, honey, and cream. • Spoon the filling into the cups and let cool completely.

Pastry

1¼ cups (180 g) all-purpose (plain) flour

⅛ teaspoon salt

¼ cup (50 g) granulated sugar

Finely grated zest of 1 orange

¼ cup (60 g) butter, cut up

1 large egg yolk

Nutty Filling

¼ cup (50 g) granulated sugar

1 tablespoon water

¾ cup (75 g) finely chopped pecans

¼ cup (30 g pine nuts

2 tablespoons honey

1 tablespoon light (single) cream

Makes: about 24 cakelets
Preparation: 45 minutes
Cooking: 10–15 minutes
Level: 2

BUCKWHEAT COOKIE CAKES

Preheat the oven to 350°F (180°C/gas 4).
• Butter two 12-cup muffin pans. • Mix the all-purpose and buckwheat flours, cocoa, baking powder, and salt in a medium bowl. Stir in the almonds. • Beat the butter and brown sugar in a large bowl with an electric mixer at high speed until creamy. • Add the eggs, milk, and vanilla, beating until just blended. • Mix in the dry ingredients and semisweet chocolate. • Fit a pastry bag with a plain ½-inch (1-cm) tip. Fill the pastry bag, twist the opening tightly closed, and squeeze out small rounds into each prepared cup. • Bake until lightly browned and a toothpick inserted in the centers comes out clean, 20–25 minutes. • Cool in the pans for 3 minutes. Transfer to racks and let cool completely. • Melt the white chocolate in a double boiler over barely simmering water. • Spoon the chocolate into a small freezer bag and cut off a tiny corner. Pipe chocolate lines over the tops in a decorative manner. Let set for 30 minutes. • Transfer to racks to finish cooling.

⅔ cup (100 g) all-purpose (plain) flour
⅔ cup (100 g) buckwheat flour
1 tablespoon unsweetened cocoa powder
1 teaspoon baking powder
⅛ teaspoon salt
1 tablespoon ground almonds
⅓ cup (90 g) butter, softened
½ cup (100 g) firmly packed dark brown sugar
3 large eggs
2 tablespoons milk
½ teaspoon vanilla or rum extract (essence)
2 oz (60 g) semisweet (dark) chocolate, finely grated
2 oz (60 g) white chocolate, coarsely chopped

Makes: about 24 cookie cakes
Preparation: 25 minutes + 30 minutes to set
Cooking: 20–25 minutes
Level: 1

CHERRY PUFFS

Using a sharp knife, carefully cut each pastry case open around the middle. Do not detach the two halves. • <u>Cherry Cream Filling</u>: Beat the cream, sugar, and kirsch in a large bowl until stiff. • <u>Frosting</u>: Mix the confectioners' sugar and kirsch in a small bowl. • Place the filling in a pastry bag with a ¼-inch (5-mm) tip and cover the bottom half of each pastry case with filling. Cover with the top half of the pastry case. • Spread the top of each cherry puff with the frosting. Refrigerate for 15 minutes. Decorate with the candied cherries.

16 storebought choux pastry cases

Cherry Cream Filling

2½ cups (625 ml) heavy (double) cream

⅓ cup (70 g) granulated sugar

2 tablespoons kirsch

Frosting

1½ cups (225 g) confectioners' (icing) sugar

2 tablespoons kirsch

Candied cherries, chopped, to decorate

Makes: about 16 cherry puffs
Preparation: 20 minutes + 15 minutes to chill
Level: 1

APRICOT TEA CAKES

Preheat the oven to 350°F (180°C/gas 4).
• Butter and flour a 12-cup muffin pan, or line with foil or paper baking cups. • Mix the flour, baking powder, and salt in a large bowl.
• Bring the apricots and water in a saucepan over medium heat to a boil. Reduce the heat and simmer for 5 minutes. Remove from the heat and beat in the butter and sugar until the sugar has dissolved. Stir in the milk, eggs, and vanilla. Stir the apricot mixture into the dry ingredients. • Spoon the batter into the prepared cups, filling each one about two-thirds full. • Bake until a toothpick inserted into the center comes out clean, 15–20 minutes. • Cool the tea cakes on racks.

2   cups (300 g) all-purpose (plain) flour
2   teaspoons baking powder
¼   teaspoon salt
⅔   cup (70 g) finely chopped dried apricots
¾   cup (180 ml) cold water
½   cup (125 g) butter, cut up
¾   cup (150 g) firmly packed brown sugar
½   cup (125 ml) milk
1   large egg, lightly beaten
2   teaspoons vanilla extract (essence)

Makes: about 12 tea cakes
Preparation: 15 minutes
Cooking: 15–20 minutes
Level: 1

LEMON TARTLETS

Pastry: Mix the flour, confectioners' sugar, and salt in a medium bowl. • Use a pastry blender to cut in the butter until the mixture resembles coarse crumbs. • Add the egg and enough water to form a stiff dough. • Divide the dough in half. Press the dough into disks, wrap each in plastic wrap (cling film), and refrigerate for 30 minutes. • Preheat the oven to 325°F (170°C/gas 3). • Spread the hazelnuts on a large baking sheet. Toast until lightly golden, 7 minutes. • Transfer to a large cotton cloth. Rub to remove the thin inner skins. Pick out the nuts and coarsely chop. • Increase the oven temperature to 375°F (190°C/gas 5). • Set out two 12-cup muffin pans. • Roll out the dough on a lightly floured surface to ⅛-inch (3-mm) thick. • Use a 2-inch (5-cm) cookie cutter to cut out 24 rounds. • Press the rounds into the muffin pans and prick all over with a fork. • Bake until the pastry is pale gold, 8–10 minutes. • Cool completely in the pans. • Lemon Filling: Whip the cream until thick. Fold into the lemon curd. Spoon the filling into the pastry bases. • Decorate with the chopped hazelnuts and lemon zest.

Pastry

1⅔ cups (250 g) all-purpose (plain) flour

2 tablespoons confectioners' (icing) sugar

⅛ teaspoon salt

⅔ cup (150 g) butter, cut up

1 large egg

2 tablespoons water

Lemon Filling

¼ cup (60 ml) heavy (double) cream

½ cup (125 g) lemon curd

1½ cups (225 g) hazelnuts

Curls of lemon zest, to decorate

Makes: about 24 tartlets
Preparation: 40 minutes + 30 minutes to chill
Cooking: 8–10 minutes
Level: 2

PISTACHIO MADELEINES

Preheat the oven to 375°F (190°C/gas 5).
• Butter two 12-cup madeleine pans. • Mix the flour, confectioners' sugar, and salt in a medium bowl. • Stir in the pistachios.
• Beat the egg whites in a large bowl with an electric mixer at high speed until stiff peaks form. • Use a large rubber spatula to fold in the dry ingredients, followed by the butter, honey, and almond extract. • Spoon the batter into the prepared pans. • Bake until a toothpick inserted into one comes out clean, 12–15 minutes. • Cool the madeleines in the pans for 15 minutes. • Transfer to a rack and let cool completely.

$2/3$ cup (100 g) all-purpose (plain) flour

$1^{2}/3$ cups (250 g) confectioners' (icing) sugar

$1/8$ teaspoon salt

$1/2$ cup (75 g) finely ground pistachios

4 large egg whites

$3/4$ cup (180 g) butter, melted

1 tablespoon honey

$1/2$ teaspoon almond extract (essence)

Makes: 24 madeleines
Preparation: 20 minutes
Cooking: 12–15 minutes
Level: 1

CARDAMOM PALMIERS

Preheat the oven to 350°F (180°C/gas 4).
• Butter a cookie sheet. • Stir together the sugar and cardamom in a small bowl. Lightly sprinkle a surface with 1 tablespoon of the sugar mixture. • Unfold or unroll the pastry into a 10-inch (25-cm) square. • Sprinkle with 1 tablespoon of the sugar mixture. • Fold the long sides of the pastry over to meet in the center. Sprinkle with 1 tablespoon sugar mixture and fold in half lengthways. • Slice the pastry into 12 portions. • Place the palmiers cut-side down 2 inches (5 cm) apart on the prepared cookie sheets.
• Sprinkle with the remaining sugar mixture.
• Bake until just golden, 10–15 minutes.
• Transfer to racks to cool.

⅓ **cup (70 g) superfine (caster) sugar**

½ **teaspoon ground cardamom**

1 **sheet frozen puff pastry (about 8 oz/250 g), thawed**

Makes: about 12 palmiers
Preparation: 30 minutes
Cooking: 10–15 minutes
Level: 1

CINNAMON SPICE MADELEINES

Mix the flour, cinnamon, baking powder, ginger, nutmeg, and salt in a medium bowl. • Beat the eggs and vanilla in a large bowl with an electric mixer at high speed for 3 minutes. • Gradually add the granulated sugar, beating until the batter falls off the beater in ribbons. • Fold in the dry ingredients and butter. • Refrigerate for 30 minutes. • Let rest at room temperature for 15 minutes. • Preheat the oven to 375°F (190°C/gas 5). • Butter two 12-cup madeleine pans. • Spoon the batter into the prepared pans. • Bake until brown and springy to the touch, 10–12 minutes. • Cool the madeleines in the pans for 15 minutes. • Transfer to racks and let cool. • Dust with the confectioners' sugar.

1   cup (150 g) all-purpose (plain) flour
1   teaspoon ground cinnamon
½   teaspoon baking powder
½   teaspoon ground ginger
¼   teaspoon ground nutmeg
⅛   teaspoon salt
3   large eggs
1   teaspoon vanilla extract (essence)
⅔   cup (170 g) granulated sugar
½   cup (125 g) butter, melted
⅓   cup (50 g) confectioners' (icing) sugar

Makes: about 24 madeleines
Preparation: 30 minutes + 45 minutes to chill and rest
Cooking: 10–12 minutes
Level: 2

RASPBERRY TARTLETS

Set out the tartlet shells. • Process the raspberries in a food processor until puréed. • Transfer to a large bowl and stir in the confectioners' sugar, liqueur, lemon zest and juice, ricotta, and yogurt. • Sprinkle the gelatin over the water in a small saucepan. Let stand 1 minute. Stir over low heat until the gelatin has completely dissolved. • Stir the gelatin into the raspberry mixture and refrigerate until thickened. • Beat the cream in a medium bowl with an electric mixer at high speed until stiff. • Fold the cream into the raspberry mixture. • Spoon the raspberry mixture into the tartlet shells. Decorate with the extra raspberries. • Refrigerate for 1 hour before serving.

12 storebought tartlet shells (or use the pastry recipe and method on page 632)

8 oz (250 g) raspberries + about 24 extra, to decorate

2/3 cup (100 g) confectioners' (icing) sugar

1/2 cup (125 ml) raspberry (or other berry fruit) liqueur

Finely grated zest and juice of 1 lemon

2/3 cup (150 g) ricotta cheese

1 cup (250 ml) plain yogurt

1 1/2 tablespoons unflavored gelatin

1/4 cup (60 ml) cold water

1 cup (250 ml) heavy (double) cream

Makes: 12 tartlets
Preparation: 50 minutes + 1 hour to chill
Level: 1

PISTACHIO TEA CAKES

Preheat the oven to 325°F (170°C/gas 3). • Butter and flour a 12-cup muffin pan. • Stir together the ground pistachios and sugar in a large bowl. • Beat the egg whites in a large bowl with an electric mixer at high speed until stiff peaks form. • Stir the egg yolks and orange zest into the pistachio mixture. • Use a large rubber spatula to gradually fold the pistachio mixture into the beaten whites, alternating with the cornstarch. • Spoon the batter into the prepared pans, filling each about two-thirds full. • Bake until a toothpick inserted into the center comes out clean, 20–25 minutes. • Cool the cakes on racks.

1¼ cups (180 g) pistachio nuts, blanched and finely ground

1 cup (200 g) granulated sugar

4 large eggs, separated

2 tablespoons grated orange zest

½ cup (75 g) cornstarch (cornflour)

Makes: about 12 tea cakes
Preparation: 45 minutes
Cooking: 20–25 minutes
Level: 1

RED CURRANT DOTS

Pastry: Mix the flour, confectioners' sugar, and salt in a medium bowl. • Use a pastry blender to cut in the butter until the mixture resembles coarse crumbs. • Add the egg and enough water to form a stiff dough. • Divide the dough in half. Press into disks, wrap each in plastic wrap (cling film), and refrigerate for 30 minutes. • Preheat the oven to 375°F (190°C/gas 5). • Set out four 12-cup mini-muffin pans. • Roll out the dough on a lightly floured surface to ⅛-inch (3-mm) thick. • Use a 2-inch (5-cm) round cookie cutter to cut out rounds. • Place in the pans and prick all over with a fork. • Bake until pale gold, 8–10 minutes. • Cool completely in the pans.
• Filling: Bring the red currants, sugar, and water to a boil in a medium saucepan over medium heat. • Simmer until tender, 5–7 minutes. • Transfer to a food processor or blender and chop until smooth. • Mix the custard powder with enough water to form a smooth paste and stir into the purée.
• Return the mixture to the saucepan and bring to a boil over medium heat, stirring constantly. • Spoon the filling into the pastry bases and refrigerate for 1 hour.

Pastry

1⅔ cups (250 g) all-purpose (plain) flour

2 tablespoons confectioners' (icing) sugar

⅛ teaspoon salt

⅔ cup (150 g) butter, cut up

1 large egg

2 tablespoons water

Filling

2 cups (500 g) red currants

1½ cups (300 g) granulated sugar

1⅓ cups (330 ml) water

⅔ cup (100 g) custard powder

2 tablespoons water

Makes: 48 cookies
Preparation: 45 minutes + 90 minutes to chill
Cooking: 8–10 minutes
Level: 2

LEMON RAISIN ROCK CAKES

Preheat the oven to 375°F (190°C/gas 5).
• Butter a baking sheet. • Beat the flour,
butter, lemon zest, and baking powder in a
large bowl with an electric mixer at medium
speed until well blended. • Add the egg,
sugar, lemon juice, and raisins. • Drop heaped
tablespoons of the batter onto the prepared
sheet, spacing them 2 inches (5 cm) apart.
Sprinkle with the sugar. • Bake until golden
brown, 15–20 minutes. • Cool the cakes
on wire racks.

1½ cups (225 g) all-purpose (plain) flour

⅓ cup (90 g) butter, melted

1 tablespoon finely grated lemon zest

2 teaspoons baking powder

1 large egg, lightly beaten

⅓ cup (70 g) granulated sugar

2 tablespoons freshly squeezed lemon juice

⅔ cup (120 g) raisins

2 tablespoons raw sugar

Makes: about 12 rock cakes
Preparation: 10 minutes
Cooking: 15–20 minutes
Level: 1

NUTTY RUM TARTS

Mix the flour and salt in a medium bowl.
• Use a pastry blender to cut in the butter until the mixture resembles coarse crumbs.
• Mix in the hazelnuts, sugar, and vanilla.
• Mix in enough water to form a smooth dough.
• Press into a disk, wrap in plastic wrap (cling film), and refrigerate for 30 minutes. • Preheat the oven to 375°F (190°C/gas 5). • Set out a 12-cup muffin pan. • Rum Filling: Beat the butter and brown sugar in a large bowl with an electric mixer at high speed until creamy. • Beat in the whole egg, almond extract, flour, almonds, 2 tablespoons milk, and rum. • Roll out the dough on a lightly floured surface to ⅛-inch (3-mm) thick. • Use a cookie cutter or glass to cut out 12 rounds large enough to line the muffin cups. Place in the cups. • Gather the dough scraps and re-roll. Use a 1-inch (2.5-cm) star-shaped cookie cutter to cut out 12 small stars. • Drop 1 teaspoon of apricot preserves into each pastry base and spoon in the filling.
• Place the pastry stars on top. • Beat the remaining egg yolk with the remaining milk and brush over the stars. • Bake until pale golden and the filling has set, 15–20 minutes. • Cool completely before removing from the pans.

1⅓ cups (200 g) all-purpose (plain) flour

⅛ teaspoon salt

⅓ cup (90 g) butter

⅓ cup (50 g) finely ground hazelnuts

⅓ cup (70 g) granulated sugar

½ teaspoon vanilla extract (essence)

3 tablespoons water

Rum Filling

3 tablespoons butter, softened

¼ cup (50 g) light brown sugar

1 large egg + 1 large egg yolk

¼ teaspoon almond extract (essence)

⅓ cup (50 g) all-purpose (plain) flour

⅔ cup (100 g) finely ground almonds

3 tablespoons milk

1 tablespoon rum

⅓ cup (90 g) apricot preserves (jam)

Makes: about 12 tarts
Preparation: 1 hour
  + 30 minutes to chill
Cooking: 15–20 minutes
Level: 2

ANISEED CRISPS

Preheat the oven to 325°F (170°C/gas 3).
• Spread the nuts on a large baking sheet.
• Toast until lightly golden, about 7 minutes.
• Increase the oven temperature to 375°F
(190°C/gas 5). • Line 2 baking sheets with
rice paper. • Transfer the almonds to a food
processor, add the sugar, and process until
finely ground. • Mix the almond mixture and
flour in a medium bowl. • Beat the egg whites
and salt in a large bowl until stiff peaks form.
• Fold in the dry ingredients and almond
extract. • Drop spoonfuls of the batter onto
the prepared baking sheets, spacing well.
Sprinkle with the aniseed. • Bake until pale
gold, 12–15 minutes. • Let cool completely.

$3/4$ **cup (125 g) blanched almonds**

1 **cup (200 g) granulated sugar**

2 **tablespoons all-purpose (plain) flour**

2 **large egg whites**

$1/8$ **teaspoon salt**

$1/4$ **teaspoon almond extract (essence)**

1 **tablespoon ground aniseed**

Makes: 20–25 cookies
Preparation: 30 minutes
Cooking: 12–15 minutes
Level: 1

COFFEE CAKELETS

Preheat the oven to 400°F (200°C/gas 6).
• Butter a 12-cup muffin pan. • Stir together the flour and baking powder in a medium bowl. Stir in the raisins. • Beat the butter, sugar, and 2 teaspoons of the coffee extract in a large bowl with an electric mixer at medium speed until creamy. • Add the eggs, one at a time, until just blended after each addition. • With mixer at low speed, gradually beat in the dry ingredients. • Fill the muffins cups about two-thirds full. • Bake until a toothpick inserted into the centers comes out clean, 12–15 minutes. • Cool the cakelets completely on a rack. • Place the confectioners' sugar in a medium bowl and add the remaining coffee extract and enough water to make a soft frosting. • Turn the cakelets over and frost the bottom of each one. Top with a coffee bean.

2/3 cup (100 g) all-purpose (plain) flour
1 teaspoon baking powder
1/4 cup (45 g) golden raisins (sultanas)
1/2 cup (125 g) butter, softened
1/2 cup (100 g) granulated sugar
1 tablespoon coffee extract (essence)
2 large eggs
1/2 cup (75 g) confectioners' (icing) sugar
2 tablespoons boiling water
Coffee beans, to decorate

Makes: about 12 cakelets
Preparation: 10 minutes
Cooking: 12–15 minutes
Level: 1

HOLIDAY
COOKIES

CHRISTMAS TREE COOKIES

Butter Cookies: Preheat the oven to 375°F
(180°C/gas 4). • Set out two cookie sheets.
• Mix the flour and salt in a medium bowl.
• Beat the butter and sugar in a large bowl
with an electric mixer at high speed until
creamy. • Add the egg yolk, beating until just
blended. • Beat in the cream and almond
extract. • Mix in the dry ingredients to form
a smooth dough. • Insert a Christmas tree
design plate into a cookie press by sliding it
into the head and locking in place. Press out
the cookies, spacing about ½ inch (1 cm)
apart on the cookie sheets. • Bake until lightly
browned, 12–15 minutes. • Cool on the sheets
until the cookies firm slightly. Transfer to
racks to finish cooling. • Chocolate Glaze:
Stir the sugar, water, butter, and corn syrup
in a small saucepan over low heat until the
sugar has dissolved. • Remove from the heat
and stir in the chocolate chips. • Return the
saucepan to the heat and stir until the glaze is
smooth. • Dip the cookies halfway into the
glaze and decorate with the sprinkles. • Let
stand until the glaze has dried, about 30
minutes.

Butter Cookies

1 cup (150 g) all-purpose (plain) flour
⅛ teaspoon salt
⅓ cup (90 g) butter, softened
¼ cup (50 g) granulated sugar
1 large egg yolk, lightly beaten
2 tablespoons heavy (double) cream
¼ teaspoon almond extract (essence)

Chocolate Glaze

½ cup (100 g) granulated sugar
2 tablespoons water
1 tablespoon butter
2 teaspoons corn syrup (golden syrup)
¼ cup (50 g) semisweet (dark) chocolate chips

Colored sprinkles or sugar crystals, to decorate

Makes: 20–24 cookies
Preparation: 45 minutes + 30 minutes to set
Cooking: 12–15 minutes
Level: 2

VALENTINO COOKIES

Preheat the oven to 375°F (190°C/gas 5).
• Butter two cookie sheets. • Mix the flour, cornstarch, cocoa, baking powder, and salt in a large bowl. • Use a pastry blender to cut in the butter until the mixture resembles coarse crumbs. • Stir in the sugar. • Add the coffee extract and enough milk to form a stiff dough. • Turn the dough out onto a lightly floured surface and knead until smooth. • Roll out the dough to ¼-inch (5-mm) thick. • Use a heart-shaped cookie cutter to cut out the cookies. Gather the dough scraps, re-roll, and continue cutting out cookies until all the dough is used. • Use a spatula to transfer the cookies onto the prepared cookie sheets, placing them 1 inch (2.5 cm) apart. • Bake until lightly browned, 10–15 minutes. Let cool on the cookie sheets for 2–3 minutes then transfer to racks to cool completely. • Spread with the frosting. Draw the tines of a fork through the frosting to make decorative patterns.

²/₃ cup (100 g) all-purpose (plain) flour

2 tablespoons cornstarch (cornflour)

1 tablespoon unsweetened cocoa powder

½ teaspoon baking powder

⅛ teaspoon salt

¼ cup (60 g) butter

¼ cup (50 g) granulated sugar

1 teaspoon coffee extract (essence)

1 tablespoon milk + more, as needed

1 recipe chocolate frosting (see page 697)

Makes: about 25 cookies
Preparation: 40 minutes
Cooking: 10–15 minutes
Level: 1

GINGERBREAD PEOPLE

Mix the flour, baking powder, and salt in a medium bowl. • Beat the butter and granulated sugar in a large bowl with an electric mixer at high speed until creamy. • Add the milk, ginger, and egg. • Mix in the dry ingredients. • Press the dough into a disk, wrap in plastic wrap (cling film), and refrigerate for 30 minutes. • Preheat the oven to 350°F (180°C/gas 4). • Butter two cookie sheets. • Roll out the dough on a lightly floured surface to ¼-inch (5 mm) thick. • Use large gingerbread people cookie cutters to cut out the figures. • Gather the dough scraps, re-roll, and continue cutting out cookies until all the dough is used. • Use a spatula to transfer the cookies to the prepared cookie sheets, spacing well. • Bake until just golden at the edges, 10–12 minutes. • Transfer to racks to cool. • Use the candy writers to decorate the cookies.

2 cups (300 g) all-purpose (plain) flour
1 teaspoon baking powder
¼ teaspoon salt
½ cup (125 g) butter, softened
½ cup (100 g) granulated sugar
1 tablespoon milk
1 tablespoon ground ginger
1 large egg
Colored candy writers, to decorate

Makes: about 12 cookies
Preparation: 40 minutes + 30 minutes to chill
Cooking: 10–12 minutes
Level: 2

TRICK OR TREATERS

Mix the flour, baking soda, and salt in a medium bowl. • Beat the butter and brown sugar in a large bowl until creamy. • Add the egg, beating until just blended. • Melt the chocolate in a double boiler over barely simmering water. • Stir the chocolate into the butter mixture. • Mix in the dry ingredients. • Press the dough into a disk, wrap in plastic wrap (cling film), and refrigerate for 30 minutes. • Preheat the oven to 350°F (180°C/gas 4). • Butter 2 cookie sheets. • Roll out the dough on a lightly floured surface to ¼-inch (5 mm) thick. • Use a 3-inch (8-cm) cookie cutter to cut out the cookies. • Transfer the cookies to the cookie sheets, spacing well. • Bake until just golden, 10–15 minutes. • Transfer to racks and let cool. • Knead the fondant until soft. • Divide it in half. Place one portion in a bowl and mix in the orange food coloring. • Roll out the plain fondant on a surface dusted with confectioners' sugar to ⅛-inch (3-mm) thick. • Use the cookie cutter to cut out enough fondant rounds to cover half the cookies. • Brush the fondant rounds with water. • Place wet-side down on top of half the cookies. • Repeat with the orange fondant and place on top of the remaining cookies. • Use an edible black candy writer to draw spooky designs.

1½ cups (225 g) all-purpose (plain) flour
¼ teaspoon baking soda (bicarbonate of soda)
¼ teaspoon salt
½ cup (125 g) butter, softened
½ cup (100 g) firmly packed light brown sugar
1 large egg
2 oz (60 g) semisweet (dark) chocolate, coarsely chopped
8 oz (250 g) store-bought ready-to-roll white fondant
2 drops orange food coloring (or red and yellow)

Makes: 12–16 cookies
Preparation: 25 minutes + 30 minutes to chill
Cooking: 10–15 minutes
Level: 2

CHRISTMAS RINGS

Preheat the oven to 400°F (200°C/gas 6).
• Butter two cookie sheets. • Mix the flour and salt in a medium bowl. • Beat the butter and 4 tablespoons of sugar in a large bowl with an electric mixer at high speed until creamy.
• Add the egg yolk, beating until just blended.
• Mix in the dry ingredients and orange zest.
• Form tablespoons of the dough into 6-inch (15-cm) ropes. • Shape into circles with slightly overlapping ends and place 1 inch (2.5 cm) apart on the cookie sheets. • Brush with the egg white and sprinkle with the remaining sugar. • Decorate with the cherries.
• Bake until lightly browned, 10–12 minutes.
• Cool on the sheets until the cookies firm slightly. Transfer to racks and let cool.

1⅓ cups (200 g) all-purpose (plain) flour

⅛ teaspoon salt

½ cup (125 g) butter, softened

6 tablespoons granulated sugar

1 large egg, separated

1 teaspoon finely grated orange zest

3 green candied cherries and 3 red candied cherries, finely chopped, to decorate

Makes: about 24 cookies
Preparation: 40 minutes
Cooking: 10–12 minutes
Level: 1

CAT FACE COOKIES

Beat the butter and sugar in a large bowl with an electric mixer at high speed until creamy. • Beat in the honey, flour, cocoa, and egg white. Add the rum and vanilla extracts. • Refrigerate for 1–2 hours. • Draw the outline of a cat's face and ears (about 3 inches/8 cm) on a acetate square or plastic lid. Cut along the outline to make a stencil. • Preheat the oven to 325°F (170°C/gas 3). • Line three cookie sheets with parchment paper. • Place the stencil on the parchment at the top corner of the cookie sheet. • Hold the stencil in position and spread a thin layer of the mixture across it with a rubber spatula, making sure the ears are filled in! • Carefully lift the stencil and place on the parchment next to the cat face you just made, spacing 2 inches (5 cm) apart. • Do not place more than eight cookies on one sheet. • Bake until the edges are firm, 6–8 minutes. • Cool on the sheets until the cookies firm slightly. • Transfer to racks to cool. • Decorate with the chocolate chips to resemble eyes and noses.

2 tablespoons butter, softened
¼ cup (50 g) granulated sugar
1 tablespoon honey
3 tablespoons all-purpose (plain) flour
1 tablespoon unsweetened cocoa powder
1 large egg white
¼ teaspoon rum extract (essence)
¼ teaspoon vanilla extract (essence)
¼ cup (45 g) semisweet (dark) chocolate chips

Makes: 20–24 cookies
Preparation: 30 minutes + 2 hours to chill
Cooking: 6–8 minutes
Level: 2

CHRISTMAS NIGHT COOKIES

Cookies: Mix the flour and salt in a medium bowl. • Beat the butter in a large bowl until creamy. • Mix in the dry ingredients and milk to form a smooth dough. • Refrigerate for 30 minutes. • Preheat the oven to 375°F (190°C/gas 5). • Set out three cookie sheets. • Roll out the dough to ¼-inch (5-mm) thick. • Use a 2-inch (5-cm) tree-shaped cookie cutter to cut out the cookies. Continue cutting out cookies until all the dough is used. • Dip the cookies in the sugar and place 1 inch (2.5 cm) apart on the cookie sheets. • Bake until just golden at the edges, 8–10 minutes. • Let cool completely. • Filling: Beat the butter and vanilla in a medium bowl until creamy. • Beat in the confectioners' sugar and milk. • Add the green food coloring. • Stick the cookies together in pairs with the filling.

2 cups (300 g) all-purpose (plain) flour

¼ teaspoon salt

1 cup (250 g) butter, softened

⅓ cup (90 ml) milk

¾ cup (150 g) granulated sugar

Filling

½ cup (125 g) butter, softened

½ teaspoon vanilla extract (essence)

2 cups (300 g) confectioners' (icing) sugar

1½ tablespoons milk

   Few drops green food coloring

Makes: about 24 cookies
Preparation: 30 minutes
  + 30 minutes to chill
Cooking: 8–10 minutes
Level: 1

SWEETHEART COOKIES

Sweetheart Cookies: Mix the flour, baking powder, cinnamon, and salt in a medium bowl. • Beat the butter and granulated and brown sugars in a large bowl with an electric mixer at high speed until creamy. • Add the egg, vanilla, and lemon zest, beating until just blended. • Mix in the dry ingredients to form a smooth dough. • Press the dough into a disk, wrap in plastic wrap (cling film), and refrigerate for 30 minutes. • Preheat the oven to 350°F (180°C/gas 4). • Butter two cookie sheets. • Roll out one-third of the dough on a lightly floured work surface to 1/4-inch (5-mm) thick. • Use a 3-inch (8-cm) heart-shaped cookie cutter to cut out the cookies. • Gather the dough scraps, re-roll, and continue cutting out cookies until all the dough is used. • Use a spatula to transfer the cookies to the prepared cookie sheets, placing them 1/2 inch (1 cm) apart. • Bake until pale golden brown, 8–10 minutes. • Let cool on the sheets for 2–3 minutes, then transfer to racks to cool completely. • Cranberry Topping: Process the cranberries, granulated sugar, and preserves in a food processor or blender until smooth

Sweetheart Cookies

- 2¼ cups (330 g) all-purpose (plain) flour
- 1½ teaspoons baking powder
- ½ teaspoon ground cinnamon
- ¼ teaspoon salt
- ¾ cup (180 g butter, softened
- ½ cup (100 g) granulated sugar
- ½ cup (100 g) firmly packed dark brown sugar
- 1 large egg
- ½ teaspoon vanilla extract (essence)
- Finely grated zest of 1 lemon

Cranberry Topping

- 1 cup (250 g) fresh or frozen cranberries
- ¼ cup (50 g granulated sugar
- ¾ cup (200 g) raspberry preserves
- 1 cup (150 g) confectioners' (icing) sugar, to dust

and puréed. • Transfer to a saucepan and simmer over medium heat until the mixture is reduced to about 1 cup (250 ml), about 8 minutes. • Remove from the heat and let cool for 15 minutes. • Use a thin metal spatula to spread the cranberry topping over the tops of the cookies. • Dust with confectioners' sugar just before serving.

Makes: 20–24 cookies
Preparation: 1 hour
    + 30 minutes to chill
Cooking: 8–10 minutes
Level: 1

CHRISTMAS CHERRY COOKIES

Preheat the oven to 350°F (180°C/gas 4).
• Butter two cookie sheets. • Sift the flour,
baking soda, and salt into a large bowl.
• Beat the butter and brown sugar in a large
bowl with an electric mixer until creamy.
• Add the eggs one at a time, beating until
just blended after each addition. • Mix in the
dry ingredients. • Stir in the dates, walnuts,
raisins, and whiskey to form a stiff dough.
• Drop teaspoons of the dough 2 inches
(5 cm) apart onto the prepared cookie sheets.
Top each cookie with a half cherry. • Bake
until pale golden brown, 8–10 minutes.
• Transfer the cookies to racks to cool.

1½ cups (225 g) all-
purpose (plain) flour
½ teaspoon baking soda
(bicarbonate of soda)
⅛ teaspoon salt
½ cup (125 g) butter,
softened
¾ cup (150 g) firmly
packed light brown
sugar
2 large eggs
1½ cups (150 g) coarsely
chopped pitted dates
1½ cups (150 g) coarsely
chopped walnuts
½ cup (90 g) golden
raisins (sultanas)
¼ cup (60 ml) whiskey
18 maraschino cherries,
drained and cut in half

Makes: about 35 cookies
Preparation: 20 minutes
Cooking: 8–10 minutes
Level: 1

CHRISTMAS BUTTER COOKIES

Preheat the oven to 325°F (170°C/gas 3).
• Set out two cookie sheets. • Mix the flour, cinnamon, and salt in a large bowl. • Use a pastry blender to cut in the butter until the mixture resembles coarse crumbs. • Stir in the sugar and coffee mixture. • Press the dough into a ball and knead it lightly. • Place the hazelnuts on a large plate. • Form the dough into balls the size of walnuts and roll in the hazelnuts until well coated. • Place the cookies 1 inch (2.5 cm) apart on the cookie sheets, flattening them slightly. Sprinkle with the remaining sugar. • Bake until faintly tinged with brown on top and slightly darker at the edges, 20–25 minutes. • Cool on the sheets until the cookies firm slightly. Transfer to racks to finish cooling.

1½ cups (225 g) all-purpose (plain) flour

½ teaspoon ground cinnamon

⅛ teaspoon salt

¾ cup (150 g) granulated sugar + 2 tablespoons extra, to sprinkle

2 teaspoons instant coffee granules, dissolved in 1 tablespoon hot water

1 cup (250 g) butter, cut up

2 cups (200 g) coarsely chopped toasted hazelnuts

Makes: 30–35 cookies
Preparation: 25 minutes
Cooking: 20–25 minutes
Level: 1

PINK SWEETHEART COOKIES

Preheat oven to 350°F (180°C/gas 4).
• Line two baking sheets with parchment paper. • Mix the flour and cornstarch in a medium bowl. Rub in the margarine. Add sugar and stir in beaten egg with vanilla to make a stiff consistency. • Roll out thinly on a floured surface. use a heart-shaped cookie cutter to cut out the cookies. • Transfer to the prepared baking sheets. • Bake until pale golden brown, 10–12 minutes. • Transfer to wire racks and let cool completely. • Prepare the pink frosting and use it to sandwich the hearts together. Prepare the vanilla frosting and use it to frost the cookies. • Finish with your preferred decoration.

$2/3$ cup (100 g) all-purpose (plain) flour

$1/4$ cup (30 g) cornstarch (cornflour)

$1^1/2$ oz (45 g) margarine

$1^1/2$ oz (45 g) granulated sugar

1 large egg, lightly beaten

$1/2$ teaspoon vanilla extract (essence)

To Finish

1 recipe pink frosting (see page 698)

$1/2$ recipe vanilla frosting (see page 699)

Colored sugar sprinkles, chocolate vermicelli, or hundreds-and-thousands, to decorate

Makes: about 12 cookies
Preparation: 25 minutes
Cooking: 10–12 minutes
Level: 1

4TH OF JULY COOKIES

Preheat oven to 375°F (190°C/gas 5).
• Line two baking sheets with parchment paper. • Mix both flours with the sugar in a medium bowl. Rub the margarine in finely.
• Beat the egg yolk and bind the mixture with this and the cream to make a very stiff paste.
• Roll out to ¼-inch (5-mm) thick and use a star-shaped cutter to cut out cookies.
• Transfer to the prepared baking sheets, spacing well. • Bake until pale golden brown, about 15 minutes. • Transfer to wire racks and let cool completely. • Prepare the vanilla glaze. Divide evenly among 3 small bowls. Color one bowl with red food coloring, one bowl with blue food coloring, and leave one plain. Decorate the cookies with the colored glazes so that they recall the American flag.

1 cup (150 g) all-purpose (plain) flour

⅔ cup (100 g) rice flour

¾ cup (150 g) superfine (caster) sugar

½ cup (125 g) butter

1 large egg yolk

2 tablespoons heavy (double) cream

1 recipe vanilla glaze (see page 696)

Red food coloring

Blue food coloring

Makes: about 35 cookies
Preparation: 15 minutes
Cooking: 15 minutes
Level: 1

VANILLA SUGAR

Fill a glass jar with the sugar. • Add the vanilla pods, seal tightly, and set aside for 7–10 days. When you open the jar, the sugar will be flavored with vanilla. • As the pods have a long aromatic life, just add more sugar as needed.

2 **cups (400 g) granulated sugar**

2 **vanilla pods, cut into 2 or 3 pieces**

Makes: about 2 cups (400 g)
Preparation: 7–10 days
Level: 1

VANILLA GLAZE

Place the confectioners' sugar in a medium bowl. • Add the vanilla extract and enough boiling water to obtain the desired consistency, from a thin glaze that can be drizzled, to a thick frosting that can be spread.

2 **cups (300 g) confectioners' sugar**

½ **teaspoon vanilla extract (essence)**

2 **tablespoons boiling water, + extra, as needed**

Makes: about 1 cup (250 g)
Preparation: 5 minutes
Level: 1

CHOCOLATE FROSTING

Stir together the confectioners' sugar and cocoa in a double boiler. Add the butter, vanilla, and enough of the water to make a firm paste. Stir over simmering water until the frosting has a spreadable consistency, about 3 minutes.

2 **cups (300 g) confectioners' (icing) sugar**

⅓ **cup (50 g) unsweetened cocoa powder**

2 **tablespoons butter**

1 **teaspoon vanilla extract (essence)**

About 2 tablespoons boiling water

Makes: about 1 cup (250 g)
Preparation: 5 minutes
Level of difficulty: 1

CHOCOLATE GLAZE

Place the confectioners' sugar and cocoa in a medium bowl. • Add the vanilla extract and enough boiling water to obtain the desired consistency, from a thin glaze that can be drizzled, to a thick frosting that can be spread.

2 **cups (300 g) confectioners' sugar**

½ **teaspoon vanilla extract (essence)**

3 **tablespoons unsweetened cocoa**

2 **tablespoons boiling water, + extra, as needed**

Makes: about 1 cup (250 g)
Preparation: 5 minutes
Level: 1

ITALIAN BUTTERCREAM

Stir the water and sugar in a saucepan over medium heat until the sugar has dissolved. • Cook, without stirring, until the mixture reaches 238°F (114°C), or the soft-ball stage. • Beat the egg yolks in a double boiler with an electric mixer at high speed until pale. • Gradually beat the syrup into the beaten yolks. • Place over barely simmering water, stirring constantly with a wooden spoon, until the mixture lightly coats a metal spoon. Plunge the pan into a bowl of ice water and stir until cooled. • Beat the butter in a bowl until creamy. Beat into the egg mixture.

½ cup (125 ml) water
¾ cup (150 g) granulated sugar
3 large egg yolks
1 cup (250 g) butter, softened

Makes: about 2 cups (500 g)
Preparation: 25 minutes
Level: 2

PINK FROSTING

Place the confectioners' sugar and butter in a medium bowl. • Add enough boiling water to obtain a thick frosting and mix until the butter is no longer visible. • Stir in a few drops of red food coloring. • Use green or other food colorings to obtain other colored frostings.

2 cups (300 g) confectioners' sugar
2 tablespoons butter
Red food coloring
½ teaspoon vanilla extract
About 2 tablespoons boiling water

Makes: about 1 cup (250 g)
Preparation: 5 minutes
Level: 1

COFFEE BUTTERCREAM

Stir the coffee and sugar in a saucepan over medium heat. • Cook, without stirring, until the mixture reaches 238°F (114°C), or the soft-ball stage. • Beat the egg yolks in a double boiler with an electric mixer at high speed until pale. • Gradually beat the syrup into the beaten yolks. • Place over barely simmering water, stirring constantly with a wooden spoon, until the mixture lightly coats a metal spoon. • Immediately plunge the pan into a bowl of ice water and stir until cooled. • Beat the butter in a large bowl until creamy. Beat into the egg mixture.

¼ cup (60 ml) very strong coffee, lukewarm

¾ cup (150 g) granulated sugar

3 large egg yolks

1 cup (250 g) butter, softened

Makes: about 2 cups (500 g)
Preparation: 25 minutes
Level: 2

VANILLA FROSTING

Place the confectioners' sugar and butter in a medium bowl. • Add enough boiling water to obtain a thick frosting and mix until the butter is no longer visible. • Stir in a few drops of red food coloring. • Replace the vanilla extract with almond, mint, orange, or other extracts to obtain frostings with other flavors.

2 cups (300 g) confectioners' sugar

½ teaspoon vanilla extract (essence)

2 tablespoons boiling water, + extra, as needed

Makes: about 1 cup (250 g)
Preparation: 5 minutes
Level: 1

Index